Addison-Wesley

Computer Literacy

AWARENESS, APPLICATIONS, and PROGRAMMING

Gary G. Bitter
Arizona State University

ADDISON-WESLEY PUBLISHING COMPANY

Menlo Park, California   Reading, Massachusetts
Wokingham, Berkshire UK   Amsterdam   Don Mills, Ontario   Sydney

About the Author
Dr. Gary G. Bitter is Professor of Computer Education at Arizona State University at Tempe. He is the Acting Director of the ASU Computer Institute and Director of the Microcomputer Research Clinic. Dr. Bitter has extensive experience as a teacher and as a consultant in the field of computers, mathematics, and curriculum development. Active as a lecturer, researcher, and author of numerous articles and books, he is also involved in many aspects of community service.

Design and Production: Design Office, San Francisco
Illustrations: Phyllis Rockne, Zahid Sardar

This book is published by the Addison-Wesley INNOVATIVE DIVISION.

Portions of this work have originally appeared in *Computers in Today's World* and are reprinted with the permission of John Wiley & Sons, Inc.

Apple is a registered trademark of Apple Computer, Inc.
Macintosh is a trademark licensed to Apple Computer, Inc.

Copyright © 1986 by Addison-Wesley Publishing Company, Inc. All rights reserved. No part of this publication may be reproduced, stored in a retrieval system, or transmitted, in any form or by any means, electronic, mechanical, photocopying, recording, or otherwise, without the prior written permission of the publisher. Printed in the United States of America. Published simultaneously in Canada.

ISBN 0-201-20274-3

EFGHIJKL-VH-89876

Contents

CHAPTER ONE The Computer: Wizard of the Modern Age   1

What Is a Computer   2
The Age of Computers   3
How Are Computers Helpful?   4
Why Are Computers Popular?   5
Uses of Computers   7

Careers and Computers: Overview   8

History of Computers   15

People and Computers: Charles Babbage   19

Four Generations of Computers   22

New Ideas and Computers: Liquid Crystals   24

The Future and Computers: Overview   28

What You Have Learned in Chapter One   29

CONTENTS

CHAPTER TWO   Chips, Boards, and Plastic: Computer Hardware   35

The Three Basic Operations   36
Input Hardware   36

New Ideas and Computers: The Cybernetic Interface Device   44

Processing and Storage Hardware   46
Output Hardware   50
How the Computer Works   56

People and Computers: Lady Lovelace, Ada Augusta Byron   58

Different Types of Computers   61

Careers and Computers: Operations Personnel, Farmers   63

The Future and Computers: The Next Generation of Computers   66

What You Have Learned in Chapter Two   67

Photo Essay: **THE MAKING OF A CHIP**   72

CHAPTER THREE   Getting Down to Business: Software and Applications   77

Software Basics   78
Two Types of Computer Software   79

Careers and Computers: System and Programming Personnel, Software Designers, Technical Writers, Law Enforcement Officers   81

Integrated Software   87
Planning a Computer Program   90

The Future and Computers: Artificial Intelligence   91

Programming and Authoring Languages   94

CONTENTS

New Ideas and Computers: Human-to-Machine Language Translation   95

People and Computers: Seymour Papert   101

What You Have Learned in Chapter Three   104

CHAPTER FOUR   Word Processing: Writing Made Easier   109

What Is Word Processing?   110

People and Computers: Samuel W. Soule   111

Word Processing and Typewriting   112
Tasks a Word Processor Can Do   115

New Ideas and Computers: User-Friendly Computers   122

Four Kinds of Word Processors   123
Who Uses Word Processing?   124

Careers and Computers: Computer Consultants, Secretarial Services Employees   127

The Future and Computers: Telecommunications   129

What You Have Learned in Chapter Four   130

Photo Essay: **INSIDE A COMPUTER FACTORY**   134

CHAPTER FIVE Data Bases: Finding Information Fast 139

What Is a Data Base? 140
How a Data Base Is Organized 143
Why Data Bases Are Better than Paper Files 145

The Future and Computers: Satellite Telecommunications 146

Setting Up and Using a Data Base 147

People and Computers: George Tate and Hal Lashlee 150

Where Are Data Bases Used? 151

Careers and Computers: Data Base Specialists, Media Specialists/Librarians, Airline Reservation Clerks 153

New Ideas and Computers: Computer Graphics in the Movies 155

What You Have Learned in Chapter Five 162

CHAPTER SIX Spreadsheets: Tools for Decision Making 167

What Is a Spreadsheet? 168

New Ideas and Computers: Computer Simulations 171

Advantages of Using a Spreadsheet 172
Setting Up a Spreadsheet 174

CONTENTS

People and Computers: Clive Sinclair   176

Uses of Spreadsheets   177

Careers and Computers: Programmer/Analysts, Athletes   178

The Future and Computers: The Political Spreadsheet   182

What You Have Learned in Chapter Six   184

Photo Essay: **THE MANY USES OF COMPUTERS**   188

CHAPTER SEVEN   Programming: Taking Steps to Solve Problems   193

Problems and the Steps to Solve Them   194

People and Computers: Jean Sammet and Grace Murray Hopper   195

What Is Programming?   196
Planning a Problem Solution   198

New Ideas and Computers: Talking with a Computer   199

Careers and Computers: Application Programmers, Engineers, Scientists and Laboratory Technicians   206

Programming in BASIC   208

The Future and Computers: True BASIC   211

Solving a Problem by Programming   212
What You Have Learned in Chapter Seven   221

CHAPTER EIGHT Computers in Our Society 225

The Roots of Our Present Society 227
The Age of Information 230

New Ideas and Computers: Computers in Medicine 232

People and Computers: Steven Paul Jobs 234

Careers and Computers: Computer Technicians, Training Specialists, Technical Support Specialists, Weather Forecasters 237

Daily Life is Changing with Computer Skills 240
Problems in the Age of Information 245

The Future and Computers: Employment Data Bases 246

What You Have Learned in Chapter Eight 250

Photo Essay: **COMPUTERS IN THE FUTURE** 254

CHAPTER NINE Computer Ethics 259

What Are Ethics? 261
Ethics in the Computer Field 262

Careers and Computers: Marketing Personnel, Sales Representatives, Computer Lawyers 263

Computer Fraud 264

The Future and Computers: Biochips 266

Computer Piracy 269

CONTENTS

New Ideas and Computers: Electronic Publishing   271

Computer Abuse   272
Invasion of Privacy   274
Preventing Computer Misuse   277

People and Computers: Marvin Minsky   279

What You Have Learned in Chapter Nine   282

CHAPTER TEN   The Future and Beyond   287

The Fifth Generation of Computers   288
Artificial Intelligence   290

New Ideas and Computers: Intelligent Computers   291

People and Computers: Donald Knuth   300

Applications of AI   302

Careers and Computers: Computer Scientists, Architects   303

Future Applications of Robotics   305

The Future and Computers: Microprocessors in Cars   306

The Future and Beyond   308
What You Have Learned in Chapter Ten   308

GLOSSARY, INDEX, ACKNOWLEDGMENTS   313

Glossary   315
Index   323
Photo Acknowledgments   335

WHAT YOU WILL LEARN IN CHAPTER ONE

By the end of this chapter, you will be able to:

1. Tell what a computer is.
2. Explain why computers are popular.
3. Explain how computers are used in business, schools, engineering, science, government, and the social sciences.
4. Briefly describe the history of the computer.
5. Tell the differences between the four generations of computers.

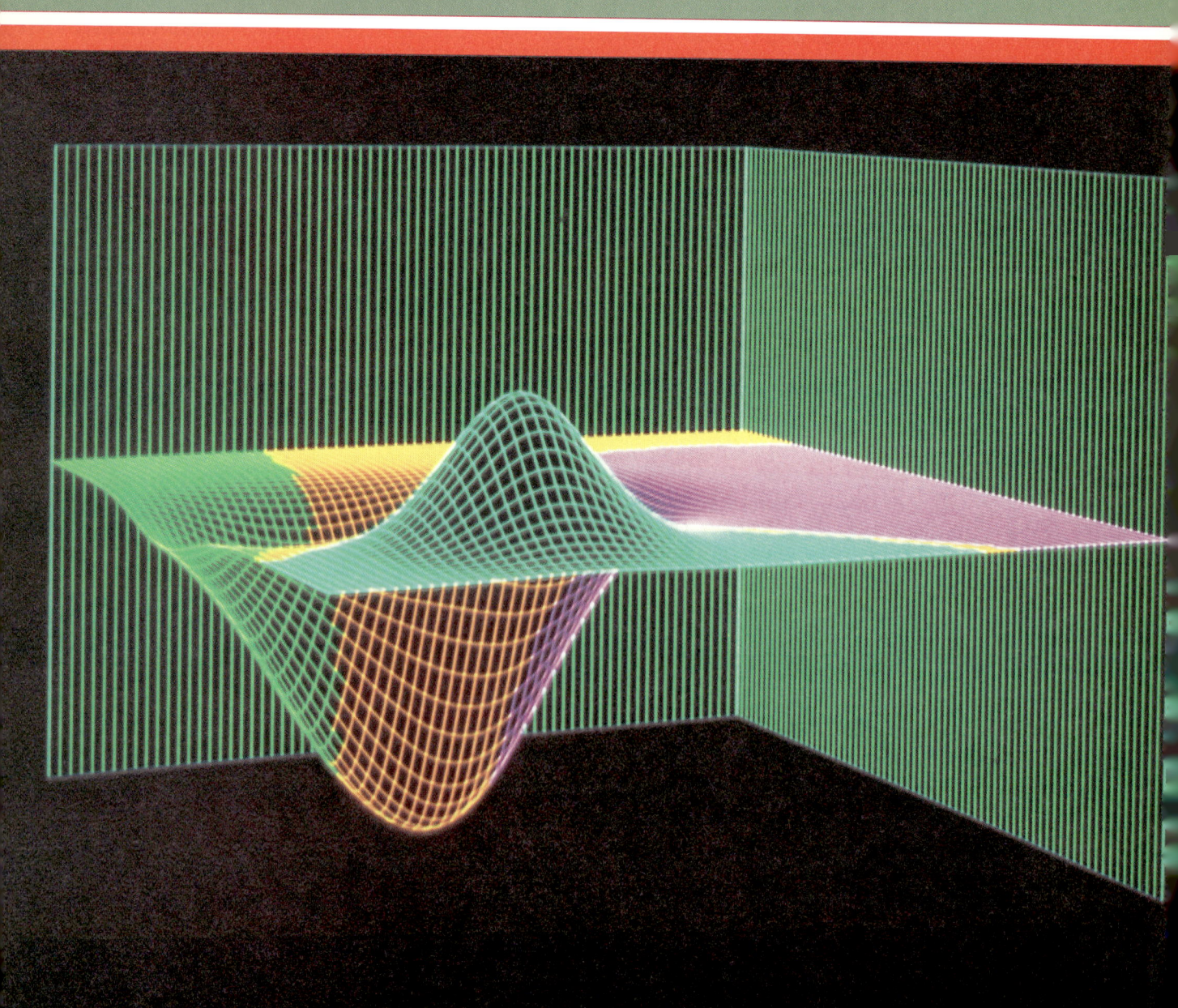

The Computer: Wizard of the Modern Age

WORDS YOU WILL LEARN

abacus
chip
computer
computer-aided design (CAD)
computer-aided instruction (CAI)
computer-managed instruction (CMI)
keypunching
large-scale integrated circuitry (LSI)
magnetic core memory
memory
nanoseconds
printout
processing
program
prototype
programming language
simulation
software
statistics
very large-scale integration (VLSI)

CHAPTER ONE

Examining a computer printout of a program is an important step in processing information.

If you call a friend in another state, if you cash a check, or if you go to the library, you will probably use a computer. If you need complicated medical help or if you run a business, the computer will help you. If you become a composer or a teacher, you will probably use a computer in your work. The computer has become an important part of our lives, and it will become even more important in the future. What is a computer, and why is it so important? How can it be helpful in so many ways? What ideas and machines were developed to produce the computers of today? In this chapter we will explore and answer these questions, and look to the future of computers in our world.

What Is a Computer?

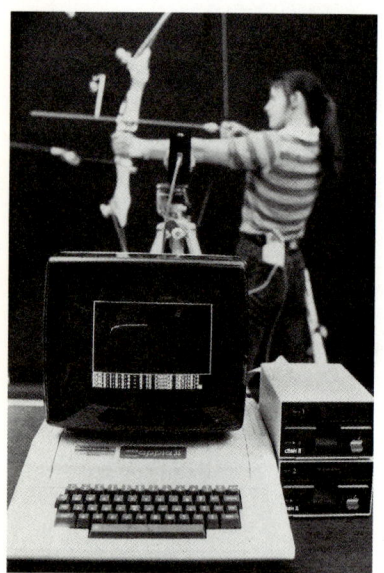

Analog computers measure an archer's movements, and this information is changed to numbers for the digital computer.

A **computer** is a machine that takes in information (called data) and processes it in some way. **Processing** is the handling, changing, and storing of information. For example, when we add two numbers, we are processing them in a specific way. We may store the answer in our memories or we may write it down. The information that a computer processes may be numbers, letters, or even sounds. It is turned into electrical impulses so that the computer can sort it, change it, or do arithmetic with it. The computer cannot decide for itself what to do with the information. It is a machine. People must decide what they want the computer to do, and they must give orders to the computer as part of its information. Most computers are electronic. They process information very quickly.

People give computers their orders. They write **programs** to tell computers what to do. A program is a set of instructions that the computer follows when it is processing information. Some of the programs used by the computer are stored inside the computer. (The part of the computer that stores information is called its **memory**.) People who operate the computer never see this programming. Other programs are written by the computer user. The user may have different needs. He or she can write a program to make the computer process the information to meet these needs. When many different users have the same needs, programs are developed and sold that may help them. For example, many offices need a program to process payroll information. Instead of hiring a computer programmer to write a program to process payroll information, offices can buy software (a program that has already been written) to use with their computers.

THE COMPUTER

Computers can perform the arithmetic that is asked for in a program. Even if the formula is long or difficult or time-consuming, computers follow instructions to do mathematics. They do addition, subtraction, multiplication, and division. Computers can also compare statements. They can see if a statement matches the information they have in their memories. In this way, they can make decisions about whether or not a statement is true.

The Age of Computers

We are living in an age of excitement and promise. Computers have become very common—almost as common as typewriters or televisions. Computers are helping businesses make a profit, teaching young children to read or do mathematics, keeping records for the government, and improving the lives of the disabled. These are only a few of the things that computers do today.

But computers are really very young. The first computers were developed in the mid-1940s. Most computer scientists believe that we cannot even imagine what computers will be able to do in twenty or fifty years. Much of what they will do will be decided by you. You are the designers and users of future computers.

Although we may not be able to imagine all of the changes computers will introduce, we do know that they will continue to change our lives. We know that they will become even more common than they are today. It is probable that in the future almost every home will have at least one computer in it. The computer may help us to shop, to vote, and even to "go to work" without ever leaving our home.

In the 1940s, it was probably not important that many people learn about computers. Today, however, computers are used in almost every job. They are helping to make new and better cars and airplanes. They are helping to develop and use new medical techniques. They are helping to write new songs and new books. They are helping to find better ways to teach. In fact, it is hard to think of jobs where an understanding of how to use computers will not be important. Today, between 55 and 85 percent of all jobs involve computers. In tomorrow's world, the computer will play an important role in processing increased amounts of information. With more information available, the computer will help in the development of more new ideas than ever before.

Plotters can make drawings of architectural designs. Pens of different colors can be used to illustrate various parts of one design.

CHAPTER ONE

How Are Computers Helpful?

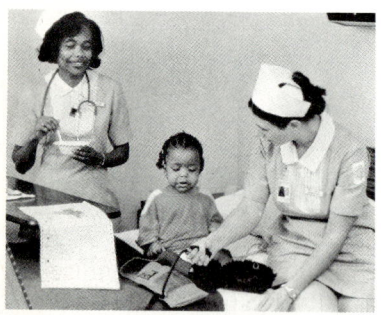

Computers are becoming an integral part of the medical examination.

Because they help us work with information, computers have become very important to our lives. Many people today make their living helping to gather, process, or store information. Others may use this information for their work.

A good example of this is in medicine. If you are sick, a doctor may enter your symptoms into a computer. The computer can compare your symptoms to those recorded in its memory. It can help the doctor to diagnose your disease. If you need surgery, a doctor can enter possible surgical techniques into the computer. The computer can tell her or him which technique would be the safest and most effective for you. If you need exercise, the computer can help decide what exercise program would be best for you.

Computers also process words. As a person types on a keyboard like a typewriter keyboard, the words are shown on a television screen above the keyboard. The computer can set or change the margins, can insert words, or can move paragraphs before the document is ever printed on paper. The computer can even check the spelling. When the document is exactly the way the user wants it to be, the computer can print it on paper. Many offices use computers rather than a typewriter to process words.

Computers are used to plan, test, and make new products. Designers use computers to draw and test their plans, and manufacturers use computers and robots to help build them. Sometimes computers are built into the products to make sure that they keep running well.

We are living in a world where we are surrounded by computers. Today, they help us train athletes, organize books, teach children, and write letters. In fact, it is difficult to think of anything that we do that is not helped in some way by computers. Because they are such an important part of our lives, we need to know a little bit about how they work and how to use them.

CHECK WHAT YOU HAVE LEARNED

1. Name three ways that we use computers.
2. Name five jobs that use computers.
3. What is a computer?
4. What is processing?
5. What does a computer program do?

Why Are Computers Popular?

Computers are used by many people in many different ways. What makes them so popular? How can the same tool help a homemaker, a farmer, a doctor, and a librarian? Several things about computers explain their popularity.

Computers Can Manage Huge Amounts of Information

Large corporations use computers for many applications. This is a computer-aided design laboratory.

Computers process great quantities of information that would otherwise be very difficult to manage or calculate. Having information available is always important, not only for educational purposes but also in the world of work. The more information we have, the more ways we can use it effectively. Large amounts of information can be organized very efficiently by a computer, and the computer makes it possible to find easily the information we want.

Computers Are Fast

Computers process information (often called data) so quickly that even the words used to describe the amount of time it takes them to do it may be new to you. For example, one second contains one million **microseconds**, or one billion **nanoseconds**. Information that may take days or weeks for a human being to calculate can be calculated in nanoseconds on a computer. New computers are much faster than their predecessors. The same information that took several hundred nanoseconds to process twenty years ago now takes only a few nanoseconds. This means that the work is done so quickly that it doesn't seem to take any time at all. (Processing time can also be calculated in **picoseconds**—or one-trillionth of a second!)

Computers Are Accurate

Computers do exactly what they are told to do. Sometimes they are told to do the wrong thing. That is, sometimes the programmer makes a mistake when he or she writes the program. Then the computer does not give correct results. If a program does not contain the right information and directions, the results will not be correct. But errors are very rarely the computer's fault.

This robot removes stacked parts from a bin and places them on a conveyor. Each part weighs over 200 pounds. A laser sensor system detects when the bin is empty.

Computers Can Work 'Round the Clock

Computers don't have to sleep or rest. They can work all night to process information while their operators are at home in bed. Computers in Japan operate robots that build automobiles all night long. They don't need lights to help them see, so electricity costs are low.

Computers Don't Get Bored

A good program can be run over and over with large amounts of data. The computer may have to repeat calculations many times. It does not get tired, bored, or frustrated with this work. It never asks for a coffee break to relieve the monotony of its work.

Computers Don't Feel Afraid or Uncomfortable

The computer in the spaceship that flew past Saturn did everything it was programmed to do. It did not worry about how it would return to earth.

In the same way, computers that work in areas that are very hot or very cold do not complain about how they feel. Computers that control machinery or that are built into the machinery make it possible to perform difficult or dangerous procedures. It is sometimes an advantage to have a task that involves very high furnace temperatures or toxic chemicals performed by a computer, rather than to have a human's safety endangered.

Computers Are Becoming Smaller, More Convenient, and Less Expensive

Some computers are now so small that you can hold them in your hand or wear them on your wrist. Computers that used to be room-sized are now easy to place on a desk top.

Computers that used to cost $25,000 can be bought for $5000 or less. Some computers are priced so that many families can afford to buy them for their homes. Computers were once owned only by the government or very big businesses. Now you can see them in schools, libraries, and small offices. You may know several people who own computers, or your family may own one. It is likely that computers will become even more common in future years.

THE COMPUTER

CHECK WHAT YOU HAVE LEARNED

1. When do computers make mistakes?
2. How many nanoseconds are in one second?
3. Name five reasons why computers are popular tools.
4. Name two ways that computers save time.
5. Why are computers better than people when they have to repeat calculations over and over again?

Uses of Computers

We mentioned some of the many uses of computers earlier. Computers are used in schools, in science, in engineering, in business, in government, and in the social sciences. We'll take a closer look here at some of these uses.

In Schools

There are many ways that computers help teachers and other school workers to do their jobs. When computers are used to help teach, this is called **computer-aided instruction** or CAI. When they are used to grade papers or keep track of grades, this is called **computer-managed instruction** or CMI. Computers can also be used in the library or office to keep track of school records or books.

The computer can be an excellent teacher. It is very patient. It can repeat the same lesson dozens of times in the same day without becoming bored or angry. Also, the computer can teach lessons in interesting ways. For example, many students play computer games to learn reading or arithmetic. In addition, the computer can test students on the material they just learned.

There are three basic types of **software** used for teaching. (Software is a set of instructions, or program, that is part of the computer system—it directs the computer to do a particular job.) These are drill-and-practice, tutorial, and simulation software. In drill-and-practice software, the computer asks a question and then the student answers. If the student is correct, the computer asks another question. If the answer is wrong, the computer may give the student another chance to answer. Computers are very

Computers are used to keep records of most library transactions.

good at drill-and-practice because they don't get bored. The problem is that the student may become bored easily with just questions and answers.

With tutorial software, the computer is more active. It actually presents the lesson before it asks questions. The computer does this by presenting a text or pictures to explain the subject. Tutorial software is more interesting to students than drill and practice software.

Careers and Computers

As you learn more about how computers work and the ways that they are used, you may become interested in a career in the field of computers. This is certainly a growing field. The number of opportunities will grow even more by the time you decide on a career.

In fact, experts are predicting that in the next ten years there will be a huge shift in the U.S. labor force. Half of all the people who now work in factories and other businesses will move into jobs in which they work with computers. Most of these people will have to be trained to work with computers. But you can begin now to prepare for a career in this field.

When you think of careers in the field of computers, you probably think of computer programmers and operators. But there are many other careers that involve computers. Professionals with all types of skills are part of the computer industry.

Computer careers can be divided into four broad categories: systems and programming, operations, development and retailing, and technical support services. Systems and programming workers decide how the computer can do certain work. They write the instructions that the computer follows. Operations personnel run the computer. They make sure that it has the information and the supplies it needs to do its work. Development and retailing workers design and produce computers and then sell their products to computer users. Technical support workers train users to operate computers and programs. They can help users whenever problems arise.

Within each of these categories, there are several different jobs that people do. In each chapter of this book, we will explore some of these jobs in the computer field. For some, we will see what these people do, what their working conditions are, what training they must have, and what these jobs may be like in the future. Other careers will be mentioned that involve using the computer outside the computer field. As you read about different careers, keep in mind your own skills and interests. This way, you can see if one of these careers seems suited to you.

Some of the most exciting software is **simulation** software. With this software, the computer is merely the vehicle that creates an environment in which something is happening. The student can see what it feels like to be part of what is happening. For example, a history simulation might give the student a chance to pretend being a soldier in the Civil War. Or the computer can teach driving by simulating driving a car on the freeway. Most students enjoy simulation software. They find it exciting to pretend to do things they cannot really do. They also learn a great deal about a subject by actually participating in it. Drill-and-practice, tutorial, and simulation software are all used for computer-aided instruction.

A teacher does much more than just give lectures or spend time with students. Most teachers must do a lot of paperwork. This is where computer-managed instruction can help. The computer can be used to grade papers or keep track of grades. Also, the computer can give and score tests. From the test results, the teacher can see what areas a student has mastered or needs help in. Computer-managed instruction can be very useful to help the teacher understand which lessons are being learned faster or slower than others.

Computers can be helpful in many other parts of a school as well. In the library, computers can be used for checking out books or keeping book collections organized. They can be used to keep track of inventory in school cafeterias or to make menus for school lunches. They can help in registering students for classes, keeping track of field trip money, or making budgets for the school.

In Science

Computers can be used in many ways to help scientists. One of the most important ways a computer can be used is as a research tool. Scientists must often gather a great deal of data. The process of comparing the data may take a long time if it is done by a human being. The computer can do this work quickly. It can also be used to make observations. Some computers have sensory devices like thermometers so that they can gather data such as temperature. A robot can be used to do experiments that might be dangerous or impossible for a person to perform.

Doctors and medical researchers use computers in many interesting ways. For example, a doctor can now "take a trip" through a patient's heart! He or she uses a computer that makes a three-dimensional movie of the heart. The computer makes the movie based on the patient's x-rays. The doctor can stop the movie at

Medical records processed by a computer provide information in seconds to the doctor.

any point. This is very important, because it allows the doctor to decide what is wrong without having to perform surgery. Computers can also be used to analyze the information gathered from an electrocardiograph or EKG. The EKG measures a patient's heart rate. Computers can read the results of the EKG and compare it to the EKG of a normal heart. They can analyze the EKG in a few seconds.

Computers are also used with simulation to do experiments. Sometimes they can replace laboratory animals in experiments. Scientists use computer simulation to see what would happen to the animals under certain conditions. This is helpful to the scientist because it is quicker than experiments with animals. It also often saves the lives of the animals that would be experimented on. Scientists can also simulate chemical experiments with computers. They can "combine" chemical compounds on the computer without actually having to mix elements and chemicals.

In a very real way, computers have made space travel possible. Space travel would be more dangerous without computers. Each space mission is carefully planned and prepared for with the help of computers. Before human astronauts go into space, NASA scientists test every system and activity with computer simulation. This way, the computer can tell what will happen if any system fails. Also, the astronauts are trained with computer simulation while they are safely on the ground. During a space launch, computers monitor the fuel, speed, and path of the rocket or shuttle. They monitor the condition of the spaceship and the astronauts during the mission. Sometimes they even repair equipment during a mission without the help of the astronauts. Computers can also gather information from space in the form of pictures or soil samples gathered by a computer-controlled robot.

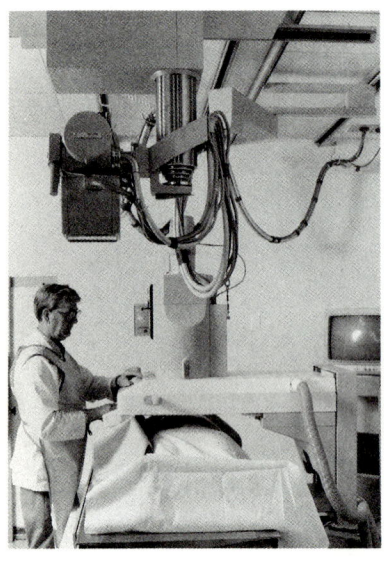

Some radiation machines depend on computers to analyze the information collected.

CHECK WHAT YOU HAVE LEARNED

1. Name two reasons that a computer can be a good teacher.
2. Name three ways that computers have helped in space exploration.
3. What does CMI stand for?
4. Explain how a doctor "takes a trip" through a patient's heart.
5. Name two advantages of simulation software.
6. Explain how a computer can be used as a research tool to help scientists.

In Engineering

Engineers invent and design new products. The computer helps in every stage of the engineer's job, except perhaps for coming up with new ideas. With a good idea in mind, the engineer uses the computer to help him or her plan. This is called **computer-aided design** or CAD. The engineer may use a light pen to draw an image on the computer's screen. Or the computer may be programmed to make an image that reflects the engineer's plans. Either way, a plan can be drawn exactly the way the engineer wants it. With CAD, the drawing can be changed every time the engineer makes a change in his or her plan. This can be done in a matter of seconds, as the engineer simply draws over the old image. The engineer may decide to design several variations of his or her plan and test them to see which one works best.

CAD applications include basic designs, drafting of these designs, and three-dimensional representation of design models.

Once the plans are drawn, testing begins. A few years ago, this was done by building a **prototype**, or model, from the plans. The prototype was used to see if the object or machine would operate correctly and safely. Whenever the engineer wanted to change his or her plan, a new prototype had to be built. Now the computer can simulate a prototype for testing. This is sometimes much safer than testing a real prototype. A pilot testing a new airplane, for example, could be badly hurt. But no pilot has ever been injured or killed while testing an airplane with computer simulation. In the design of automobiles, computer simulations are used to test fuel intake, exhaust emissions, and road safety.

The computer also helps the engineer plan how the object or machine will be built. It can determine what is the most efficient process of making the object or machine. It also helps calculate the number of parts necessary and the amount of time it will take to make the object. Some computers can even order the parts needed to build the object. Once the object has been planned and tested, the computer can be used as a tool in manufacturing. When it is attached to a robotic device, the computer can actually help in the building process. For example, robots are replacing human workers in automobile factories very quickly. This is because much of the work of building a car is very routine and can be done by robots working around the clock.

Once an object is built, the computer can make sure that the object is of good quality by testing it. For example, computers help make tiny computer parts by testing them to see if they operate properly. Computerized robots compare each tiny part to an image of a perfect one stored in their memory. If the new part matches, it is approved. Sometimes a computer can keep testing a product even after it has left the factory. Some cars have computers built into them. These computers keep an electronic "eye" on different systems in the car. When they detect problems, the computers let the car owner know that the car needs to be repaired.

In Business

In the business world, people have different kinds of work to do. Computers can help with most of this work. This is because computers can work with information much more quickly than humans can. Also, they can work at solving complicated problems for hours without having to rest. They make fewer mistakes than humans. For these reasons, more and more businesses are using computer systems to help them do their work.

The computer has three basic skills that make it useful in business. First, it can store a lot of information in a small space. A common use for this skill is in keeping track of products stored in a warehouse. Second, it can add, subtract, multiply, and divide numbers very quickly. Businesses need to calculate employee salaries, and other expenses, and money earned from sales, Third, it can be used to write, edit, store, and print words very quickly and easily. This skill is used to write business letters, make reports, and keep accurate records. Although each business uses computers in a different way, they all rely on computers to make their work faster and simpler.

Business applications can be analyzed by computers. This screen shows several types of information.

In Government

The government relies on computer power to do the huge amount of work it must do in order to keep running smoothly. Government agencies must store and process huge amounts of information each year. They need computers with large memories that work at the fastest speeds possible.

One of the first major organized data collections was developed to tabulate the 1890 census. The census is a collection of information on all the people in the U.S. that is taken every ten years. Before 1890, taking the census had been a very time-consuming process. Computers have saved a great deal of time. The census is used for many things by state and federal government. For example, state and federal monies are given to counties and cities according to their populations. The population is found through the census data. The computer also uses census data to find out how cities or populations have grown, how work patterns have changed, or how much money most people make. The census has become a more useful tool because the computer allows the data to be presented through reports, lists, and data information systems.

Computers have also become an important part of the election process. Registered voters are now listed on a computer report called a **printout** (information printed on a piece of paper) and their names are checked on the list before they are allowed to vote. Once a person has voted, that vote is entered into the computer and counted very quickly. In some areas, voting is done by computer and votes are entered directly into the system by the voter. Computers help candidates before voting day by putting together mailing lists. Candidates can use these mailing lists to send out their political literature. The computer can also keep track of the money raised to support a candidate. In the future, it is possible that we will use our home computers to vote. If it were possible to register and vote from home, perhaps many more people would vote. Computers may help us to become a more active democratic society.

The task of calculating income taxes can be a big headache for many taxpayers. Computers make this easier in a number of ways. The individual taxpayer can figure out how much he or she owes on a personal computer. There are many software packages on the market to help personal computer users complete their income tax returns. Professional accountants use these programs to make their work faster and more accurate. State and federal governments also use computers to organize the tax returns. The government must usually refund some part of the taxes that have been paid or collect additional taxes. Millions of checks must be written or received. This is a huge task, and it must be completed once a year! Computers allow the tax analysts to make sure the tax returns are correct in a short period of time. Computers also automatically print the refund checks and store the tax records on magnetic disks or tapes for future use.

The military services of the U.S. and many other countries use computers to provide training and to keep records of huge amounts of information. Training is accomplished using CAI and CMI. It is much less dangerous to teach a new pilot how to control a $24 million airplane through computer simulation than with the actual airplane. The computer can simulate many different weather conditions for flying. Pilots can learn to apply their training without the danger of a real crash. The computer also

The Cray-2 supercomputer is one of the fastest computers in the world. It is very compact in size—this student is able to walk into the center of the U-shaped computer.

aids surveillance. Computers keep track of our military and civilian aircraft to ensure no accidents result from one not knowing where the other is. Through computer simulation, an officer in training may control personnel carriers, jets, helicopters, and other machinery or equipment. The computer presents battle commanders with simulated action situations. The Army believes that this simulation will train commanders to make fast and accurate decisions.

In the Social Sciences

Computers also help us to take a closer look at people and how they live. They are used by researchers in the social sciences such as sociology and psychology. Sometimes they are used to help collect information about people. They can ask questions and conduct surveys. Sometimes people answer questions more honestly or with less embarrassment if they are just "talking" to a machine. The computer can store their answers and can later count the different answers or compare them to each other.

Most research in the social sciences uses **statistics**—this means it deals with collecting and analyzing numerical information. For example, the statement "10 percent of the population of the U.S. have college degrees" is a statistic. To arrive at this statement, a social scientist must find out how many people there are in the U.S. and how many of them have college degrees. Then he or she must calculate what percentage of the population is made up of people with college degrees. This is a fairly simple example of research, but much research is very complicated. Calculating statistics is a very difficult mathematical process. The computer can do this quickly and accurately.

CHECK WHAT YOU HAVE LEARNED

1. What is a prototype? What is it used for?
2. Name two basic skills that make a computer useful in business.
3. Give one reason that a computer might be used to ask people visiting a clinic if they have stayed on their diets.
4. Name two things that computers help governments to do.
5. What is CAD?

History of Computers

In a way, the idea of computers is not so new. People have always looked for ways to make calculating easier. In this section we will look at the ideas and machines that led up to the computers of today.

The Earliest Calculators

Thousands of years ago, people needed to count what they owned. Probably the first way they did this was by using their fingers and toes. On their fingers, people could keep track of ten items at one time. We probably use our modern base-10 number system as a result of this ancient custom of using one finger for each object. The base-10 number system has digits from 0 through 9. If people used their toes as well, they could count twenty objects.

Because people sometimes had to count to more than twenty, they began to use other methods of counting. They may have used stones for this. For example, a shepherd could pick up one stone for each of his sheep in the morning. When he counted the sheep again at night, he could throw one stone away for each sheep. If he had no stones left, he would know that he had not lost any sheep.

Later, people used a table covered with sand or dust. They drew marks to represent numbers. The problem with this was that it was difficult to carry a table around. People needed something that was smaller so that they could use it wherever they needed to do their counting.

The first small counting machine was the **abacus**. The abacus is a wooden frame on which thread is strung. Beads are strung onto the thread to represent numbers. To count with the abacus, people moved the beads up and down on the thread. Different threads could represent different place values.

Some cultures still use an abacus to help them calculate. The Chinese abacus has vertical rods to hold the beads. The rods represent ones, tens, hundreds, and thousands. The position of the beads at the top and bottom of each vertical rod gives the value of that rod. The Japanese use a similar abacus. The Romans developed an abacus made of a grooved table with stones placed in the grooves. The stones were called calculi. This is where our word *calculate*, which means to count or compute, comes from. During the Middle Ages, people in Western Europe invented a type

The abacus was one of the first tools used to help people calculate numbers.

of abacus known as a counting board. The board was marked with horizontal lines, and counters were placed on the lines or in the spaces between them to represent numbers. We do not know who invented these various counting devices. They were all used before careful historical records were kept.

The First Mechanical Calculators

In more recent times, many inventors and historians have left careful records. Sometimes an idea may not seem important at the time, but it makes possible later developments that do seem important. For instance, John Napier lived during the late 1500s in Scotland. He wanted to make mathematics easier for people to perform. His most memorable invention was the use of sets of rods called Napier's rods. They were used in sets of two. When they were placed side by side, they could be used to do difficult multiplication problems. Have you ever seen or used a slide rule to do multiplication or division? A slide rule is a modern version of Napier's rods.

Napier's rods are also important because they work on the basis of **logarithms**. Logarithms make it possible to do multiplication and division by doing a series of additions and subtractions. Other scientists have been able to apply logarithms to their work. Computer scientists today still use logarithms. John Napier is also known for inventing the decimal point to show parts of a whole number. Although he lived 400 years ago, Napier's ideas are still important today to scientists and mathematicians.

John Napier invented this calculating machine to solve difficult multiplication problems through the use of logarithms.

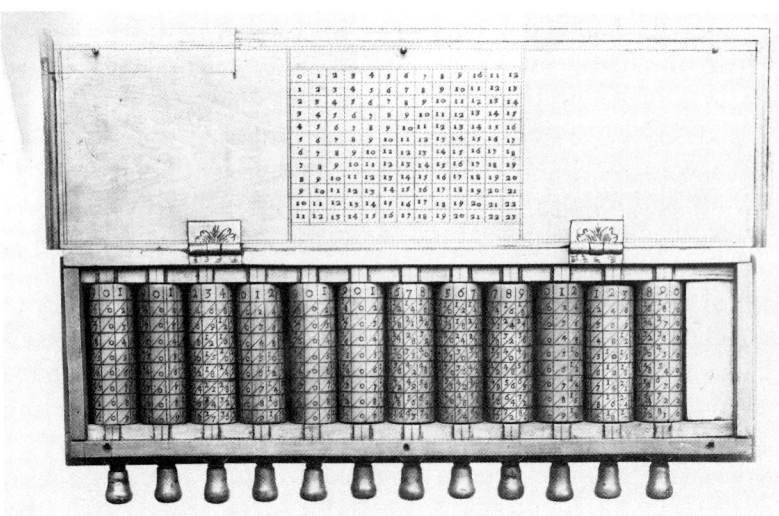

THE COMPUTER

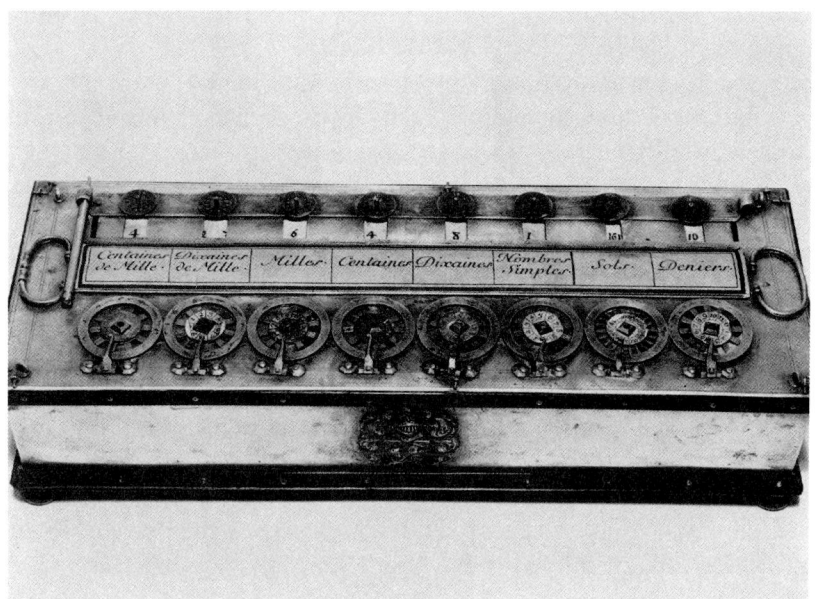

This mechanical device was invented by Blaise Pascal and was capable of doing bookkeeping. Many machines that we use today are based on the same principles as this device.

Six years after Napier died, Blaise Pascal was born in France. In 1642, he invented a mechanical device to make his father's bookkeeping easier. He is credited as the man who built the first mechanical calculator. The machine was made up of wheels and gears. Each wheel was marked with the digits 0 through 9. As the wheels and gears turned, numbers were added or subtracted. The machine was not popular because it broke easily. But it was still a very important development for two reasons. First, it was the first machine built to do mathematics. Second, the system of wheels and gears is still used today in instruments such as car odometers and gas and electric meters. Pascal has been honored by having a computer programming language named after him. The language Pascal is popular with many programmers today.

Another European mathematician who influenced the development of computers was Gottfried Wilhelm von Leibnitz. Leibnitz was born in Prussia in 1646, one year after Pascal developed his calculating machine. Leibnitz used some of Pascal's ideas when he built his calculator. Leibnitz's model could perform multiplication and division as well as addition and subtraction. Leibnitz's machine did not become popular either. He was not recognized as an important mathematician until many years after he died in 1716. Today he is credited with having begun the study of formal logic. This is the basis of computer programming and operation.

Liebnitz's calculating machine could do multiplication and division as well as addition and subtraction.

CHAPTER ONE

The Industrial Revolution

Perhaps you have studied a period in history called the Industrial Revolution. During this time, many people were trying to make their work faster and easier to do. Machines were built to do many jobs. People moved to cities in large numbers to work with machines in factories. The need to control machines brought about by the Industrial Revolution led to some ingenious inventions. These inventions had a great deal to do with the development of the computer.

For example, Joseph Marie Jacquard was a weaver born in Lyon, France in 1752. He wanted to find a way to make the job of silk-weaving easier. In 1801, he made an attachment to the weaving loom. This attachment could produce patterns in fabric without requiring humans to change the thread. The system that Jacquard used involved cards in which rectangular holes were punched. Hooks on the loom could reach through the holes to grab the thread underneath. Where there were no holes, the hooks did not grab the thread. This way, patterns were woven into the fabric automatically. This system is similar to the process of computer data entry known as **keypunching**. A keypunch operator works on a machine that punches small holes in cards. These holes represent numbers and letters to the computer. The computer gets its instructions from punched cards in much the same way that Jacquard's loom did.

We now come to the man who is often credited with having built the first computer. Charles Babbage was born in England in 1791. He studied mathematics at Cambridge University. There, he became interested in inventing a machine to produce astronomical tables for navigation. Babbage designed what he called an analytical engine, which was a complex calculating device. The analytical engine used cards like Jacquard's loom, but it used two sets. One set gave the machine instructions while the other set recorded the numbers to be used in calculation. This is similar to the computers developed later in the 1940s that get instructions from punched cards. Babbage divided the analytical engine into two parts. One unit was the store unit, where instructions and numbers could be kept. The other part was the mill unit, where mathematical functions were performed. This is also similar to later computers. Babbage never completed his analytical engine.

In his work, Babbage had a close associate. He was helped by Ada Augusta Byron (Lady Lovelace), the only child of the famous British poet Lord Byron. She became interested in Bab-

The Jacquard loom used a system of cards with holes punched in them to weave patterns automatically.

Babbage's analytical engine was never completed, but it would have worked in much the same way as modern computers do.

bage's work when she translated an article about him from French into English. After that, she worked closely with him. Ada Byron wrote a demonstration program for use on the analytical engine. For this reason, many people consider her the first computer programmer. Like Pascal, Ada Byron was honored by having a modern computer language, ADA, named after her. She died in 1852.

People and Computers

Charles Babbage

Charles Babbage became interested in inventing a machine that could produce astronomical tables to be used in navigation. After working on what he called the difference engine, he received a grant from the British government to help him build a mechanical calculator, or analytical engine. This machine could receive instructions, process and store information, and print the results, much as computers would later do. Babbage knew what a computer should do, and how to build one, but the people of his time could not build the thousands of gears and moving parts for his machine accurately enough so that it would work. However, because of his work on the analytical engine, Babbage is known as the Father of Computers.

During this time, the Industrial Revolution was also active in the United States. People were moving from small towns to work in larger cities. One of the problems in the U.S. was to keep track of its increasing population. When the U.S. census was taken in 1880, the information was not completed for seven years. The process of gathering and calculating the data was an enormous task. To simplify this task, the U.S. Census Bureau had a contest to find ways to make its work faster and easier. There were a number of machines entered in the contest, but the winner was Herman Hollerith's punched-card tabulating system.

Herman Hollerith's tabulating system saved the U.S. Census Bureau years of work.

Herman Hollerith was born in New York in 1860. He worked for the U.S. Census Bureau during the 1880 census. For the contest, he designed a system by which cards were punched to represent census information. These cards were fed into a tabulating machine, which then calculated the information it received. It took less than three years to tabulate all the information from the 1890 census, compared to the seven to ten years needed for the 1880 census. Hollerith's machine was obviously very fast. After winning the U.S. Census Bureau contest, Hollerith rented his machines to the government. He also formed his own company. Hollerith's company joined with other companies to form what is known today as IBM (International Business Machines).

Early Electronic Computers

The first electronic computer was built in 1939 by John Atanasoff and Clifford Berry. It was called the ABC, or the Atanasoff-Berry Computer. The computer required forty-five vacuum tubes to perform calculations. Vacuum tubes are devices that can stop or send electrical current without the need for a mechanical switch. They are large, get very hot, and wear out quickly. The ABC was not a very popular computer, but its design influenced other computers.

By this time, it was easier and less expensive to make the parts needed to build computers. Also, with the beginning of World War II, many scientists worked to build machines that could be used in that military effort. During this time, computer development advanced very quickly.

At the same time that Atanasoff and Berry were developing the ABC, a group of scientists at Harvard University were building a computer too. The leader of the group was Howard Aiken. Their computer, the Mark I, was finished in 1944. It was electromechanical—that is, it operated by a series of mechanical switches turned on and off by electricity using magnetic principles. It used paper tape on which instructions were coded. The Mark I was 51 feet long and 8 feet high. More than 1 million parts, 500 miles of wire, and 3000 switches were needed to build it. It took up all the space in a large room, but it was the best calculating machine that had ever been built. The Mark I could add three large numbers in one second.

Two years later, John W. Mauchly and John Presper Eckert, Jr., introduced their computer, the ENIAC. ENIAC stands for Electronic Numerical Integrator And Computer. Like the Mark I, the ENIAC operated electromagnetically and was very large. It

THE COMPUTER

21

weighed more than 30 tons (60,000 pounds) and contained nearly 20,000 vacuum tubes. All of these vacuum tubes needed a great deal of electricity and gave off a lot of heat. But the ENIAC was more than 1000 times faster than the Mark I. The ENIAC could add 5000 numbers in one second.

Another person who was very important to the development of computers was John von Neumann. Von Neumann had a photographic memory. In other words, he could remember every book he ever read and could even recite passages from them. He worked

The Mark I was the first electro-mechanical calculator. It took 0.3 seconds to add or subtract, 4.0 seconds to multiply, and 12 seconds to divide.

ENIAC could do as much work in one hour as the Mark I could do in a week. To reprogram ENIAC, computer scientists had to manually change the wires connecting the vacuum tubes.

with the designers of the ENIAC computer. He defined what a computer should do. He said that computers should be made up of three parts. One part should do the arithmetic. One part should control (or operate) the computer. The third part should store information (in the computer's memory). He thought that the computer could work best by having instructions coded as numbers and stored in the memory of the computer.

During this same period of time, Europeans were also working on the development of computers. Because of the World War II effort, Konrad Zuse built a number of relay connectors, used to more effectively link parts of the machine to expand its capabilities. Zuse formed his own company to build computers. In England, Andrew Booth and Kathleen Britten were also working on relay connectors. They also developed the concept of magnetic core, which is a way of making computer memory faster and more efficient. You will learn more about magnetic core memory in the next section.

CHECK WHAT YOU HAVE LEARNED

1. How did a weaver contribute to computer development?
2. Who was the first computer programmer?
3. Who made the first mechanical calculator? Why wasn't it popular?
4. Why was the 1890 U.S. census so much easier to tabulate than the 1880 census?
5. How big was the Mark I?

Four Generations of Computers

When we discuss computer history, we usually talk about the different generations of computers. Think about your own family. You are one generation, your mother is another generation, and your grandmother is yet another generation. Each one is born from the last. This is similar to what we mean when we talk about computer generations. Each new computer development is born from the technology that was used to build earlier computers. That is why we use the word **generations** to talk about the history of computers.

THE COMPUTER

The First Generation: Vacuum Tubes

We have already discussed two of the computers that were in the first generation of computer development. These were the ABC and the ENIAC. These computers, and all first generation computers, used vacuum tubes to operate. A vacuum tube is a glass tube inside of which is an empty space, or vacuum. Electrical current flows through the empty space. This works in a computer because the current is controlled by the vacuum tube. The flow of the current represents numbers to the computer. The computer recognizes these numbers as instructions or information.

Most first-generation commercial computers were produced from 1951 to 1959. Computers built before that time were electromechanical. This means they worked with a series of switches. In comparison, first-generation computers used vacuum tubes and did not need moving parts to work. First-generation computers were the first electronic computers.

First-generation computers used **magnetic core memory** to store information and instructions. Magnetic core memory is made of some magnetic material that can hold electrical charges. The computer can read electrical charges as numbers. It then translates these numbers into instructions or information. This is different from computers that used punched cards or paper tape to store instructions.

The first-generation computers were better and faster than the computers that came before them, but they still had a number

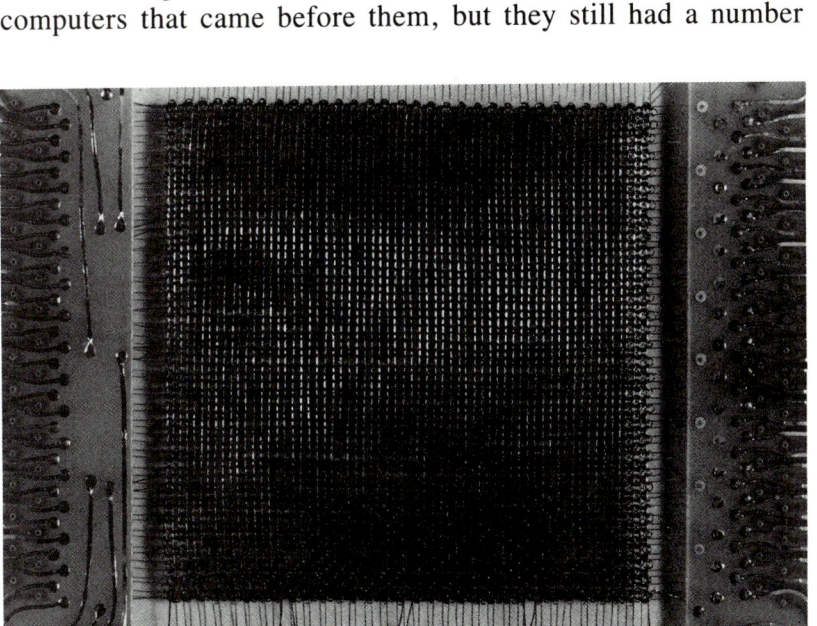

Vacuum tubes were used in first generation computers to control electrical currents. Vacuum tubes were very big, gave off a great deal of heat, and used a huge amount of electricity.

Magnetic core memory was used during the first and second generations of computers.

New Ideas and Computers

Liquid Crystals

Liquid crystal displays (LCDs) are what you see when you read the numbers from digital watches and calculators. For a long time, they were displayed only in one color (black) and were not very clear when used for anything but numbers and letters. New technological advances, however, are making it possible for LCDs to appear in many colors and in advanced graphics. This means that it is now or will soon be possible to make pocket color television sets, portable computer displays, and electronic color display panels for cars and airplanes.

Much of the technology is still in development. But this is a rapidly changing area, as companies are competing to produce smaller displays that still have high quality.

---

of problems. First, a large amount of heat was produced. The excessive heat made it necessary for computer owners to make specially air-conditioned rooms for their computers. The great amount of heat also made the computers break down often. In the early days of computers, a repair technician had to be highly trained. At that time, there were not many technicians who could repair these machines. Also, vacuum-tube computers required a great deal of electricity. Size was another disadvantage of the first generation of computers. They were very big. Computer owners often built entire rooms just for their computers!

For these reasons, and because of the high prices of computers, not many people could afford their own computer systems. It was more practical to rent computers from the people who owned them. Computer owners repaired computers for the people who rented the computers from them.

During the first generation, there were several important computers besides the ABC and the ENIAC. In 1946, the EDVAC was designed by the same people who made the ENIAC. EDVAC stands for Electronic Discrete Variable Computer. The EDVAC was an important computer because it could store data and instructions using a special code called binary code. Three years later, in 1949, the EDSAC (Electronic Delayed Storage Automatic Computer) was introduced. The EDSAC was able to store instructions in units; this feature made it very practical to change one set of instructions for a different set.

First-generation computers were also designed for business. The UNIVAC-I (Universal Automatic Computer) was introduced in

1951. It was the first computer to be made in large quantities. The UNIVAC-I used the binary code, stored its instructions and information on punched cards, and ran one program at a time. It was used to correctly predict the results of the election for President in 1952. IBM was also very active in computer design during this time.

Computers were beginning to grow faster and more powerful during the first generation. Still, computer scientists wanted to solve the problems of overheating, large size, and slow speeds.

The Second Generation: Transistors

The second generation of computers used transistors instead of vacuum tubes. A transistor is an object that allows some electricity to flow through it but stops some other electricity at the same time.

The use of transistors had several advantages. First, they were much smaller than vacuum tubes. Two hundred transistors could fit into the same amount of space that one vacuum tube could fit into. This made it possible to build computers that were much smaller than first-generation computers. Second, they required much less electricity to operate. This made them much less expensive to use. Also, second-generation computers did not produce the great amounts of heat that first-generation computers did. Because of this, they did not break down as often.

Transistors marked the beginning of the second generation of computers.

Second-generation computers were still very expensive to buy, though. This is because it took a long time to build them. A large number of parts were needed to perform even very simple calculations. And second-generation computers were still not fast enough to satisfy computer designers. For a computer to work faster, the distance between the parts must be shorter. Wires connect the parts of a computer. The longer the wire is, the slower the computer. In the second generation, there were still fairly long wires between the parts.

An important event during the second generation of computers was the development of computer **programming languages**. Programming languages are special languages that help humans communicate with computers. Computer programmers use these languages to write instructions for computers to follow.

The Third Generation: Integrated Circuitry

Third-generation computers used **integrated circuitry**. Integrated circuitry means that many tiny transistors were put together on a very small piece of silicon (a complex material manufactured from sand). The small piece resembles a thin wafer, and is called a **chip**. The integrated circuits on the chip took the place of the separate transistors. The distance between the circuits on a chip was much shorter than it was between transistors in second-generation computers. For this reason, third-generation computers were much faster.

Third-generation computers also had a different kind of

The chip has revolutionized computer technology. Pictured here are a wafer containing many chips and one chip packaged as an integrated circuit. One chip, smaller than your fingertip, is probably more powerful than the first generation Mark I computer that filled an entire room.

memory, called semiconductor memory. Semiconductor memory became possible with the invention of integrated circuits. In semiconductor memory, integrated circuits remember data by storing information as electrical charges. The computer can read the code of electrical charges. Semiconductors can store much more information in a smaller space than magnetic core memory can store. Semiconductor memory also allows the computer to read data from its memory faster, and it is less expensive to use.

Programming languages were used more widely in the third generation than in the second. Human operators were learning better and easier ways to give instructions to machines. And during the third generation, more than one person could use a computer at the same time. This made it possible for people who could not afford to buy a computer to share the cost and use of a computer system.

The Fourth Generation: LSI and VLSI

The fourth generation of computers began in the mid-1970s. It used **large-scale integrated circuitry** or LSI. As in integrated circuitry, many tiny transistors were put on a chip. But with LSI, the circuits were smaller and more of them could be put on a single chip. Also, each chip could now do a number of different jobs.

Semiconductor memory was made possible with the invention of integrated circuits in third generation computers— the circuits remember information by storing it as electrical charges.

The Future and Computers

People have been developing different systems for counting and calculating the objects around them since prehistoric times. This development has been gradual, but each new invention has built upon the inventions before it. Even the early counting systems depended upon the counting systems that preceded them. Until recently, development was slow, and new systems were rare even during the Industrial Revolution.

The last forty years or so have seen a sudden burst of development as computers have been born and new systems have been developed. Forty years ago, for example, computers were enormous systems that were used by only a few highly trained specialists. Most people were unlikely to ever see a computer, much less use one. Today we see small computers all around us. We use them at home and at school and in business. And the change in computers has brought about a change in the way we live. Computers have changed our lives in more ways than we can really know.

This sudden burst of technology has just begun. Computer scientists are changing and refining computers very quickly. There are many more ways that computers may be used in the future as they become even smaller, faster, and less expensive. For example, we may use a computer to monitor all of the appliances in our houses. We may simply tell our cars where we want to go. We may use robots to do most unpleasant chores. And when we are sick, we may tell our computer our symptoms before we tell our doctor.

Each chapter in this book will highlight a view of the future. If we use our imaginations, we can think of many other things that may change as computers become more a part of our day-to-day lives.

Putting several jobs on one chip was a big change. Many new inventions appeared that had not been possible before. One of these was the "calculator on a chip." It contained 6000 transistors and could do addition, subtraction, multiplication, and division. Other inventions that use the LSI chip are the digital watch and video games.

One result of LSI technology was that the price of electronic equipment dropped very quickly. In fact, computers are still becoming less expensive all the time. In the first generation of computers, 100,000 calculations cost about $1.25. With LSI, the same 100,000 calculations cost less than a penny! Computer power is one of the few things in the world that has gone down in price since the mid-1940s.

However, LSI was still not efficient enough for the computer scientists. They tried to make computers even smaller than those

THE COMPUTER

built with LSI. The result was VLSI—**very large-scale integration**. Greater numbers of microscopic circuits were put onto chips. With VLSI, chips contain as many as 300,000 units. VLSI made the microcomputer possible. If you have a microcomputer in your school or in your home, you can thank VLSI technology.

The fourth generation has also brought about a new kind of computer—the supercomputer. Supercomputers are the largest and most powerful computer systems. They have very large memories for storing information and instructions. They operate at very fast speeds. Supercomputers are used by the government and by big businesses. Although the price of these supercomputers is in the millions, the price per single calculation is much lower than similar computer systems could produce in the 1950s.

Some people say that we are already in the fifth generation of computer development. Others say that we are still in the fourth. It will probably take a few years before we can be sure. What do you think the fifth generation will be like?

CHECK WHAT YOU HAVE LEARNED

1. What made first-generation computers so expensive?
2. Why are chips faster than transistors?
3. During what generation of computers were programming languages first used?
4. Name two disadvantages of second-generation computers.
5. What is the difference between LSI and VLSI?

WHAT YOU HAVE LEARNED IN CHAPTER ONE

A computer is a machine that takes in information and processes it in some way. The information that it processes can be numbers, letters, or even sounds. The computer can sort the information, change it, or do arithmetic with it. The computer cannot decide by itself what to do with the information. People must give it orders. Programs are written to tell computers what to do. A program is a set of instructions that the computer follows.

Computers are used in many ways and for many jobs. They

help people to collect information, store it, print it, change it, and work with it. They are very popular because they can process information very quickly and accurately. They can work all night without becoming tired. Sometimes a computer must repeat calculations many times, but it does not get bored or frustrated. Also, computers do not know when they are in danger. For this reason, they can be used in situations that might be impossible for a human being. Computers are becoming smaller and less expensive, so more people are able to use them.

In schools, computers are used for many things. When they are used to help teach lessons, this is called computer-aided instruction (CAI). Probably the most interesting type of CAI is that in which the computer "pretends" that a situation is happening. The student tells the computer what he or she would do in that situation. This is called computer simulation. Computers are also used to grade papers and keep track of grades. Computers are used in schools to keep records of the students, make menus for lunches, make budgets for the school, or to keep book collections organized.

Scientists use computers to help gather, store, and compare information. Doctors and medical researchers can use computers to study patients, make diagnoses, or even simulate experiments. Computers have also made space travel possible.

Engineers use computers to help them plan new products. This is called computer-aided design (CAD). With CAD, the plans can be changed very quickly and easily. The plans can be tested using computer simulation. This is far easier and less expensive than building a model of the planned product. The computer can also help in the manufacturing and testing of the final product.

Computers are used in business for many different things. They can be used to store information, write, edit, and store words, and do mathematics very quickly. Government agencies also use computers for a number of purposes. Computers help gather census information. They also help count votes during elections. Military services can use computers to store information and to simulate situations.

The first electronic computer was built in 1939 by John Atanasoff and Clifford Berry. It was called the ABC computer. Most of the first generation of computers were commercially built between 1951 and 1959. These computers used vacuum tubes to transmit electricity. The vacuum tubes produced a lot of heat, and computer owners had to provide air-conditioned rooms for their computers. The first generation computers were also very big and expensive to operate.

THE COMPUTER

Second-generation computers used transistors instead of vacuum tubes. This made the computers smaller and less expensive to operate. But they were still very expensive to buy and were not fast enough.

Third-generation computers used integrated circuitry. This means that many tiny transistors were put onto a chip. Third-generation computers were faster than second-generation computers.

Fourth-generation computers have chips that are made of even smaller transistors. More transistors can be put onto one chip. Also, each chip can do many different jobs. Computers are now much less expensive than they once were. They are also much smaller. Microcomputers, or computers small enough to fit on a desk, have been introduced during the fourth generation of computers.

1. Name three ways in which a school can use a computer.
2. What is a computer simulation?
3. Why were first-generation computers very hot?
4. Name one way in which CAD makes a designer's job easier.
5. What is a computer?
6. Why does a computer need to be programmed?
7. In what way(s) were second-generation computers better than first-generation computers?
8. Name three reasons why computers are popular.
9. What is it called when a computer is used to teach students?
10. Where are the transistors in fourth-generation computers?

USING WORDS YOU HAVE LEARNED

1. A computer is a machine that takes in information and _____ it in some way.
2. One second contains a billion _____.
3. If the computer presents a lesson to the student and then tests the student on the material presented, it is using _____ software.
4. A less dangerous way to test a new airplane is by using computer _____.
5. A model of a new product is called a _____.
6. First-generation computers used _____ _____ memory to store information and instructions.
7. Second-generation computers used _____ instead of vacuum tubes.
8. Integrated circuitry means that many tiny transistors are put together to form a _____.
9. Most research in the social sciences is based on collected information, called _____.
10. The first small counting machine was the _____.

UNDERSTANDING WHAT YOU HAVE LEARNED

MULTIPLE CHOICE

1. A program is a set of:
   a) priorities
   b) information
   c) instructions
   d) word processing
2. Computer-assisted instruction helps the teacher to:
   a) teach
   b) keep track of grades
   c) give final exams
   d) keep track of books
3. People probably first counted by using:
   a) an abacus
   b) sand or dust on a table
   c) stones
   d) fingers and toes
4. The man who built the first mechanical calculator was:
   a) Joseph Marie Jacquard
   b) Gary Bitter
   c) Blaise Pascal
   d) Howard Aiken
5. First-generation computers used:
   a) magnetic core memory
   b) semiconductor memory
   c) transistors
   d) integrated circuitry
6. Astronauts are trained using:
   a) semiconductor prototypes
   b) computer simulation
   c) magnetic core memory
   d) an abacus
7. A computer cannot:
   a) perform calculations
   b) carry out instructions
   c) save time
   d) act without instructions
8. Computers do not:
   a) get bored
   b) work quickly
   c) do what they are told
   d) work accurately
9. VSLI was first used with:
   a) third-generation computers
   b) fourth-generation computers
   c) second-generation computers
   d) first-generation computers
10. With computer simulation, the military can train soldiers to:
    a) pilot airplanes
    b) react to possible dangerous situations
    c) make fast decisions
    d) all of the above

TRUE OR FALSE

1. The safest way to test a new airplane is by using a prototype.
2. Some programs are stored inside the computer.
3. Computers rarely make mistakes.
4. With CAD, an engineer needs several days to change a design.
5. Most research in the social sciences uses statistics.
6. The keypunch system was first developed by Howard Aiken.
7. Third-generation computers were very hot.
8. Transistors are located far apart in fourth-generation computers.
9. Computers can be built into other products.
10. Computers were used to help predict the election for president in 1852.

SHORT ANSWER

1. Name three ways that computer simulation can be helpful.
2. What contribution did a weaver make to computer development?
3. What is magnetic core memory made of?
4. Name three reasons why computers are popular.
5. What is tutorial software?

THE COMPUTER

6. Who won the U.S. Census Bureau's contest in 1880?
7. How was the second generation of computers different from the first?
8. In what generation of computers was the supercomputer first introduced?
9. How big was the Mark I?
10. Name two ways that computers can help teachers.

EXERCISING YOUR WRITING SKILLS

Ask five adults and five students what they think about computers. Record the results.

	AGREE	DISAGREE	DON'T KNOW
1. Computers are human.			
2. Computers can speak.			
3. Computers hate people.			
4. I would like to own a computer.			
5. Computers are all-powerful.			
6. Computers make few mistakes.			
7. Computers are frightening.			
8. Computers are expensive.			
9. Computers can think.			
10. I like computers.			

Write a short paper telling about the results of your survey. Did the adults answer differently from the students? Why do you suppose they did or did not?

WHAT YOU WILL LEARN IN CHAPTER TWO

By the end of this chapter, you will be able to:

1. Define input, processing, and output.
2. Describe at least three methods of computer input.
3. List at least three methods of computer output.
4. Tell what the two major components of a computer processor are.
5. Explain the differences between primary and secondary storage.
6. Define bits and bytes.
7. Name the major types of computers used today.

Chips, Boards, and Plastic: Computer Hardware

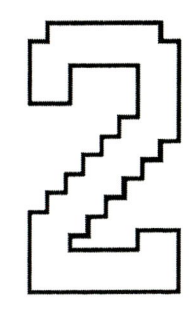

2

WORDS YOU WILL LEARN

assembler
assembly language
binary
bit
byte
cathode ray tube (CRT)
central processing unit (CPU)
compiler
cursor
cybernetic interface device
disk drive
diskette
hard disk
hardware
high-level language
input
keypunch
kilobyte (K)
machine language
magnetic ink character recognition (MICR)
magnetic tape
mainframe
microcomputer
minicomputer
modem
mouse

networking
optical character recognition (OCR)
output
peripheral
plotter
printer
random-access memory (RAM)
read-only memory (ROM)
tape drive
terminal
voice recognition device

35

You have probably seen a computer at work and watched it turning out numbers and letters at lightning speeds. You may have thought that it was very complicated and that you would never be able to understand how it worked. If you thought this, you were only half right. The computer *is* a very complicated machine. But once you know a few simple ideas and terms, you will understand how computers operate.

In this chapter, we will discuss the **hardware** that makes up the computer system. Hardware is the physical equipment of the computer. Terminals, keyboards, disk drives, tape drives, printers, and the computer's brain—the central processing unit—are all hardware. We will find out how these parts work together in the computer system.

The Three Basic Operations

The whole point of computer hardware is to make possible three basic operations: input, processing and storage, and output. Remember from Chapter One that the computer cannot work without instructions from a program and information such as numbers to calculate. The instructions and information that the computer needs are put into the computer by way of **input** hardware. Once the instructions and information are in the computer, it must have processing and storage hardware to perform its work. After the computer has finished its work, it must have **output** hardware. This allows it to display its work in some way that humans can understand and use. These hardware devices that attach to a computer are called **peripherals**.

All computer systems must include hardware to do these three operations. But different computers use different kinds of hardware to input, process and store, and output information. Let us look next at the hardware that has been designed to serve those purposes.

Input Hardware

Without instructions and information to tell it what to do, the computer cannot do anything. Human programmers must write

COMPUTER HARDWARE

instructions for the computer. They need to have a way to send their instructions into the computer so that it knows what to do. This is the purpose of input hardware. The term *input* simply means to put information into the computer. You will read and hear this term often in connection with computers. Sometimes input is referred to as data entry.

Keypunch Machine

One of the first machines used to input data was the **keypunch** machine. The keypunch system of data entry is fairly simple. The keypunch operator puts a thin cardboard card into a machine. Then the operator types in information. Keypunch machines punch tiny holes into the card. The holes make up a code that the computer can read. Inside the computer, the holes are passed over by beams of light or by brushes. These tell an electrical system, or circuit, when to turn on and off. This is how the computer "reads" the cards.

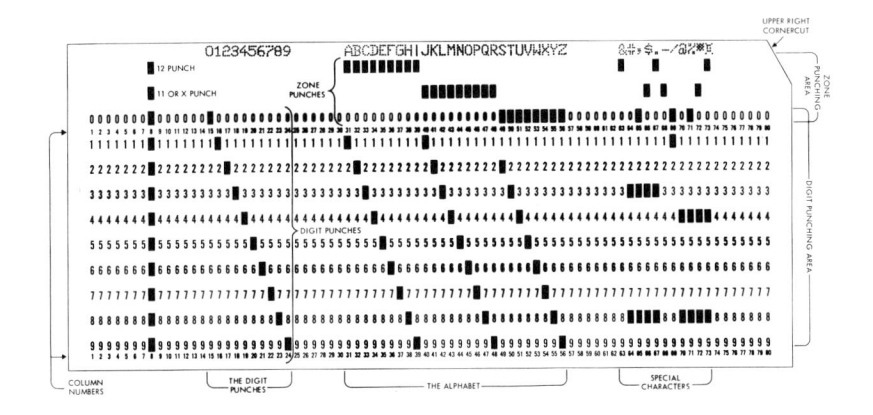

Keypunch cards were used with early computers to input or store data. The punched holes make up a code that the computer can read as they are passed over by a light or by tiny brushes.

Keypunch was once a very popular way to input data, but it is not used very much in business today, for several reasons. The cards are hard to handle in large numbers, and they take up a great deal of room to store. They cannot be used more than one time because it is impossible to erase the holes punched in the cards. Cards are fragile because they are thin, so it is easy to damage or destroy them when they are handled. Most important, the computer takes a long time to read keypunch cards, and this wastes time.

Magnetic Tape

During the 1960s people began to see the problems with keypunch data entry. Then key-to-tape data entry came into use. With key-to-tape data entry, the operator still types information using a keyboard similar to a typewriter keyboard. But instead of punching holes into cards, the key-to-tape operator records data onto **magnetic tape**. Next the tape is played into the computer by a machine called a **tape drive**. The tape drive is very much like a tape recorder and player that you may use to listen to music. By "reading" the electrical impulses stored in magnetic spots on the tape, the computer knows when to turn electrical currents on and off. The pattern of electrical currents makes up a code that the computer translates into instructions and information.

It is much faster for the computer to read electrical impulses from magnetic tape than to scan—or pass over—holes punched in cards. In fact, it may be as much as 600 times faster for the computer to read magnetic tape. Imagine how much time this could save in a busy office!

Electrical impulses may be stored on magnetic tape and read into the computer. The pattern of electrical impulses makes up a code that the computer can translate into information and instructions.

Although magnetic tape stores more information in a smaller space than punched cards, it still may take up a great deal of room.

Magnetic Diskettes

Another method of data entry that has become more popular in recent years is the use of **diskettes**. Diskettes are round platters made out of a plastic called Mylar. The diskette looks very similar to a 45-rpm record that you might play on your stereo. On the outside of this diskette is a substance that makes the surface magnetic, just like the magnetic tape. Another word for diskette is disk. Disks come in different sizes and are sealed inside special envelopes or cases that protect them from damage. Information stored on a magnetic disk is put into the computer by a disk drive.

Diskettes are becoming more and more popular, especially with people who use small computer systems. There are several reasons for this. First, diskettes are smaller and easier to handle than cards or tape. Second, diskettes take less room to store since they are smaller and hold more data than other types of materials used to put information into a computer. Third, it takes less time for the computer to read data from diskettes than from cards or tape. This saves a lot of valuable time.

Magnetic diskettes store more information in a smaller space than do cards or tape. Diskettes look like small phonograph records, but are permanently encased in special envelopes that protect them from damage.

The Mouse

Recently, a new device called a **mouse** has been developed for use with some computers. The mouse looks like a little box about the size of a real mouse. It is used instead of a keyboard for inputting data and instructions into the computer. The user rolls the mouse on a desk top. This moves a pointer of light, called a **cursor**, on the computer's screen. The cursor can be pointed at various pictures on the screen, each of which represents a different job for the computer to do. When the cursor is pointing at the desired job, the user pushes a button on the mouse and the computer immediately begins to do that job. This means that the computer operator does not need to know a lot of special commands—or even how to type—in order to have the computer do its job.

This computer uses a mouse to input instructions and data into the computer. The mouse is connected by a cord to the computer. To move the cursor on the screen, the user rolls the mouse on the desk top, and then pushes the button on top of the mouse when the cursor points to what the computer is to do.

Terminals

Another device that is often used for entering instructions and information into the computer is the **terminal**. A terminal is a typewriter-like keyboard and comes in many different designs.

This device is similar to those we have just discussed. The operator types information on the keyboard. Often the keyboard is part of the terminal, or it may be connected by a wire or even "connected" without a wire by using wireless communication. The keyboard looks like a typewriter keyboard, but it may also have some special symbols for giving the computer instructions. Some keyboards also include number keys arranged like a calculator so that the operator can enter numbers quickly and easily.

After the operator has entered information into the terminal through the keyboard, the information may go directly to be processed. Or, instead, it may go to a magnetic tape or disk so that it can be stored for use later.

A computer keyboard looks like a typewriter keyboard, but may include special function keys. This keyboard, for example, has arrows to move the cursor up, down, or sideways, a delete key, an escape key, and other keys that perform special functions.

The operator must be able to see information as it is being entered. Some terminals include a screen to display whatever is typed in. The most common screen used for computers is the **cathode ray tube**—or CRT. A CRT is also referred to as a **monitor**. The CRT looks very much like a television set, and it is used for the same purpose—viewing. The screen may show characters in black and white, green, amber, or full color. Another type of terminal that is used for data entry, the hard-copy terminal, has no screen. Instead, this terminal includes a **printer**. The operator can print a paper copy (called a *hard copy*) of the information entered into the hard-copy terminal. For example, some grocery stores use a hard-copy terminal. Computerized cash registers print out sales tickets that show what has been bought.

COMPUTER HARDWARE

CHECK WHAT YOU HAVE LEARNED

1. Name two problems with using a keypunch system for inputting data.
2. What are the three main operations performed by every computer system?
3. Give two reasons why diskettes are a popular way to store data.
4. What is a CRT?
5. What does a mouse do?

The Modem

Another common data input peripheral is the **modem**. It is a small box that connects to, or is built into, a computer and has a place to put a telephone handset or to attach a telephone cord. Over telephone lines, data from one computer can be sent to or received from another computer having a modem. The data are sent in a series of electrical impulses. These impulses can be used and processed directly by the computer connected to the modem.

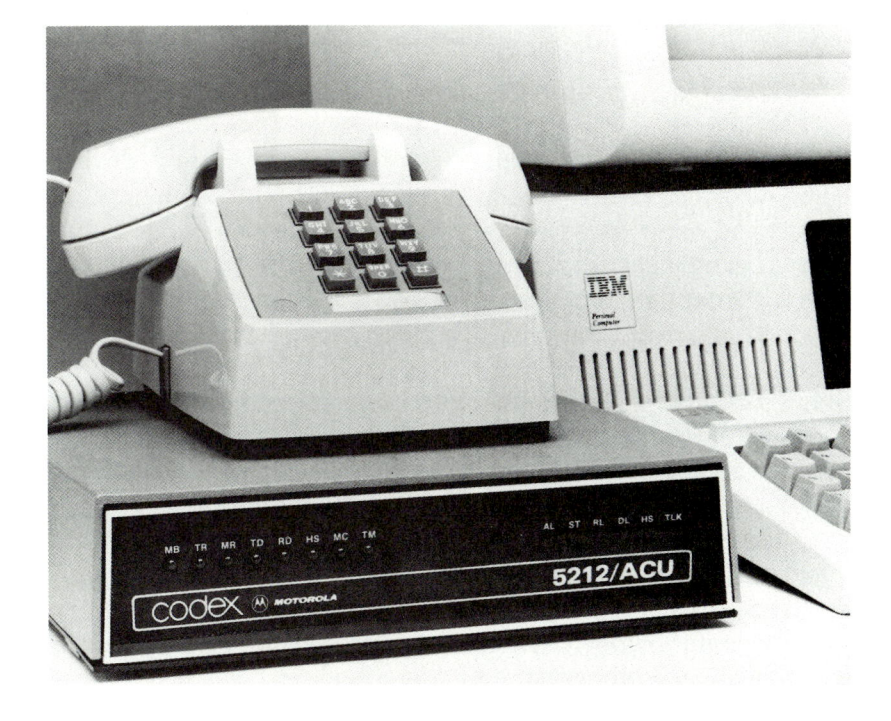

A modem can be connected to a computer to allow it to communicate with another computer by phone.

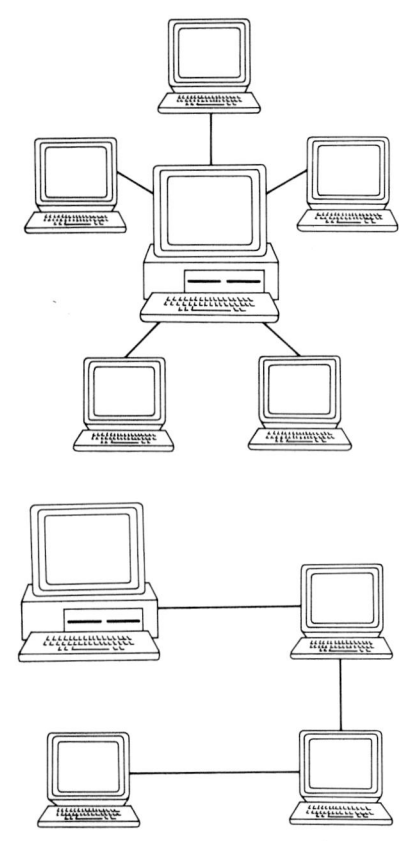

Networking is a connection of computer systems at different locations that exchange data. A star network (top) has many terminals connected to a central computer. In a bus network (bottom), several terminals share a single connecting line to the main computer. Some situations use *intelligent* terminals to process data.

The modem is an important business tool. Companies that have several branches in one city or hundreds of branches across the country use them. They can process all of their data in one central location by sending the data from distant—or remote—terminals by way of modem to the main computer. Large companies use data sent through modems to keep track of how each branch is doing and to write reports about the entire company.

Modems can save businesses a great deal of money. Instead of buying expensive computers for each branch office, many businesses buy just one powerful computer to place in a central office. An inexpensive approach is to put *dumb* terminals in the branch offices. Dumb terminals can input or output information but cannot process it in any useful way. At the end of each business day or week, branch offices input their data into dumb terminals. The data is sent through a modem to the central computer to be processed. This can cost less than purchasing many computers to compute data for each individual branch.

Sending data through a modem also keeps the main office up to date on what is happening with each branch. Without modems, branch offices would have to make reports of their business data and then mail or deliver the reports to a main office. Writing the reports and mailing them might take weeks. In the meantime, the main office would not know how each branch was doing. The same data can be sent through modems in a matter of seconds.

The Voice Recognition Device

Another exciting input device is the **voice recognition device**. The voice recognition device accepts data that is spoken rather than typed or recorded on disk or tape. With this type of input device, people can literally talk to computers and be understood. Voice recognition devices work by assigning numeric values to vocal signals. When the computer hears a voice pattern (or speech), it compares the numeric values of the speech to numeric values for other vocal signals stored in its memory. When it finds a pattern that matches the speech it has heard, it can use the pattern in its memory to understand the signal it has just received. Then it carries out the instructions it has been given.

Voice recognition devices are handy for a wide range of uses. They are convenient to use when a person is doing other work that requires the use of the hands. For example, stores can use voice recognition devices to make taking inventory easier. Taking inventory is the process of counting all of the items in a store or warehouse and keeping records of these items. It is a bother for a person to have to pick up items to count them and then put them down to write down the number of items counted. With a voice recognition device, the person can keep counting and handling items while simply saying the number out loud to the voice recognition device. The device makes note of the number and then sends its data to a computer to be calculated.

People with disabilities have also been helped by voice recognition devices. A person who cannot use his or her hands to type commands into the computer can use a voice recognition device to tell the computer what to do. A person who is paralyzed can tell a computerized robot to pick up an object, read a book, write a letter, and do many other tasks that the disabled person cannot do alone. This allows the disabled person to lead a more normal life. One example of the way that computers have changed the lives of disabled people is the story of Rob Marince, who lives in Hopewell Township, Pennsylvania. When he was seventeen, Rob was in a serious automobile accident that left his body paralyzed. Rob's brother put together a complex computer system that included a voice recognition device. Rob can tell his computer to find a channel on his television set, to dial a telephone number, to adjust the angle of his bed or the brightness of a light in his bedroom, to write letters or computer programs, and to play games. When he gives the computer a verbal order, it even answers with "Yes, Master." The voice recognition device has helped Rob lead a more active life.

Because it recognizes voice patterns, the voice recognition device can be used for another important job. Voice patterns—or voice prints, as they are sometimes called—are like fingerprints. Everyone has a different print. No two voice prints are exactly alike. Therefore, the voice recognition device can be used to positively identify a person whose voice pattern has been registered in the computer's memory. For example, voice recognition can be used to make sure that only authorized people have access to a computer. In the same way, voice recognition can be used to keep homes and other buildings secure. Some experts say that in the near future we will no longer carry keys. Instead, we will tell our doors to open for us, and the computer controlling the doors will recognize us and let us in. People we do not want in our homes will not be allowed to enter. This will make our homes and offices more secure.

Optical Character Recognition

Just as the computer can "hear" voice patterns, it can also "see" written or printed characters. It does this by using **optical char-**

New Ideas and Computers

The Cybernetic Interface Device

Computer scientists want to take the voice recognition device one step farther in development. The next step is the **cybernetic interface device**, which will be able to understand our thoughts without our even having to say them out loud. Imagine being able to write a letter without ever having to write, type, or even dictate it! The cybernetic interface device works by recognizing brain waves as we think and translating the brain waves into words for us. The system shown here (for stress reduction) is in a related field of computerized sensory perception. The cybernetic interface device is a promising new technology being developed today.

acter recognition, or OCR. OCR devices work like the human eye to "see" characters and marks. OCR devices have many uses. One of the most common is the bar code reader used in stores. You have probably seen cash registers in stores that do not require that prices of items be typed in. Instead the cashier passes the item over an OCR device. The OCR device reads the bar code of the item. The bar code is the series of heavy black lines you've seen on some items you have bought. The bar code can be used for different purposes. It can indicate to the cash register how much the item costs. It can also tell how many items have been sold. This helps the store manager to make sure that items are reordered when the supply is low. Bar code information is useful in many important business decisions.

Bar code does not look like much to humans, but to computers that have OCR devices, each line has a meaning. In many supermarkets, bar code is used to indicate to the cash register how much an item costs, and it can help the computer keep track of items sold.

COMPUTER HARDWARE 45

An optical character recognition device is used in supermarket checkout counters to record the product description and price on a printed receipt, as well as to keep inventory. When the clerk passes the code over the OCR, it registers the code in the computer.

Magnetic Ink Character Recognition

Magnetic ink character recognition—or MICR—devices are similar to OCR devices. Like OCR devices, they "see" and interpret printed characters. The MICR device works by recognizing characters printed with a special magnetic ink. It compares these characters to pictures of characters stored in its memory.

MICR is useful in banking. Magnetic ink can be used on bank checks, for example. The MICR device scans the checking account number printed in magnetic ink. Then it can tell the computer which account to subtract money from to pay for the check. Another use of MICR is the magnetic stripe character reader, which is popular in many stores. This device can be used to read and record credit card account numbers. The numbers are printed on a magnetic stripe, usually on the back of the card. This is faster than writing down the number by hand. It also prevents the chance of writing down the wrong number and charging the wrong account.

The magnetic numbers at the bottom of checks or on credit cards enable banks and stores to automatically deduct amounts from the correct account. Because this is done by the computer, fewer errors are made and much time is saved.

As you can see, there are many types of input devices for use with computers. These peripherals enter data into the computer quickly and in correct form. Once the data is entered, it can be processed by the computer's processing hardware.

CHECK WHAT YOU HAVE LEARNED

1. Name one way that a modem can help a business save money.
2. In the future, our doors may open as soon as we say "Open Sesame." What input device will the doors use to be sure it's us and not Ali Baba?
3. I have a friend who says she's going to think a book when she grows up. What hardware is being developed that will help her to do that?
4. What do you call the series of heavy black lines you see on some items at the supermarket?
5. How can voice recognition devices help people with disabilities?

Processing and Storage Hardware

After the instructions and information have been entered, the computer is ready to do its work. The place where it does its work is called the **processor**. The processor does several jobs. It receives the information that has been entered. It "remembers" or stores the information. It also processes the data in some way. The processor is made up of two parts: the **central processing unit**—or CPU—and main storage.

The CPU

The CPU in a microcomputer is called a microprocessor (*micro* means tiny). The CPU (or microprocessor) also has two different sections. One section is the **control unit**. The control unit acts like a supervisor in an office. It controls the other parts of the computer system and regulates the work they do. The other section of the CPU is the **arithmetic logic unit,** or ALU. The ALU does all of the calculating for the computer. It can perform arithmetic very quickly.

Main Storage

The main storage area stores instructions and information that have been entered into the computer. It's like the way you remember things that you have learned. In fact, computer storage is often called memory. The computer has to remember or store instructions and data before it processes them and after it processes them. Memory keeps the information inside the computer as long as it is needed.

As you learned in Chapter One, some of the earlier computers used a method of main computer storage called magnetic core memory. Magnetic core memory has now largely been replaced by semiconductor memory, which is faster and smaller. Still, there is a problem with some types of semiconductor memory. When the power is turned off, all of the information stored in semiconductor memory is lost. So there is a need to store information outside of the computer's memory. Devices that store data outside the computer are called secondary storage devices. We'll discuss more about them later in this chapter, but first we'll learn more about computer memory.

"Remember when hardware meant a hammer and nails?"

The age of computers has changed not only our lives but our language as well.

RAM and ROM

You may be curious about how the memory of a computer works. Basically, it can do two jobs: read and write. When the memory reads, it gets the information stored in a word. When the computer writes, it creates a word in which to store information. This is very much like the process you go through when you read a book to get information about a subject or write a letter to give information to someone else.

We have already said that most computers use semiconductor memory and that this kind of memory is made of integrated circuits. Today's computer memory is made of very large-scale integrated circuits. Integrated circuits are put together to form a chip. There are several different kinds of memory chips.

One kind of chip is a ROM chip. ROM stands for **read-only memory.** This means that the computer can only read information from the ROM chip. It cannot write information onto the chip. The manufacturer of the ROM chip puts information onto the chip. This information is usually a program that tells the computer how to perform a specific job.

The PROM chip is similar to the ROM chip. PROM stands for **programmable read-only memory**. Remember that the computer cannot write instructions or programs onto the ROM chip. This is not true of the PROM. The PROM can be programmed, but this type of chip can usually be programmed only once. It usually cannot be erased. However, there are some PROM chips that can be erased and written over with the use of special equipment.

Another kind of chip is the RAM chip. RAM stands for **random-access memory**. This chip is the opposite of the ROM chip. The manufacturer does not write any programs onto the chip. The person who buys the chip puts programs onto it. Also, the instructions and information stored on a RAM chip can be erased and rewritten whenever the user needs to store different information.

Secondary Storage

Two popular types of secondary storage are magnetic tape and magnetic disks. Remember that tape and disks record data in spots on their surface that are electrically charged. The computer reads these charges like a code that stands for the data that has been stored.

When you store data on tape or disk, you have to have some way of finding the data again. Finding the data is called accessing. There are two types of access: **sequential access** and **random** or **direct access**. When you want to find data by sequential access, you must sort through all of the data that has been stored from beginning to end, even if the data you want is near the end. Sequential access may take a long time. This is one of the problems with storing data on magnetic tape.

In contrast, data stored on magnetic disks is located by random or direct access. This means that the computer figures out where the data that you want is and goes immediately to that spot to find it. This is a much faster way to find data that has been stored. This is one reason why magnetic disks are very popular.

Memory Boards

As computer technology has developed, computer scientists have designed smaller computers with larger memories. This is why each new model of computer works faster and can solve larger

COMPUTER HARDWARE

problems than the models before it. In fact, the smallest microcomputer on the market today works at lightning speed compared to the first, huge computers of the 1940s.

The memory of computers today can be enlarged fairly easily. The most common way a user enlarges computer memory is with a **memory board**. The memory board is a card onto which many integrated circuits or chips have been placed. Each of these chips plays a part in storing or "remembering" data and programs inside the computer. Some boards are RAM (random-access memory). The user can store data or programs in this memory.

There are also memory boards that contain programs to do specific tasks. These boards are called ROM (read-only memory) because the user cannot change the information they store. The computer can only read the data stored in ROM. It cannot write new information onto the board.

Memory boards are very popular because they are easy to install. To install a memory board, the user slides it into slots connected to the CPU. These slots hold the board in place. With memory boards, the computer can grow as the user's needs increase.

This computer technician is working in a semiconductor factory. Because the devices being made are easily damaged by dust, the room is kept completely dust-free. He is wearing a "bunny suit" to keep his clothes from spreading dust.

Memory boards must be assembled very carefully. Here, an automatic insertion machine inserts the memory chips into printed circuit boards.

Memory boards are placed directly inside the central processing unit, by sliding them into slots. Several memory boards can be placed inside the computer to enhance the computer's memory.

Hard Disks

Another type of memory technology that increases the size of the computer's memory and allows it to work faster and better is the **hard disk**. The hard disk, as its name implies, is rigid. It is usually fixed inside the computer by the computer manufacturer. Some hard disks are separate pieces of hardware that can be added to a computer that uses floppy disks. The hard disk is useful because it can store a great deal more information than can a floppy disk. Because the computer has more memory, it can load and run much larger programs with more data much faster from a hard disk than from floppy disks.

The hard disk has another important advantage over other types of memory. With most types of main memory, the information and data stored in memory are lost when the computer is turned off. But this is not the case with a hard disk. With a hard disk, data and programs are stored until the user changes or erases them. Many computer systems operate with a combination of hard and floppy disks.

CHECK WHAT YOU HAVE LEARNED

1. I want to add a memory board to my computer that will allow me to store my own data. Should I get a RAM board or a ROM board?
2. What are some advantages of hard disk memory over floppy disk memory?
3. What is secondary storage?
4. When data is stored on tape or disk, how can you find that data again?
5. How does PROM differ from ROM?

Output Hardware

We have seen how data is entered into the computer and how the processor works with data. But there is one more step. After the computer has finished processing the data, it needs to have some way of sending its work back out to the operator. Otherwise, we would have no way of knowing what the computer had done and

COMPUTER HARDWARE

A COMPUTER SYSTEM

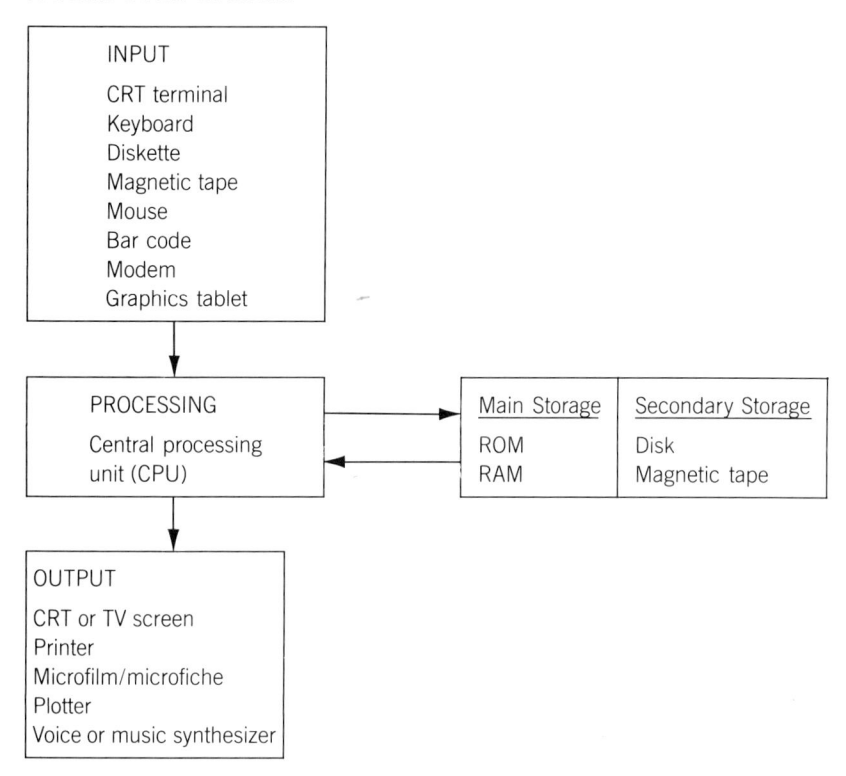

```
INPUT
  CRT terminal
  Keyboard
  Diskette
  Magnetic tape
  Mouse
  Bar code
  Modem
  Graphics tablet
       │
       ▼
PROCESSING          ──▶   Main Storage  │  Secondary Storage
Central processing         ROM          │  Disk
unit (CPU)          ◀──    RAM          │  Magnetic tape
       │
       ▼
OUTPUT
  CRT or TV screen
  Printer
  Microfilm/microfiche
  Plotter
  Voice or music synthesizer
```

A computer system, showing various types of input, processing, storage, and output devices.

computers would be useless to us. Sending the data from the computer back to the operator is referred to as outputting data. This is the opposite of inputting.

A number of devices can be used to output data. The kind of device that the operator chooses depends on what kind of output she or he needs. If the operator needs only to see the data, then a terminal with a CRT can be used. If the operator wants to have a permanent copy, usually printed on paper, then a printer can be used. We will also look at other ways to output the data that the computer has processed.

Terminals

As discussed earlier, a terminal usually includes a CRT or even a television set. The terminal displays on a screen the information the computer processes. The computer usually processes the information much faster than a human can follow on a terminal. But the terminal is a very convenient way for a person to immediately see the output.

Printers

Probably one of the most common types of devices used to output data is the **printer**. Printed books help us to remember a great deal of information on all different subjects. If we did not have books, we would probably forget much of this information. This is the same case with computer output. Unless we print a permanent record of computer output, it is easy to lose or forget it.

Basically, there are two ways to print. One method is impact printing. Think of the way a typewriter prints characters on paper. When you strike a typewriter key, the key moves up and hits the ribbon against the paper. This causes the ink from the ribbon to rub off on the paper in the shape of the character you typed. This is impact printing. The other method of printing is non-impact printing. In non-impact printing, no key strikes the ribbon against the paper to print a character. Instead, the letters are sprayed or chemically burned onto the paper. Intense beams of light such as lasers are now being used by some printers to burn letters on paper.

Printing devices can create two kinds of images: dot matrix characters and formed characters. Formed characters are similar to those printed by a typewriter. In other words, the whole character is formed at one time. Dot matrix characters are made up of

Printers allow the computer user to keep a paper or "hard" copy of the computer output. Some printers use impact printing, like a typewriter, and others use lasers or chemicals to burn the characters onto paper.

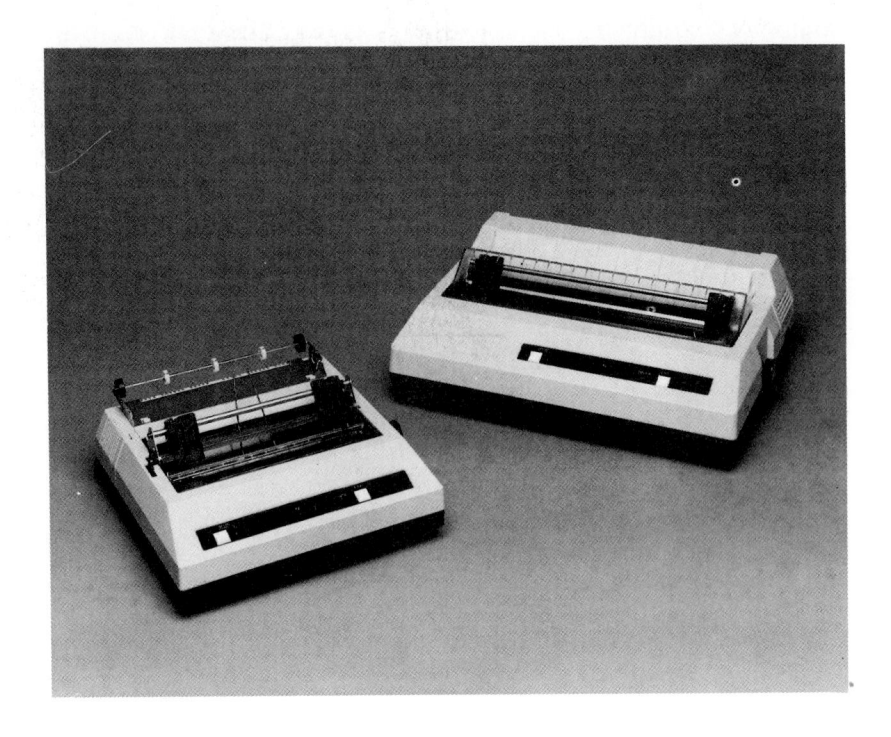

COMPUTER HARDWARE   53

many small dots. For this reason, dot matrix characters may be harder to read than solid or formed characters.

Formed characters are easy to read.

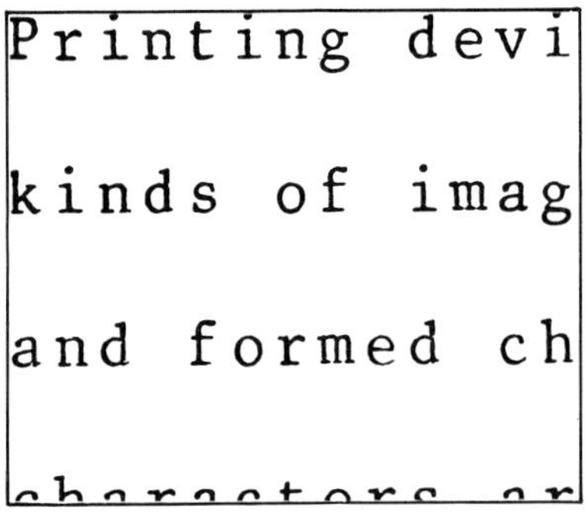

Dot matrix characters are made up of a series of tiny dots.

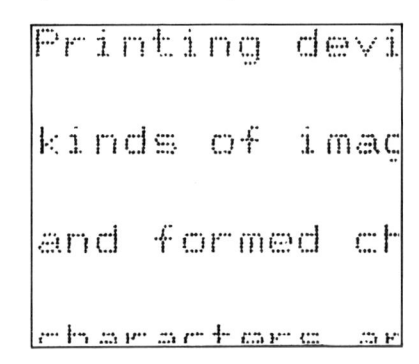

Laser printers use dot matrix characters, but the dots are so close together the characters appear to be formed.

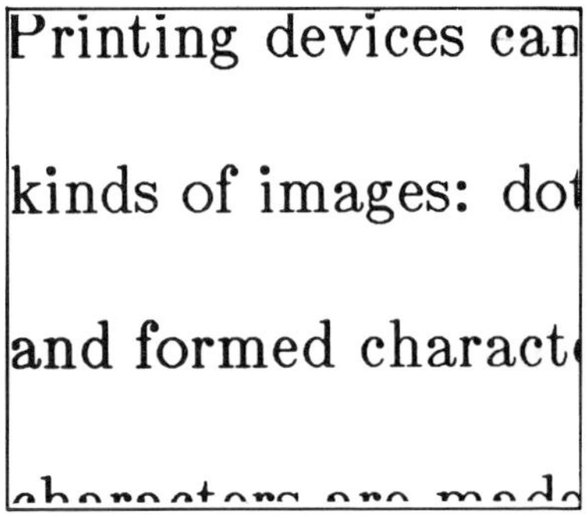

Microfilm and Microfiche

As more and more hard copy has been produced, the need to better handle and store it has also increased. Two popular ways of keeping permanent, readable copies of output are with **microfilm** and **microfiche**. Data is reduced in size and photographed onto thick film. Microfilm is stored in long rolls like filmstrips. Microfiche is stored as flat cards. The information that used to fill hundreds of sheets of paper can now be read from a single card or roll.

Plotters

The **plotter** is another device that prints hard copies of processed information. Plotters use data from the computer to guide pens across paper to draw images. Plotters can have various numbers of pens and these pens can be of several different colors. Some even combine two or more colors of ink to produce a spectrum of shades in complex drawings. Plotters are often used with computer graphics to make illustrations. Printers are more often used to print letters and numbers.

A plotter is especially useful for drawing graphs or pictures.

Voice Synthesis

Sometimes, though, the user may not require a paper copy of processed data. Data can be output in many other forms besides paper copies. With voice synthesis, for example, the computer can output information in spoken words rather than written or printed words. Voice synthesis is the opposite of voice recognition. The term *synthesis* means the process of making something artificially. For example, synthetic fabric is manmade, unlike cotton or wool, which are natural fabrics. The term *voice synthesis*, then, means that the computer, which has no natural voice, is making the sounds of the human voice artificially.

You have probably heard a computer "talk" through voice synthesis. If you dial a telephone number that has been changed recently, you may be given the new number by a computer that speaks each number separately. The computer is programmed to respond to a call to the old number by looking up the new number in its memory and telling you the number aloud. The computer does this task at a smaller cost than human workers do.

Voice synthesis is used in many different computer applications. It is often used in schools where young children are learning to use the computer. Talking to computers and having them talk back keeps students interested in their work on the computer. Through voice synthesis, the computer can help a student learn to read by pronouncing words that the student has trouble with. Or it can teach a student to speak a foreign language by carrying on a conversation in the new language.

Voice synthesis is also a valuable tool for the disabled. A person who cannot speak can type words into the computer and then command the computer to say the words. This enables the person to communicate with others. A sight-impaired person can use a special computer that can recognize letters in a book and read the book aloud. With this special device, blind people can read any book in a library rather than being limited to books that are printed in Braille.

Music Synthesis

Along with voice synthesis, computers can also synthesize music. No doubt you have heard songs in which computerized music synthesizers are used to produce unusual futuristic tones and special effects. Music synthesizers can also reproduce the sounds of most instruments in an orchestra. Some synthesizers can imitate many different instruments at once, and they do it so well that you may not be able to tell that it is a computer you are listening to and not a violin.

Music synthesizers can be used to perform and record music.

COMPUTER HARDWARE

They are also used by composers who want to hear what they have written and make changes to the music as they compose. And music synthesizers are very useful in teaching music theory. Students can learn to read music, for example, by programming notes into a computer and then playing the notes back on a music synthesizer.

Photo at left: Voice synthesis can make learning much more fun as the computer "talks" to the user. The computer may say aloud the words that a child has spelled, it may correct the child, or it may give some verbal encouragement.

Photo above: With a music synthesizer, a computer may produce what sounds like an entire orchestra through the use of one keyboard.

Robotics

Sometimes computers send data to other machines that use the information to do specific tasks. This is often the case with **robotics**. The computer can process data and then send the data to a robot. The robot then uses the data to do welding, moving, or lifting of objects. The robot can even use the data to adjust what it is doing so that it will do a better job.

CHECK WHAT YOU HAVE LEARNED

1. My robot never talks to me. What output device does it need if I want it to hold a conversation?
2. What are two common output devices that make hard copies of computer information? How are they different?
3. How does a dot matrix printer print one letter (character)?
4. Name two ways of printing where keys do not strike the paper.
5. What two things can computers synthesize?

How the Computer Works

How does the computer work? To understand this, you need to know a few simple things. You need to know about binary numbers, bits and bytes and buses, and computer languages.

Binary Numbers

The numbering system we normally use is the decimal system. The decimal system has ten digits—0 through 9. To portray large numbers, we show these digits in columns that represent ones, tens, hundreds, thousands, and so on. This system developed from human beings counting and calculating numbers by using their ten fingers.

The **binary** system is different because it uses only two digits—0 and 1. Instead of representing ones, tens, hundreds, thousands, and so on, the columns of a binary number represent ones, twos, fours, eights, sixteens, and so on. Another way to think of

COMPUTER HARDWARE 57

the columns is 1 times 1, 1 times 2, 2 times 2, 2 times 4, 2 times 8, and so on. For example, the decimal number 4 would look like 100 in binary. The 1 is in the fours column followed by 0 in the twos column and 0 in the ones column. Let us look at several more examples:

Decimal number	Binary number				
	8 (2 × 4)	4 (2 × 2)	2 (1 × 2)	1 (1 × 1)	
0				0	
1				1	
2			1	0	(one 2, zero 1s)
3			1	1	(one 2, one 1)
4		1	0	0	(one 4, no 2s or 1s)
5		1	0	1	(one 4, no 2s, one 1)
6		1	1	0	(one 4, one 2, no 1s)
7		1	1	1	(one 4, one 2, one 1)
8	1	0	0	0	(one 8, no 4s, 2s, or 1s)
9	1	0	0	1	(one 8, no 4s or 2s, one 1)
10	1	0	1	0	(one 8, no 4s or 1s, one 2)

As you can see from the examples, it takes more places to represent larger amounts in binary than in decimal. The decimal number 9, for example, is only one digit, but it takes four digits to show the numeral 9 in binary.

The binary numbering system is very important to computers because computers must use numbers as their language. A numbering system with only two digits is easy for an electronic machine to use. This is because the numbers 0 and 1 can be seen by the computer as either the presence of an electrical current (1) or the absence of an electrical current (0). In other words, as electrical current passes through the computer, the computer "reads" a 1 whenever it senses an electrical current and a 0 whenever there is no electrical current. The computer can read many of these signals in a very short time, so it is easy and quick to enter large numbers into the computer.

Bits, Bytes, and Buses

To the computer, 0 and 1 are the smallest pieces of information that can be read. These small pieces of information are called **bits**. Bits can be put together in many different ways to represent numbers, letters, and special symbols. This is similar to the way that letters of the alphabet can be put together to form words that we can read.

A bit is a single piece of information, but it takes a great number of bits to represent all of the information and instructions that the computer needs to do its work. Bits are organized into bigger units called **bytes** (pronounced like "bites"). A byte is usually made up of eight bits, although it can be larger or smaller.

Bits are entered into the computer memory to be stored and processed. In the computer's memory are divisions called **words**. A word can be one or more bytes. Each time the computer moves bits from one place to another, it takes one word at a time. Before the computer can move a word, though, it has to know where to find it. For this reason, each word has its own address within the

People and Computers

Lady Lovelace, Ada Augusta Byron

The Countess of Lovelace, born Ada Augusta Byron in 1815, was the only child of the famous English poet Lord Byron and his wife Annabella. As an adult, Lady Lovelace became a mathematician like her mother, and also became the close friend of Charles Babbage.

In addition to being a mathematician, Lady Lovelace had extraordinary verbal talent. She was able to explain Babbage's ideas much better than he could. It is because of Lady Lovelace that we have detailed accounts of Babbage's work. She also worked on the development of instructions for doing calculations on Babbage's analytical engine.

Ada Augusta Byron died at the age of thirty-six and was buried next to her father in Newstead, England. Because of her valuable work in the history of the computer field, the computer language ADA is named after her.

COMPUTER HARDWARE

memory of the computer. This is similar to the way we use an address to find the house where a friend lives. Each word has two parts: its address and the information that its bits contain.

When the computer is almost ready to use a word, it moves the word into a **register**. A register is a tiny memory space the size of one word. This gives the computer a place to store the word until it is ready to use it. The word does not stay in the register, though. When the computer is ready to use the word in the register, it moves the word to a different place and the register is empty for the next word.

The computer must also include some way for messages to go back and forth between the supervisor and other parts of the computer. Messages are sent back and forth by **buses**. Buses in the computer work something like public city buses. City buses travel along a route, stopping to pick up passengers and drop off passengers. Buses in the computer are circuits that pick up messages from parts of the computer and deliver them to other parts. One big difference between city buses and buses in the computer is that computer buses work at the speed of light. That is, they travel at 186,000 miles per second!

Buses carry messages inside the computer. But it is also necessary to get messages from devices outside the computer to the processor inside the computer. This is done through **interfaces**. An interface is a connection by cable between the computer input and output devices. Without it, people could not put information into computers or get information out of them.

Interfaces are usually built to do one specific job, such as send information out to the printer. However, some interfaces can be used with several different kinds of machines. With interfaces, the computer owner can add new devices to the computer so that it can perform all sorts of tasks. Interfaces can also allow computers to be connected to terminals, printers, and other devices that are many miles apart. This is important to businesses that have offices in different cities.

Computer memory is usually measured in **kilobytes**. A kilobyte (or K) consists of 1024 bytes of information. A byte is usually eight bits of information. So a computer with a memory of 512K can store more than 500,000 bytes of information.

Computer Languages

Now that you understand how the computer records the information it receives, you may be curious about how humans can communicate with computers in the first place. Keep in mind that the computer's language is made up of numbers: 0s and 1s. Since humans do not speak in numbers but in words, some way for humans to "talk" to machines had to be developed.

There are basically three types of languages for communicating with computers: machine language, assembly language, and high-level language. **Machine language** is made up of different arrangements of bits. This type of language, which is really made of numbers, is easy for the computer to understand. In fact, the computer understands machine language directly. Most machine languages use the binary numbering system we have just learned about. There is one problem with machine language. Although it is easy for the computer to understand, it is difficult for humans to write programs in this language. Therefore, other types of programming languages were developed.

Assembly language uses letters of the alphabet to represent the different arrangements of bits in machine language. Using letters as symbols is easier for humans to do. This makes programming in assembly language faster than programming in machine language. But because the computer understands only numbers, assembly language has to be translated into machine language in order for the computer to be able to interpret the instructions. Programs called assemblers translate programs from assembly languages into machine languages.

The third type of language is the **high-level language**. High-level languages are more similar to our regular language than machine language or assembly language are. So it is simpler to write in high-level languages. However, the computer cannot understand high-level language until it has been translated into machine language. Programs called **compilers** (or interpreters) translate programs from high-level languages into machine language. Some high-level languages are BASIC, COBOL, Pascal, FORTRAN, Forth, and ADA. We will talk about these languages and others in more detail in the next chapter.

CHECK WHAT YOU HAVE LEARNED

1. My mother is 100000 years old in binary. How old is she using the decimal system?
2. I saw 14 people walk 20 miles to raise $28 dollars for a local charity. How could I say that using binary numbers?
3. What do we call the smallest piece of information that can be read by the computer?

4. How many bits are usually in a byte?
5. How fast does a computer bus work?

Different Types of Computers

Now that you have a better idea of how the computer works, you are ready to learn about the different types of computers. If you have seen several computers, or pictures of computers, you have probably noticed that they are very different from each other. Some are very big and others are quite small. How can you tell the difference between the computers?

There are basically three types of computers: mainframes, minicomputers, and microcomputers. Sometimes experts do not agree on the differences among computers, but usually a computer is classified by its size.

Mainframe Computers

The largest and fastest computers in use today are **mainframes**. Mainframes have been in use for only a few years. Several features are usually mentioned in describing the mainframe. First, it has a very large memory so that it can store a great deal of information. Second, it does its work at very fast speeds. Third, it can use more than one input and output device. Fourth, it uses tapes or disks for secondary storage. Last, it is a very expensive computer, sometimes costing millions of dollars.

Mainframe computers can store millions of bytes of information. Also, they can do their work at a rate of more than 100 million computations per second. That speed is far too great for us to imagine! Mainframes are built to work as fast as possible since they are used by people who need to handle a great deal of information in the shortest time possible.

The biggest mainframes are known as supercomputers or number crunchers. Some common uses of supercomputers are for government and military purposes, for oil exploration, for forecasting weather, and for manufacturing airplanes. Supercomputers have also been used to create computer graphics for movies.

Not all mainframes are supercomputers, though. There are also smaller-sized mainframes. These mainframes do not have as

Mainframe computers are large, complex, powerful, and expensive. Supercomputers, or "number crunchers," are used by the government, by oil companies, for weather forecasting, and even to create the graphics for movies.

much memory as supercomputers or large mainframes have. More businesses and organizations use the small or medium-sized mainframes because they are not as expensive as larger mainframes. Even though they do not cost as much as larger mainframes, these mainframes are quite powerful and can work with large amounts of information. Smaller mainframes are becoming more popular all the time.

Minicomputers

You have just discovered what the largest computers available can do. There are other computers in the middle range of computer power. Such computers are called **minicomputers**. Minicomputers are smaller than mainframes, but they are bigger than microcomputers, which will be discussed later in this chapter.

The machinery of the minicomputer usually takes up less space than mainframe hardware. The minicomputer has a smaller memory than a mainframe computer has. It also has a smaller price tag. Like small mainframes, the minicomputer came into use in the 1960s and has become more and more popular since that time. Its use is very helpful to many businesses. Minicomputers are used to perform mathematical calculations. They are also used in factories to make sure that the products being made are all of good quality.

Careers and Computers

Operations Personnel

After instructions have been written to tell a mainframe computer how to do its work, someone has to actually run the computer. Someone is needed to turn the computer on, and to mount tapes or disks that contain data and information. Someone needs to keep it supplied with printer paper and other supplies it requires, and call in a computer technician if the computer breaks down. In addition, someone needs to enter the data that the computer uses to process information. The people who do these jobs are referred to as operations personnel. They are very important workers wherever computers are used.

In fact, many people begin their careers in the computer field as operations personnel. The main reason for this is that operations jobs usually do not require a great deal of training and experience. Most operations personnel are trained on the job by the company that has hired them. With the hands-on experience they get from their jobs, they can learn about computers and prepare themselves for other computer-related jobs.

COMPUTER OPERATORS

Computer operators are those people who actually run the mainframe computer. It is their responsibility to turn the computer on at the beginning of a workday and to turn it off at the end of the day. They also load programs by mounting disks or tapes and giving the computer a command to read the programs on the disks and tapes. In large computer installations, the computer operator must keep track of the schedule of jobs to be done on the computer. This way, all of the work is done when it needs to be finished.

The computer operator also keeps the printer supplied with paper and ribbons. This is important so that the computer can output data, information, and reports. It is also the computer operator's job to keep a close eye on the computer to make sure that it is working properly. When something goes wrong, the computer operator must notify someone who knows how to repair the computer. Many computer operators have little formal training in computers. They are usually trained on the job. Often, after learning how the computer works, the computer operator takes classes to become a programmer or other computer professional. This job is a good starting point for other computer careers.

DATA ENTRY OPERATORS

Data entry operators type information into the mainframe computer so that it can do its work. Data entry is usually done on a keyboard with a CRT, and the data entry operator must be able to type quickly and correctly. It is important that the data entered into the computer be correct. If the input is incorrect, then the output will also be incorrect.

Like the computer operator, the data entry operator is often trained on the job. Good typing skills are required. This job may also lead to other computer careers.

Farmers

Farmers are using computers in many aspects of their lives. Like many people in small business, farmers find computers useful for calculating how much they have spent and how much is owed to them. With a computer, the farmer is able to calculate what his or her budget will be like if an investment is made for new equipment. The additional growth in the business which the new equipment might allow can be compared to the cost of the equipment. In this way, the farmer can make an informed decision about making the investment.

In addition to this function, some farmers are using computers to monitor other aspects of their farms. For example, electronic eyes in the feed bins for cows and transistorized sensors around the cows' necks can tell dairy farmers exactly how much food the cows have eaten. Their diet can be carefully controlled so that the cows eat exactly the right amount of food for each pound of milk that they give.

During the 1970s, minicomputers grew more popular as businesses began to computerize their work. Designers of minicomputers began creating minicomputers that met specific needs of small businesses, and this made minicomputers more popular. Like mainframes, minicomputers are very useful in business. In recent years, minicomputers have become more powerful. At the same time, the cost of minicomputers has dropped.

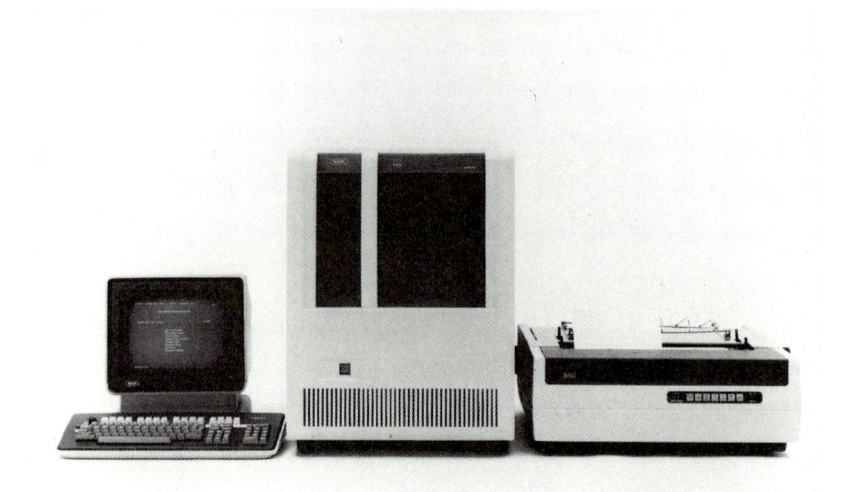

Minicomputer systems may include a computer and several terminals and printers. They are very useful in large offices, where many people may need to do work on the computer at the same time.

Minicomputers can be used by more than one person at the same time. This makes them very useful in large offices where many people need to do work on the computer. For secondary storage, most minicomputers use magnetic disks or tapes.

Microcomputers

Of the three common types of computers, the one you are most familiar with is probably the **microcomputer**. Microcomputers are almost everywhere—in schools, homes, offices, hospitals, and libraries, for example. Wherever people have work to do, the microcomputer can be found. Today there are more than 100 different brands of microcomputers being sold. Microcomputers first appeared on the market in the 1970s.

The most obvious difference between microcomputers and other computers is size. The microcomputer system is designed to fit on a desk top. This is quite a contrast to the old computers of the 1940s and 1950s that took up entire rooms! The microcomputer's small size makes it very convenient to use in offices or homes.

Another obvious difference between microcomputers and other computers is cost. Microcomputers cost much less than other computers. In fact, the price of microcomputers seems to be decreasing all the time. Depending on the brand of microcomputer

You may have a microcomputer in your home or school. Because it can fit on a desk top and is relatively inexpensive, the microcomputer is becoming a very popular computer for small businesses, schools, and homes.

and the additional peripherals used with it, microcomputers usually cost under $10,000. Compared to the cost of a supercomputer, that is not very expensive.

However, we must remember that microcomputers are not as powerful or as fast as supercomputers. Microcomputers usually have much smaller memory sizes than larger computers. Since the microcomputer does not usually have a very large memory, it is important to use secondary storage devices. The two most common types of storage devices used with microcomputers are tapes and disks.

The Future and Computers

The Next Generation of Computers

Most computer scientists believe that computers will become even smaller in the future. We already have computers that will fit easily in your hand. Compare that to the early, room-sized computers, and you will see how far we have come. As computers become smaller, they usually become faster as well. This will be important to us as we do more and more of our work on computers.

One way to make computers faster is to improve the memory they use. A type of memory that computer scientists are working on is **bubble memory**. Bubble memory is made up of magnetized crystalline materials. Memory cells form a series of bubbles from the crystalline materials. These contain tremendous amounts of magnetized material that holds data and programs. Bubble memory allows the computer to store more information and instructions in less space, as well as using less electrical energy. And bubble memory units are usually less than 2 inches square in size. Once it is fully developed, bubble memory may very well replace other kinds of memory.

Computer scientists will also try to develop new and different computerized robots in the future. You have probably seen robots in movies, but remember that not all robots look like mechanical people. Many robots are simply machines that do hard or boring work that humans cannot do or do not want to do. Artificial intelligence will give machines the ability to figure out solutions to problems by themselves, unlike the computers of today that need human programmers to tell them how to solve problems.

Computers have developed rapidly during recent years. They have become faster, more reliable, smaller, and less expensive. Now that you know more about computers, perhaps you can make some guesses of your own about what computers will be like in the future. After all, those are the computers that you will be using to manage your office and your home.

COMPUTER HARDWARE

Microcomputers can be programmed in a variety of programming languages, and this makes them very useful to those who want to write their own programs. The language that is most commonly used with microcomputers is BASIC. BASIC is one of the easiest programming languages to learn. It is a popular choice for microcomputer programming, since it is often done by people who are not computer experts. Other languages such as COBOL, FORTRAN, Pascal, Logo, and PILOT can be used with some microcomputer systems.

CHECK WHAT YOU HAVE LEARNED

1. What are two major differences between a mainframe and a minicomputer?
2. What kind of computer should a small neighborhood business get? Why?
3. What are some uses of supercomputers?
4. Name one reason why BASIC is a popular programming language for microcomputers.
5. Which is more powerful: a computer with a memory of 2K or one with a memory of 64K? Why?

WHAT YOU HAVE LEARNED IN CHAPTER TWO

Every computer system performs three basic operations: input, processing and storage, and output. Input hardware lets the operator tell the computer what to do. Processing and storage hardware is where the computer does its work. Output hardware allows the computer to show what it has done.

Input hardware is used by the operator to put information and data into the computer. The most common input device is a keyboard like a typewriter keyboard. Magnetic tapes or diskettes can also enter material already stored on them. A modem allows computers to communicate by phone, entering the information from one computer into another. Optical character recognition lets the computer read printed characters such as bar codes. Magnetic ink character recognition sends data to the computer by reading characters printed in magnetic ink. Voice recognition devices allow the computer to understand the spoken word.

Once the computer has the information, it must do its work in the processor. The processor includes both the central processing unit (CPU) and the main storage area. The CPU has two parts. A control unit acts like a supervisor and controls the other parts of the computer system. An arithmetic logic unit (ALU) does all of the calculating for the computer.

The main storage area, or memory, is where the computer keeps the information that it must remember. This can be enlarged by adding special memory boards. A memory board is a card onto which chips (integrated circuits) have been placed. Another way to increase the computer's memory size is by adding a hard disk. A hard disk is usually inside the computer. It stores a greater amount of information in a smaller space than can be stored on diskettes. The hard disk does not lose its data even when the computer is turned off. Hard disks, diskettes, and tapes are called secondary storage because the information is not a part of the computer's main memory.

After the computer has done its work, it must send the information back to the operator. This is called outputting the data. Usually, data is shown on a CRT screen, printed on a paper, or stored on a diskette or tape. Additional components might include voice or music synthesizers. Voice synthesizers allow the computer to output data in spoken words. Music synthesizers output data in musical tones. Users choose output devices based on the form in which they need data.

The computer uses the binary number system (0s and 1s). Information coded in binary is stored in a memory made up of integrated circuits. The integrated circuits are put together to form a chip. There are several different kinds of memory chips: RAM (random-access memory), ROM (read-only memory), and PROM (programmable read-only memory).

We are able to communicate with computers with the help of three types of programming languages: machine language, assembly language, and high-level language. Some examples of high-level languages are BASIC, COBOL, Pascal, and ADA.

There are three major types of computers: mainframes, minicomputers, and microcomputers. Mainframes are the largest and fastest computers, and are used by the government and large businesses. Minicomputers, used by businesses, are smaller and have a smaller memory than mainframes. Microcomputers are small (to fit on a desk top) and are used in schools, homes, offices, and hospitals.

COMPUTER HARDWARE

1. What does the CPU allow the computer to do?
2. Name one way to increase a computer's memory.
3. Name two common output devices.
4. What are computer chips made up of?
5. Name two popular types of secondary storage.
6. What does the ALU help the computer to do?
7. What are the two main parts of the CPU?
8. What does a modem allow the computer to do?
9. Who is most likely to use a mainframe computer?
10. What number system is used by computers?

USING WORDS YOU HAVE LEARNED

1. Storing data on magnetic disks or tape is known as _____ storage.
2. The printer is a common device used to _____ data.
3. A _____ is used to allow computers to communicate over telephone lines.
4. The largest mainframes are known as number crunchers or _____ .
5. The ALU is located in the _____ _____ unit.
6. A person who is paralyzed might use a _____ _____ device to input data into his or her computer.
7. When a computer outputs with spoken words it is using a _____ _____ .
8. A keyboard is sometimes used to _____ data.
9. One way to increase the speed of a computer is to put a _____ board in the CPU.
10. The smallest piece of information that can be read by a computer is called a _____ .

EXERCISING YOUR MATH SKILLS

Look at the five cards in the next column. They are named by the number in the upper left-hand corner: the #1 card, the #2 card, and the #4, #8, and #16 cards.

Ask a friend to think of any number between 0 and 32 without telling you the number. Then have your friend point to the cards that show that number. By adding up the numbers (1, 2, 4, 8, or 16) of all the cards your friend points to, you can find the secret number.

#1 Card	#2 Card	#4 Card
1 3 5 7	2 3 6 7	4 5 6 7
9 11 13 15	10 11 14 15	12 13 14 15
17 19 21 23	18 19 22 23	20 21 22 23
25 27 29 31	26 27 30 31	28 29 30 31

#8 Card	#16 Card
8 9 10 11	16 17 18 19
12 13 14 15	20 21 22 23
24 25 26 27	24 25 26 27
28 29 30 31	28 29 30 31

Suppose your friend points to the #1 card, the #8 card, and the #16 card. Add those numbers. Do you get 25? Your friend's number is 25. Now suppose the secret number is 14. Where does 14 appear? It appears on the #2 card, the #4 card, and the #8 card. These numbers—2, 4, and 8—add up to 14.

The numbers in the upper left-hand corners of the cards—1, 2, 4, 8, and 16—are multiples of 2 by itself. These types of numbers make up the binary number system. A computer can register 0 and 1 easily by means of an on-off switch (or light, or electrical charge): on equals 1; off equals 0. The more switches a computer has, the more capability it has for processing numbers. Think of these cards as switches. Each card either contains the number we guessed or it doesn't. Write a 1 if the number is on the card and a 0 if it isn't. Start with the #16 card and work to the #1 card. For example, the number 27 does appear on the #16 and #8 cards, it does not appear on the #4 card, and it does appear on the #2 and #1 cards. Writing a 1 for yes and a 0 for no, we get 11011, or 27 in the binary number system. You have used the binary system to find the number!

UNDERSTANDING WHAT YOU HAVE LEARNED

MULTIPLE CHOICE

1. The actual equipment of the computer is called:
   a) input devices
   b) hardware
   c) software
   d) CPU
2. The part of the computer that processes data is called the:
   a) CRT
   b) OCR
   c) CPU
   d) MICR
3. The device that allows a computer to speak in a human voice is:
   a) a voice recognition device
   b) an optical character recognition device
   c) a cathode ray tube device
   d) a voice synthesis device
4. To input data into the first computers, operators used:
   a) keypunch machines
   b) terminals
   c) cybernetic interface devices
   d) modems
5. The smallest piece of information that can be read by a computer is called a:
   a) byte
   b) word
   c) register
   d) bit
6. The computer can write information onto a:
   a) music synthesizer
   b) PROM chip
   c) ROM chip
   d) CPU
7. A family is most likely to own:
   a) a number cruncher
   b) a minicomputer
   c) an MICR
   d) a microcomputer
8. It is faster to access data stored on:
   a) a magnetic diskette
   b) a magnetic tape
   c) a CRT
   d) a keyboard
9. A voice recognition device is:
   a) an output device
   b) a central processing unit
   c) an input device
   d) a storage device
10. BASIC is:
    a) a machine language
    b) an assembly language
    c) a binary number system
    d) a high-level language

TRUE OR FALSE

1. A modem allows computers to "talk" over the phone.
2. A laser dot matrix character is more difficult to read than a formed character.
3. Sequential access is faster than random access.
4. The CPU includes the control unit and the arithmetic logic unit.
5. The voice synthesizer can help people who cannot speak.

COMPUTER HARDWARE

6. Output can be done by a keyboard.
7. A magnetic disk is a secondary storage device.
8. The smallest piece of information a computer can read is called a bit.
9. Supercomputers use a keypunch system of inputting data.
10. A store might use an MICR to read bar codes.

SHORT ANSWER

1. Name two ways to store data.
2. What are the three operations performed by any computer system?
3. What output device might a composer use to help him or her write music?
4. Name two problems with the keypunch method of inputting data.
5. What does the arithmetic logic unit (ALU) do?
6. Name one way that an operator might improve his or her computer's memory.
7. What device is used by the telephone company to tell us that a telephone number has been changed?
8. What number system does the computer use?
9. What are the three major types of computers?
10. Why are floppy disks popular for data entry?

THE MAKING OF A CHIP

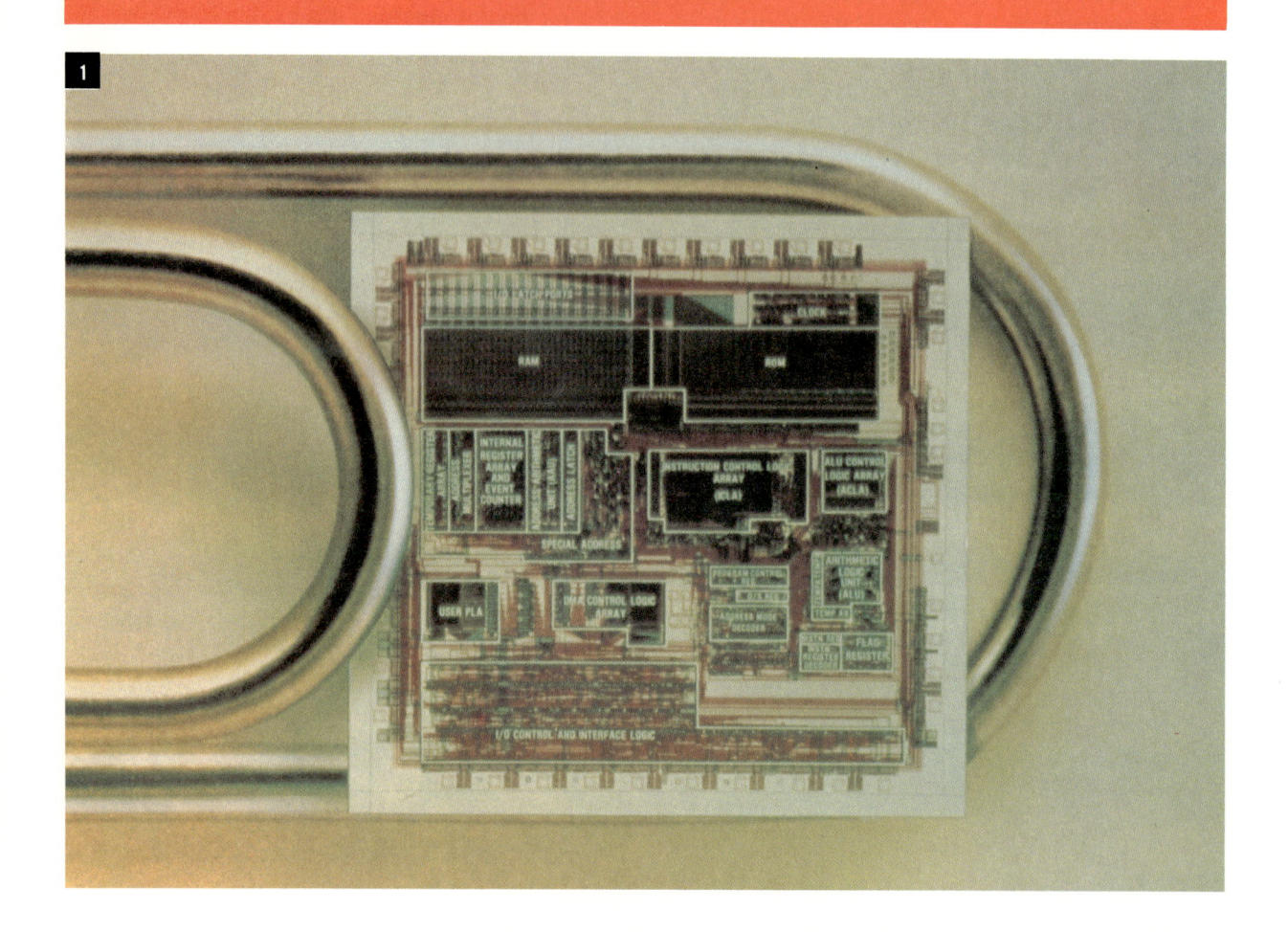

1

A very small piece of material called silicon can be transformed into an electronic circuit, capable of conducting electricity to operate the fastest of computers. The sequence of pictures on the next few pages shows the production of a chip from its planning stages to the finished product.

(**1**) A single chip, so tiny that it rests comfortably on the end of a paper clip, is capable of processing and storing large amounts of data. (**2**) When the chip is packaged in a protective case, it is still only about the size of a dime.

The planning stages in making a chip begin with drawings that are usually much larger than a road map! These drawings (**3**) consist of various electronic circuits that will perform different jobs on one chip.

THE MAKING OF A CHIP

The many different circuit drawings are put together in one final drawing (**4**)—at this stage, the drawing is 400 times larger than the actual finished chip.

A computer operator then traces over each circuit in the large drawing (**5**), "computerizing" the information, using a computer graphics system. This stage, called *digitizing*, makes it possible for a computer to store the circuit information on magnetic tape. The information on tape is used to make masks, which are patterns of the different circuits. (When finished, a chip will consist of many different layers of circuits, made from the patterns of many different masks.) At this stage, the masks are also dramatically reduced in size so the circuits will fit the final size of the tiny chip.

A chip is originally part of a silicon wafer. Silicon, one of the most available substances on earth, is the most widely used raw material for wafer fabrication. When silicon is first purified and heated in a special way, it forms a crystal that can be sliced into very thin circular pieces, or wafers. (Each wafer is about three inches in diameter, and is large enough to produce several hundred chips.)

PHOTO ESSAY

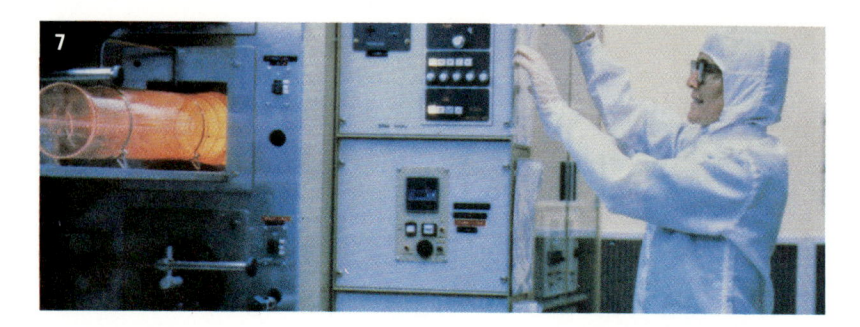

The chip-making process requires many steps that include dipping the wafer in acid baths (**6**), baking it in a furnace at extremely high temperatures (**7**), exposing it to ultra-violet light, and giving it many different washings. Many of these steps are repeated, with every step taking place in a "clean room," air-conditioned, and free of dust that may damage the process, with workers wearing special clothing, similar to suits worn in hospital operating rooms (**8**).

The wafer is carefully inspected (**9**) and tested to make sure it functions properly. Sometimes computers that can "see" check for flaws—if the wafer is not made exactly as designed, it is rejected. Because chips are made on one wafer, a cutting machine automatically and precisely cuts the wafer into separate chips (**10**). Each chip is then ready for final assembly.

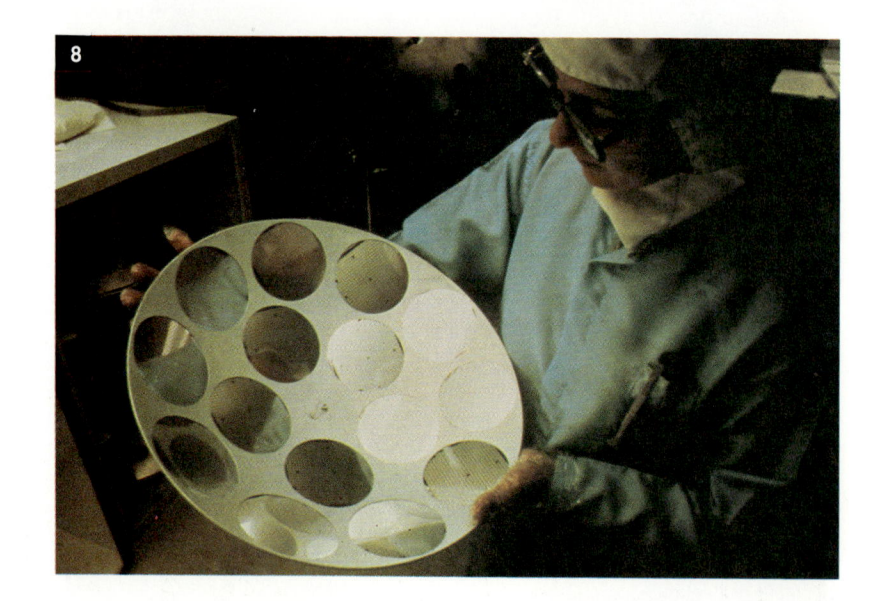

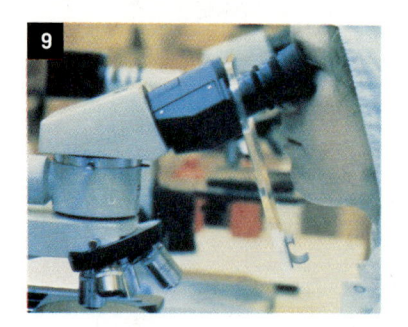

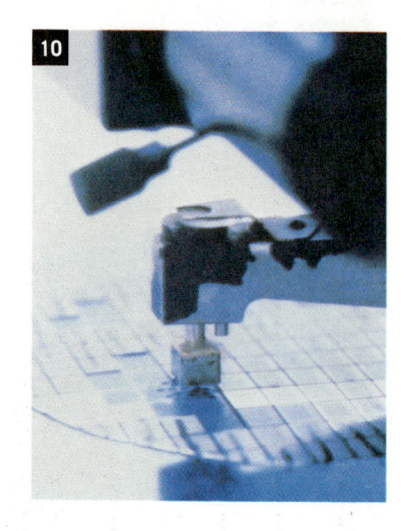

THE MAKING OF A CHIP

75

Special connective gold wires are attached to the chip (**11**), and these and other connectors are attached to the final protective packaging (**12**). The chip in this form is now a complete integrated circuit and package, and it is ready to be plugged into an electronic system within a computer.

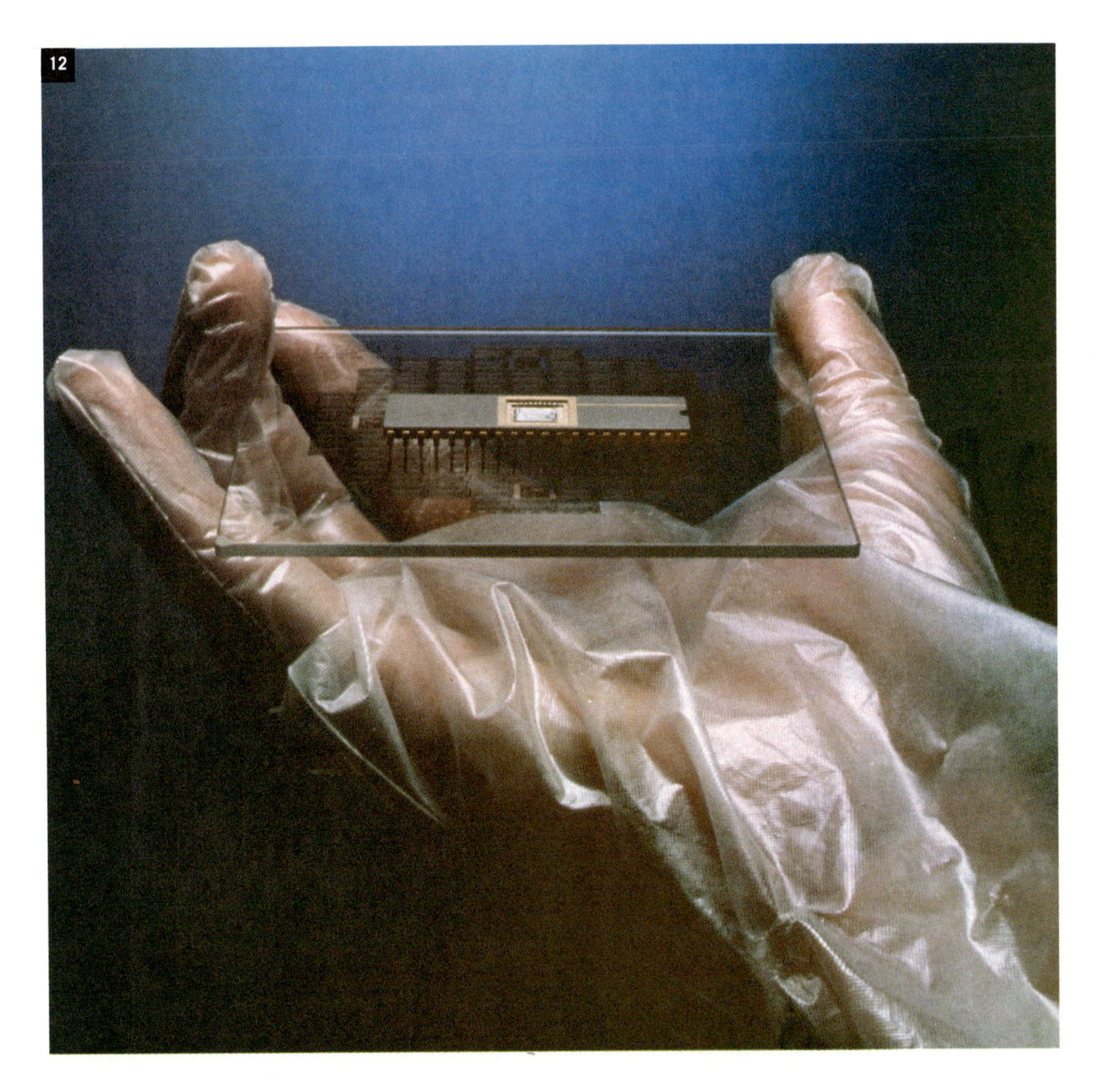

WHAT YOU WILL LEARN IN CHAPTER THREE

By the end of this chapter, you will be able to:

1. Define computer software.
2. Explain the difference between system software and application software.
3. Identify four computer applications.
4. Name three ways to plan a computer program.
5. Identify at least four computer languages and tell how they differ.

Getting Down to Business: Software and Applications

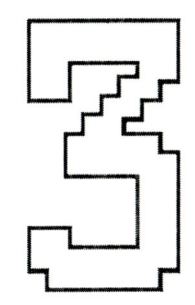

WORDS YOU WILL LEARN

algorithm
application software
authoring language
BASIC
COBOL
code
data base
debug
flowchart
Forth
FORTRAN
integrated software
LISP
Logo
Pascal
PILOT
pseudocode
software
spreadsheet
system software (operating system software)
top-down structured programming
word processing

We have looked at some of the parts of the computer itself. But now that we know about the machine, how can we tell the machine what to do? This chapter will explore some of the ways that people can give instructions to a computer. We will also learn about some of the things that people ask computers to do.

Software Basics

There are two important parts of the computer system that help it to do its work: hardware and software. As you have learned, hardware is the physical equipment of the computer itself. **Software**, on the other hand, is the instructions that humans write to tell the computer how to do its jobs. The computer needs both hardware and software in order to work properly. It needs software to tell it what to do, and it needs hardware to actually carry out the work.

Software is another word for computer programs. Programs are the actual instructions that the user gives the computer. People who write instructions for computers are called programmers. A program might tell the computer how to calculate an employee's paycheck or locate a book in a school library. Computer programs are an important link between computers and the people who want to use them.

At first, one of the problems in making computer systems was in developing ways for people to communicate with their computers. Without the right instructions, or programs, computers could not do their work. But how could people tell the computers what they needed? It was necessary to design languages that could be understood by both computers and people. This was not easy. People use words to communicate, but computers understand only numbers. Computer languages had to be developed so that words used by people could be translated into numbers that the computer could read.

Early computer languages were very complicated. It took a great deal of time for programmers to learn to use them. Writing programs in these languages was a time-consuming process. It was difficult for most people to learn to program a computer. Often, they did not want to spend the time necessary to learn a programming language. Computer experts realized that simpler languages were needed if the computer was to be used by many people. Languages were designed to be easier to use.

Two Types of Computer Software

There are two kinds of computer software. The first kind is called operating system software or just system software. The second kind is called application software.

System Software

System software is a set of rules and instructions that helps the computer's operating system. For example, a program that tells the computer how to accept input information is part of the system software. Also, a program that tells the computer how to output information is part of system software. System software is written by a system programmer. It usually comes with the computer. Sometimes the user can choose from two or more operating systems to use with the same computer.

Let us look at the operating system and what it does. The operating system is a set of programs that controls what the computer does. Without its operating system, the computer cannot do anything! The operating system controls how information and instructions are sent from one part of the computer to another.

In most computer systems, the computer seems to do several different jobs at once. Actually, the computer does not do all of them at the same time. If it did, all of the information from the different jobs would get mixed up. What it really does is move back and forth from job to job very quickly. To a human, it seems as if the computer is doing all of the jobs at once.

When a computer is doing several jobs, it needs a way to organize them. For this reason, the **supervisor**, which is part of the computer's operating system, tells the computer what order to do the jobs in. It also tells the computer how and when to accept input or send out output. This keeps all of the work of the computer organized. The supervisor also gets the instructions for a specific job from the tape or disk where they are stored. It loads the program into the main memory of the computer, where the computer can read the program. This way, the computer knows how to do the job it has been given.

The supervisor has other jobs to do as well. When a person tries to use the computer, the supervisor has to make sure that the person has permission to get into the system. Otherwise, people who are not allowed to use the computer could make problems. This is true when the computer stores private information.

Once the supervisor has made sure that the person who wants to use the computer is allowed to do so, it must follow the orders of the user. It must find out what program the user needs. Then it loads that program into the main memory of the computer. While the computer is carrying out the instructions of the program, the supervisor controls all of the activities of the computer. When the computer has finished its work, the supervisor sends a message to the user that the job is done.

It will be easy for you to remember what a supervisor of the computer's operating system does if you compare it to the human supervisor in an office. In an office, the supervisor makes sure that other workers do the work that they are supposed to do. The supervisor advises them when to do their job so that all of the jobs are finished on time. The supervisor also makes sure that everyone knows how to do his or her job.

Besides the supervisor, there are other programs included in the computer's operating system. There are language translators, for example. We have already seen that most of the programs that people write for computers have to be translated. The computer can only understand the program in machine language. Language translators are programs that translate the other programs into machine language. There are different language translators for different programming languages.

The computer's operating system also contains utility programs. Utility programs help the computer do many different things. For instance, a utility program may help the computer to copy information from one diskette to another. Or it may tell the computer how to print out a paper copy of information.

Some large computer systems also have programs that tell them when the computer needs service. There are also system programs to help the computer operator find out what is wrong with the computer when it does not operate well.

CHECK WHAT YOU HAVE LEARNED

1. Name three things that the supervisor of the computer operating system does.
2. What is system software?
3. What is another word for software?
4. Why was it difficult to write computer programs in the early days of computers?
5. What kind of program helps the computer to copy information from one diskette to another?

Careers and Computers

System and Programming Personnel

By itself, the computer can do nothing. It is a helpless machine without the people who write instructions to tell it how to do a specific job. The people who do this are called system and programming personnel. Among these people are system analysts, system programmers, application programmers, programmer/analysts, and data base specialists.

System Analysts

The system analyst is a very respected computer specialist. Without system software, application software would be useless. The system analyst must design a system for work to be done. In other words, system analysts have to invent ways for the computer to operate before the system software can be written.

If the manager of a payroll department that prepares paychecks for company employees wants to start using a computer instead of doing everything by hand, he or she calls a system analyst. The manager explains all of the steps in doing payroll to the system analyst. Then the analyst designs a process for the computer to follow in order to do the payroll. Once the system is designed, the analyst explains it to the system programmer, who will write the system software. The analyst also explains it to the application programmer, who will write the step-by-step process to tell the computer what to do.

The system analyst has a good deal of contact with other company employees who need to find ways to do their work by computer. For this, analysts need good communication skills. They must also know how to understand problems and figure out solutions. Above all, the system analyst is a problem-solver.

Many system analysts began their careers as either system programmers or application programmers. Then they are able to work into system analysis. Most companies prefer that a system analyst have a college degree, either in computer science or in a business-related field. They also prefer analysts who have had experience working with computers.

In general, system analysts earn more money than programmers do. They have a lot of contact with other people in a company. As computers are used in more areas, more system analysts will be needed. The need for system analysts will increase in the next ten years.

System Programmers

System programmers write instructions that tell the computer how to operate. These programs are the computer's operating system. The operating system is a bridge between the computer and the information and instructions that it gets. It tells the computer how to accept data, how to process information, how to send output to the printer, how to turn on disk or tape drives, and how to do other operations that are necessary to run other programs.

Like system analysts, system programmers are problem-solvers. First they are told what the computer is expected to do. Then they must write programs that tell the computer how to do this work. After they write their programs, they must test them to be sure that the programs work correctly. System programmers spend much of their time debugging system software. It is important that they like working with details. Some bugs in programs are caused by very minor details that can be easy to overlook.

Often, system programmers begin as application programmers. They can be promoted to system programmers after gaining experience in writing software. The system programmer usually has more technical knowledge about the way the computer works than the application programmer has. Most system programmers have college degrees, usually in computer science.

System programmers often earn more than application programmers. They are always faced with challenges that provide interesting work. Like all other programmers, system programmers will continue to be in demand in the future.

Software Designers

Another name for the computer programmer is software designer. This person writes programs that perform tasks many users will find helpful. The software designer who writes prepackaged software tries to make sure to write a program that can be used by many people.

Software designers may not be full-time employees of the software publisher. They may write programs independently and then sell them to the publisher. The programmer may receive a royalty for each copy of the program that is sold (a royalty is a percentage of the purchase price).

Knowledge of a programming language is essential for this job. Programmers must also be very logical and very patient. It is likely that they will have to spend some time testing and debugging the program before it is published.

Technical Writers

After a program is written but before it can be sold, the technical writer has to write a set of instructions for it. The instructions tell the user how the program works and what it can do. Without clear instructions, many users would not be able to run the program. The same is true for computer hardware. Some technical writers write instructions for operating computers and the equipment that is used with computers.

Technical writers have a variety of skills. They must have technical knowledge of the products being written about. It is also essential that technical writers be able to write clear instructions that are easy for users to follow. In addition, technical writers must work closely with engineers and programmers who are most familiar with the product.

Law Enforcement Officers

Computers are being used to make the law enforcement officer's job much easier. Vast amounts of information about crimes, criminals, and missing persons are kept in computers. Criminal records can be accessed through the National Crime Information Center (NCIC). These can help police track lawbreakers.

> For example, the name of a person who has not paid an out-of-state parking ticket may be entered into a computer that contains information about drivers' records throughout the United States. The person can then be located at the most current address, even though he or she is no longer in the state where the crime was committed.
>
> Some patrol cars are equipped with portable computer terminals. The law enforcement officer can use the computer to get information about stolen cars, previously apprehended suspects, and even gun registrations. Police work and police investigation have been dramatically changed by the addition of computers.

Application Software

The second type of software is called **application software**. These are programs that tell the computer how to do specific jobs for the user. Application means the purpose for which we use the computer. For example, using computers in the classroom to help students learn mathematics is an application of the computer.

The computer gets instructions from application software. It may find out how to write payroll checks in a business or how to calculate a student's grade in school. Application software is written by an application programmer. Application software runs under the direction of the operating system of the computer. Without an application program, the computer would not be very useful.

There are many application programs on the market today. Some application software is used in schools to help students learn many different subjects. Some programs are used in offices to process words and numbers that keep businesses operating. Others are game programs that entertain the people who use them. There is almost no limit to the number of application programs that are available to computer users.

Three important types of application programs are word processing, data base, and spreadsheet. A **word processing** program is a program that helps the user to prepare a written document. Suppose you are writing a business letter. If you use a typewriter, you must go back and correct every mistake. This takes time. If you decide that you think the last paragraph really ought to come first, you must retype the whole document. You might decide that five other people should get the same letter, and you must retype the letter with a different introduction each time. With word processing, the user types the letter using a keyboard, but the letter does not go straight to a piece of paper. The user can see the

Word processing is a very important computer function. Because a document can be revised or changed before being printed, a great deal of time and energy can be saved.

Data base systems (like the one displayed on the CRT here) help save and organize important information.

letter on the CRT, read it, correct it, and change it before he or she ever sends it to the printer. He or she can then save the letter on a disk so that it will be ready to use again, or change it slightly for later use. Word processing saves a great deal of time in offices where written reports, business letters, and memos can be very important.

A **data base** program can also save a business a lot of time. The data base is simply a method of organizing information. In this way, it is similar to a filing system. But a computer data base can be much more efficient than a paper filing system. For example, a company might enter information about all of its customers on a computer data base. In January, the user might ask the computer to list out all of the customers that have a birthday in that month. The company can send them birthday cards. Or the user might ask the computer to list all the customers who live

SOFTWARE AND APPLICATIONS 85

in Texas or all the customers who have bought a specific product over the last year. The computer can search its data base to find customers who fit certain descriptions. It can do this much more easily than a human can search a filing system. Can you imagine how long it would take a human to look through 1000 files to find out which customers have birthdays in January?

Spreadsheets keep track of and calculate important numerical information.

A **spreadsheet** is an electronic ledger (a ledger is a book containing records of financial transactions). It can help to plan and account for the finances of a business. Instead of entering the amounts that have been paid or received in a book, the business can enter those amounts into the computer spreadsheet. The spreadsheet shows amounts in specific columns. The computer can add or subtract the figures in the columns and can figure out the company's profit or loss. For example, if a company needs to find out how much it has spent on paper goods over the past year, the computer spreadsheet can figure this out very quickly. It can also tell the user what the effects would be if more or less money were spent in a certain area. This is how the spreadsheet helps with planning. When the company is considering making a new investment, the spreadsheet can tell the user how that investment might change the figures.

A spreadsheet can show other information—it is not limited to representing amounts of money. For example, a teacher can use a spreadsheet to record test scores. Once the information is in the spreadsheet, the teacher can use it to compute grade averages, print grades, and show the results in a chart or table.

Real estate investors can use a spreadsheet to analyze property to buy. For example, a spreadsheet can show the total purchase price. But it can also figure and show what monthly payments would be required over a certain number of years. The spreadsheet can help an investor make a better decision to buy or not.

Application software can be bought in computer stores or other stores. Sometimes, the software publisher can sell software electronically. For example, games can be sold to customers who get their software through cable television rather than having to go to a store. This is a fast and convenient way of buying computer programs. It is possible that much software will be purchased in this way in the future.

Another way to get computer programs is to have them written specially for the jobs that the computer must do. A scientist or engineer may hire a computer programmer to do this. This is useful for scientists or engineers who want custom programs designed to meet their own needs. Big research institutes often have a number of computer programmers who write operating system and application software to keep their scientific research running.

Small-computer users also write their own programs. Many people who buy home computers find that they enjoy writing programs. This way, they can create programs that do exactly what they want the computer to do. These people may take classes in computer programming, or they may learn to program by reading books and experimenting with their computers. Writing their own programs allows them to design software that fits their own needs and wants.

CHECK WHAT YOU HAVE LEARNED

1. What is a data base? Name three ways that a business might use its data base.
2. What do application programs tell the computer to do?
3. What is a spreadsheet?
4. How does word processing save time?
5. Why do you need application software?

SOFTWARE AND APPLICATIONS

Integrated Software

There are many different kinds of software available for computer users today. Programs can help with writing (word processors), managing information (data base), financial planning (spreadsheets), displaying information (graphics), entertainment (games), education (CAI), and many other applications. As computers have become more popular, computer software has become an important business. More and more software publishers are racing to meet the needs of computer users.

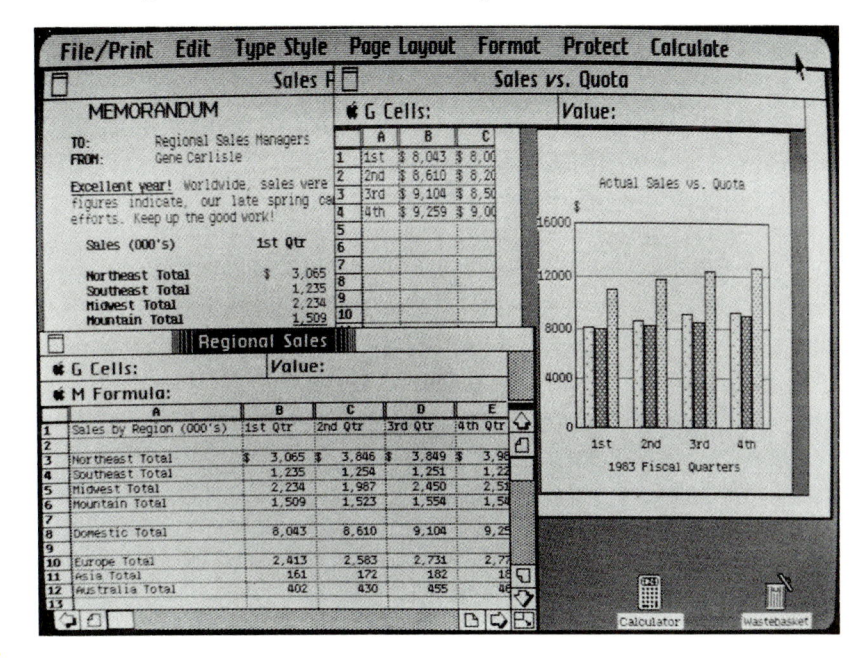

By using integrated software, a business can show a number of different items of interest at the same time.

One way that they are meeting these needs is through **integrated software**. Integrated programs are programs that can communicate with each other. Several years ago, a user could buy programs that would do almost any job that needed to be done by a computer. But each time a different program was run, the user had to change the disk or tape to load a new program on the computer. There was no easy way to use information that was in one program with another program.

For example, let's say that you are running an ice cream store. You have a microcomputer that helps you run your business. One program automatically keeps track of your inventory so that you know which flavors of ice cream are selling well. It can tell you when you need to reorder. But if you want to write a letter telling your supplier which flavors to send, you must use your word processing program to do this. The only way to use the figures from the inventory program in your letter is to type them into the document you are writing with your word processing program. This is slow and tedious. You also want to use these same inventory figures to show your main office that you are selling more mint chocolate chip ice cream than anything else. You can create a bar graph or a pie chart with your graphics program. The only drawback is that you must type the inventory figures into the computer again. If your programs could only talk to each other, you would have more time to dip and sell ice cream.

This is where integrated software can help. These programs can talk to each other. With integrated software, you could command your word processing program to read the inventory figures in from the inventory program automatically. You could command the graphics program to do the same thing. In fact, after the graphics program does its bar chart based on the inventory figures, you could read the bar chart into your word processing report. You could place the chart in the middle of the report. You could do all this without having to retype the inventory figures even one time!

With computer-aided design (CAD), engineers can develop and test computer models before building their products. Here, an engineer uses CAD to design cars. Integrated software can be used to prepare a written report that includes this graphic display.

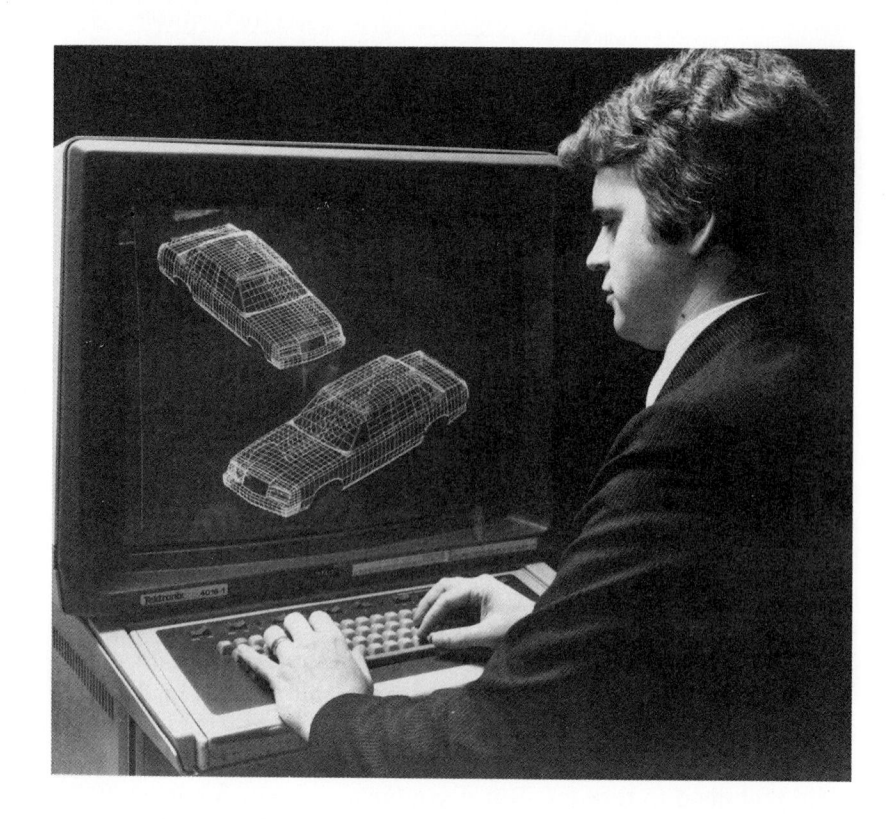

SOFTWARE AND APPLICATIONS

A display can be divided into several windows that show data from several programs at once.

Many integrated software packages have a feature known as a **window**. A window is an area of the screen that shows you information from a specific program. The screen might be divided into several windows so that you can see data from several programs at once. This is a very useful tool in business. For example, the businessperson might like to look at information from inventory programs, financial planning programs, and graphics programs all at the same time.

A computer equipped with a mouse makes it easy to use software packages that have windows as a feature. Simply by moving the mouse so that the cursor points to different areas within the windows, the user can move those items to a different part of the screen. Or a window may be increased in size, or made to overlap information in another window.

Integrated software is often designed for a specific type of computer. However, there are integrated packages on the market that can be used with many computers. Integrated software allows the user to use the same information in a number of ways. It can be used to produce reports, to create graphs and charts, to plan for the future, to build data bases and mailing lists, and to do many other important jobs.

CHECK WHAT YOU HAVE LEARNED

1. What is a window?
2. Name three ways that you could use an integrated program.
3. Why would a businessperson want to use windows?
4. What is one way that software publishers have met their customers' needs?
5. Name three career opportunities that are available to people who help make software.

Planning a Computer Program

How, exactly, do programmers create application and system programs? Writing a computer program is like writing a story or an essay. First, you must think of ideas to write about. You must either decide on a plot for your story or a topic for your essay. Then you must plan how to write the story or essay. What will be the clearest way of organizing and presenting your ideas? How much detail should your story or essay contain? After planning out your writing, you must actually write the story or essay. This means that you must choose the right words to express your ideas in a way that others can understand. After you finish writing, you must revise your story or essay to correct any mistakes that you might have made. You may need to rewrite parts of it to make it better.

This is exactly what computer programmers do. When they have an idea for a program, first they spend a good deal of time planning. They ask questions like: What do I want this program to do? What is the easiest way to do this job by computer? What problems may arise when I try to make the computer do this job? To help him or her plan, the programmer makes an **algorithm** of the program. An algorithm is a step-by-step outline of the calculations that the programmer wants the program to perform. When the algorithm is finished, the programmer writes the **code** of the program. Code is the term for actual computer instructions. It is like the sentences that make up a story.

The computer programmer is not finished with the job when the code is written. The program must be run to see how well it works. Every new program contains bugs, or instructions that

The Future and Computers

Artificial Intelligence

New software is being designed every day. Some of the most exciting developments are in the area of artificial intelligence. Artificial intelligence programs are programs that tell the computer how to think logically, like humans do. One such program has been developed by Herbert A. Simon at the University of Pittsburgh. It is called Bacon. Bacon finds patterns in data and comes up with predictable laws of nature. It has already rediscovered the laws of atomic weight, planetary motion, and electrical resistance. It is interesting to think that if Bacon could rediscover natural laws that people have already discovered, it could also discover a natural law that people have not found yet. In fact, it is possible that in the future some of our greatest scientists could be computers!

One of the biggest problems in designing artificial intelligence programs is that we are not really sure how people think. Remember that in order to write a program, the programmer must divide the jobs into tiny steps. We do not yet know enough about how people actually think to be able to give computers step-by-step instructions. For example, we can give a computer enough information to be able to recognize a drinking glass. The computer can then scan a number of objects and choose the glass. But if we tip the glass over, the computer no longer recognizes it as a glass. Human beings, even very young ones, are still able to tell that it is a glass when it is tipped over. Can you explain how you do it? Artificial intelligence is an area in which many programmers will be working in the future.

---

make the computer act differently than the programmer wants it to. Bugs are mistakes, things that the programmer has overlooked or not planned for in writing the program. When the program is run (or activated), the programmer can see what the bugs are and can **debug** the program. That is, he or she can correct the mistakes just as you correct spelling and punctuation in an essay. The program is not finished until it runs the way it is supposed to. Debugging a program can take as much or more time than writing the code.

Many programmers feel that the most important step in writing a computer program is in making an algorithm. Careful planning can prevent mistakes in later steps. There are several ways to plan a computer program. Three of these methods are top-down structured programming, writing pseudocode, and drawing a flowchart.

Top-Down Structured Programming

It sounds complicated, but top-down structured programming can be simple. The programmer decides what job the computer must do. He or she then breaks the job down into smaller and smaller steps and makes a chart. It is called "top-down" because the programmer begins at the top of the chart with what the program will do. Then he or she moves down the chart, dividing the job into smaller tasks.

For example, let's say that we want to write a program that will compute a student's grade in history. That job is at the top of our top-down structure, because that is the major job that we want the computer to do. But we cannot simply tell the computer to compute the grade. We have to tell it the steps it must go through to arrive at the final grade. So we divide the job into smaller jobs. We might list these smaller jobs as three simple steps:

1. Enter and add together all the student's grades in history.
2. Divide the total grades by the number of grades.
3. Print the result on a grade report.

We now have divided the job of calculating final grades into three simpler steps. But the computer still does not have all of the instructions it needs. We must divide these three steps into even smaller steps. The first step above, of entering and adding together all the student's grades in history, can be divided into these simpler jobs:

1. Locate a student's grade record.
2. Read a history grade into memory.
3. Read the next grade and add it to the previous grade.
4. Keep reading and adding grades until there are no more grades to read.

Now we are ready to write the code that tells the computer how to do these steps. Our code will be even more specific than the steps above. The computer must have its instructions broken down into very small units. These small units listed in a very orderly way give the program its organized structure, and help to make the program as complete as possible.

With top-down structured programming, the programmer plans each step so that no tasks are forgotten. This helps him or her to write a complete and well-organized program. No steps are left out, and the computer can move from one step to another smoothly in order to finish its work.

Writing Pseudocode

Writing **pseudocode** is another way to plan a computer program. The word *pseudo* means false or artificial. Before the programmer writes the real code, it is useful to write the instructions down in a human language. This is like writing an outline or a rough draft of an essay.

This process of writing pseudocode is like top-down structured programming because the programmer has to decide what steps will be included in the program. Then the steps are written down in a human language before they are coded into programming language. The pseudocode is a "false code" because the computer cannot really understand instructions written in a human language. But it keeps the programmer on track when he or she is writing the actual programming language code. Pseudocode helps to ensure that no steps will be left out when the program is written. It is an outline of the coded program.

In our example of a program that computes a student's history grade, our pseudocode might look like this:

> Figure a student's history grade.
>   Locate the student's record.
>   Read a grade.
>   Read another grade and add it to the total.
>   Do this until there are no more grades.
>   Divide the total grades by the number of grades.
> Print the result on a grade report.

In an actual program, the steps would be broken down into even more specific tasks than these. The computer can only do very small parts of a job at once. It performs them so quickly, though, that it appears to be doing large jobs at a very fast pace.

Drawing a Flowchart

Like top-down structuring and pseudocode, the **flowchart** is a tool that programmers use to stay organized. The flowchart is a drawing made up of different symbols. Each symbol stands for a step in the program. The symbols all have the same meaning to all programmers, so one programmer can easily read another programmer's flowchart. This is useful when several programmers are working together on a large project.

The symbols serve the same purpose as top-down structuring

or pseudocode. They show the programmer what steps must be included in a program and where they should occur. At a glance, the programmer can see what code needs to be written so that the computer can follow the steps involved in performing a job.

Flowcharting used to be an extremely popular method of planning computer programs. Many programmers still do use this system. However, top-down structured programming is becoming more popular. Whatever method a programmer uses to organize a program, the key to good programming is careful planning. Once a program is planned, it can be written in any of many different programming languages.

CHECK WHAT YOU HAVE LEARNED

1. What is at the top of the chart in top-down structured programming?
2. What word means "getting rid of the mistakes" in computer programming?
3. What is the most important step in writing a program?
4. Which planning tool uses symbols to stand for different step in the program?
5. What are the real instructions to the computer called?

Programming and Authoring Languages

A number of computing languages have been developed since the 1940s. The early languages were often difficult and time-consuming to learn. Today, we have much simpler languages that anyone can learn. In fact, there is a group of languages, known as **authoring languages**, that allow users who do not know programming languages to write programs in human language. The authoring language then translates the programs into language the machine can understand.

As we mentioned in Chapter Two, programming languages fall into three basic categories: machine language, assembly language, and high-level languages. Of all the programming languages, high-level languages are most like human languages. An instruction written in a high-level language usually stands for several lines of machine language code. This makes high-level languages faster to program with than machine language. Also,

New Ideas and Computers

Human-to-Machine Language Translation

Computer programming languages are much simpler today than they were in the early days of computers. But we still need special languages and commands to communicate with computers. Why can't we just type English words into the computer? Why can't we teach the computer to understand and translate our language? Many computer scientists are working on developing a system to do just that.

Teaching a computer to speak human language sounds easy, but it is really very complicated. The programmer must teach the computer about the rules that we use to combine words. Unfortunately, many words are used in a number of different ways. The computer has to learn how to tell not only what a word means, but also how it is being used and how it goes together with the other words in the sentence.

Some new programs have been developed that can translate human language into machine language. They are not yet able to understand language as well as a human, but they can accept and translate many orders in English. For example, the computer user might type in, "What is the average height of all the children in my class?" With a language translation program, the computer could understand the request and could answer the user's question. It might print out, "The average height of the children in your class is five feet." At present, programs that translate human language to machine language are extremely expensive. But it is possible that someday you will be able to carry on a conversation with a home computer without having to know any special languages at all.

---

high-level languages are easier to learn because they are very like the language we speak. We will be looking at several high-level languages here.

FORTRAN

FORTRAN stands for FORmula TRANslator. FORTRAN was one of the early computer languages. It is still used today for many engineering and scientific applications. FORTRAN was designed to make writing mathematical formulas easier.

FORTRAN was developed by computer scientists at IBM. It became a popular programming language in the 1950s. Before FORTRAN was introduced, most programmers were writing their programs in machine language. These programs were lengthy and slow to write. Programmers welcomed FORTRAN because it cut down on the amount of code that they had to write.

A program written in FORTRAN looks like this:

```
C       THIS PROGRAM READS FOUR NUMBERS
C       AND PRINTS THEIR PRODUCTS
     1  READ (5,10) A1, A2, A3, A4
    10  FORMAT (I2, I2, I2, I2)
C
     2  A5=A1*A2*A3*A4
C
C       THIS PRINTS THE RESULTS
     3  WRITE (6,11) A5
    11  FORMAT (1X,I16)
        STOP
        END
```

Notice that some lines are marked with *c* at the beginning. This means that these lines are comments. Other lines are marked with numbers. These lines are actual instructions to the computer.

Before FORTRAN was introduced, programmers had to write programs for the specific computer that the programs would be run on. Since FORTRAN is the same everywhere, programmers using FORTRAN can run their programs on many different computers. This was an exciting development in computer programming at the time. Now there are many languages that allow programmers to run the same program on different computers.

COBOL

Another computer programming language that has been used for many years is COBOL. COBOL stands for COmmon Business-Oriented Language. This language was designed to be used in writing programs for business. It was developed in 1959 by a group of large-computer users including the federal government and computer manufacturers. COBOL helped computers become accepted in business. Like FORTRAN, COBOL is the same everywhere so a program written in COBOL can be run on many different computers. A program written in COBOL might look like this:

```
001000  IDENTIFICATION DIVISION.
001010  PROGRAM-ID.  JF1.
001020* THIS PROGRAM READS FOUR NUMBERS AND
001030* DISPLAYS THEIR PRODUCT
001040  ENVIRONMENT DIVISION.
```

SOFTWARE AND APPLICATIONS

```
001050     CONFIGURATION SECTION.
001060     SOURCE-COMPUTER.   XYZ-1.
001070     OBJECT-COMPUTER.   XYZ-1.
001080     INPUT-OUTPUT SECTION.
001090     FILE-CONTROL.
001100         SELECT IN-FILE
001110            ASSIGN TO INPUT-DEVICE.
001120         SELECT OUT-FILE
001130            ASSIGN TO OUTPUT-DEVICE.
001140     DATA DIVISION.
001150     FILE SECTION.
001160     FD  IN-FILE
001170         LABEL RECORDS ARE OMITTED.
001180     01  IN-RECORD.
001190         02  NUM-IN     PIC 9.
001200     FD  OUT-FILE
001210         LABEL RECORDS ARE OMITTED.
001220     01  REPORT-DATA.
001230         02  PRODUCT    PIC ZZ9.
001240     WORKING-STORAGE SECTION.
001250     01  EOF-FLAG       PIC X.
001260     01  NEW-NUMBER     PIC 999  VALUE 1.
001270*
001280     PROCEDURE DIVISION.
001290*
001300     MAIN-ROUTINE.
001310         OPEN INPUT IN-FILE
001320              OUTPUT OUT-FILE.
001330         MOVE "N" TO EOF-FLAG.
001340         READ IN-FILE
001350            AT END MOVE "Y" EOF-FLAG.
001360         PERFORM MAIN-LOOP
001370            UNTIL EOF-FLAG IS EQUAL TO "Y".
001380         PERFORM PRINT-OUTPUT.
001390         CLOSE IN-FILE, OUT-FILE.
001400     MAIN-LOOP.
001410         MULTIPLY NEW-NUM BY NUM-IN
001420            GIVING NEW-NUM.
001430         READ IN-FILE
001440            AT END MOVE "Y" TO EOF-FLAG.
001450     PRINT-OUTPUT.
001460         MOVE NEW-NUM TO PRODUCT.
001470         WRITE REPORT-DATA.
```

Notice that each line of code is given a number. This quickly identifies the line, and is especially helpful when the program is being debugged. COBOL is an extremely useful language in a business setting.

BASIC

Another programming language that is useful in business as well as schools and homes is BASIC, or Beginner's All-purpose Symbolic Instruction Code. BASIC is a very popular language because it is one of the easiest programming languages to learn. In fact, when John Kemeny and Thomas Kurtz introduced the BASIC language in 1963, they said they had tried to design a computer language that could be learned in three hours!

This was an important development in computer programming because BASIC allows many people to learn to write their own programs. BASIC can be learned by people who are not professional programmers. This has been especially important as microcomputers have become more popular in homes and schools. In fact, many students learn BASIC as a first programming language.

BASIC can be used for many different applications. Like COBOL and FORTRAN, it is the same everywhere so programmers can use their programs on different computers. A program written in BASIC might look like this:

```
10   Rem  This program finds the product of
15   Rem  four numbers
20   Print "Enter four numbers"
30   Input A1, A2, A3, A4
40   Let A5=A1*A2*A3*A4
50   Print "The product ="; A5
60   END
```

The lines of the BASIC program are numbered so they can be located easily. Often the programmer leaves gaps between the numbered lines so that he or she can add more code later.

Pascal

Pascal is a programming language named after Blaise Pascal, the seventeenth-century French mathematician mentioned in Chapter One. It was designed in Switzerland by a computer scientist and introduced for some computers in the early 1970s. This makes it a fairly new computer language. Like BASIC, Pascal is easy to learn and to use. In fact, some experts think that it is better to learn Pascal first instead of BASIC. Pascal is like BASIC and COBOL, and is very structured. Program organization is very controlled, and it is very popular in computer science courses. A program written in Pascal might look like this:

SOFTWARE AND APPLICATIONS

```
program product(input,output);
  const  number=4;
  var    index, product, num :integer;
begin
  product:=0:;
  for index:= 1 to number do
    begin
      writeln('Enter number');
      readln(num);
      product:=product+num
    end;
  writeln('The product is' ,product)
end.
```

The lines of a Pascal program are not numbered like those of BASIC, COBOL, and FORTRAN. The lines of the program are separated by semicolons (;). Pascal is a fairly new language, and it is not yet the same everywhere. As it becomes more popular, however, it will be made the same so that Pascal programs can be written and run on many different computers.

Forth and LISP

The **Forth** programming language takes its name from the fourth generation of computers, which is when this language was introduced. It is especially popular in engineering and graphics applications. A program written in Forth might look like this:

```
0   (A PROGRAM TO MULTIPLY FOUR NUMBERS
    TOGETHER)
1   (THE NUMBERS ARE INPUT ONE AT A TIME)
2     : MULTIPLY 4     PAGE
3       ."ENTER FOUR NUMBERS TO BE MULTIPLED
        WHEN PROMPTED BY?"
4       CR  ." PRESS<RETURN> AFTER EACH
        NUMBER"
5       #IN  #IN  #IN  #IN
6       * * *
7       ."THE PRODUCT OF THE NUMBERS IS" CR
8       . QUIT ;
```

LISP—or LISt Programming—is a special type of computer programming language. It is used in the field of artificial intelligence (which will be discussed later). LISP is not a mathematical language. It is likely that LISP will be used more in the future as computers become more "intelligent." A program written in LISP might look like this:

```
Index of definitions:
  product . . . . . . . . . . . . . . . . . . . . . . . . 1
  product_help . . . . . . . . . . . . . . . . . . . . . 2
product

EXPR
(lambda nil  (comment ** Function to multiply N
             numbers **)
             (princ ''Number of entries: '' )
             (product_help (read) 1))

product_help

EXPR
(lambda  (max index)
         (comment ** Get next number ** )
         (terpri)
         (princ ''Enter number '' )
         (princ index)
         (princ '': '' )
         (cond ((equal index max)
                (comment ** Last number—just
               return it **)
                (read)
                (t (comment ** Else—Recurse
                  and get rest **)
                  (times read)
```

Logo

Seymour Papert and his coworkers developed **Logo** as a programming language to help very young children learn mathematics and computer programming. For example, children who are still preschool age have become successful programmers using Logo. That may seem hard to believe, but children use the Logo language to instruct mechanical devices that move on the floor. The children's instructions tell the objects how far to move and in what directions. Sometimes pens are attached to the objects and they are placed on paper so that they draw pictures as they move. This lets the young programmers see a map or picture of the instructions they have given the objects. The objects are called turtles.

Students may also enter Logo commands into a keyboard to make "turtles" on the CRT screen draw pictures. Young children

People and Computers

Seymour Papert

Seymour Papert is a professor at the Massachusetts Institute of Technology. He and some of his coworkers developed the Logo programming language for children. To design it, Papert used the suggestions of students, classroom teachers, psychologists, and computer scientists.

Papert studied mathematics and philosophy in South Africa, where he was born. Later, he went to Cambridge University in England and to France to continue his studies. While he was in Paris, he met Jean Piaget, a famous child psychologist. He became interested in how environment affects learning. He worked with Piaget for five years before he came to MIT in 1963. Seymour Papert designed Logo to be fun, but it also teaches serious programming skills.

Computers can be programmed to control robots. This robot (called a turtle) has a pen that leaves a design on a paper. Commands are given to the computer for the design, and the turtle moves and draws the design. Students of all ages find the turtle to be a useful learning tool.

Logo was developed to help children learn to use computers. By moving a "turtle" pointer around on the screen, children can create intricate patterns that can be saved or used with other programs.

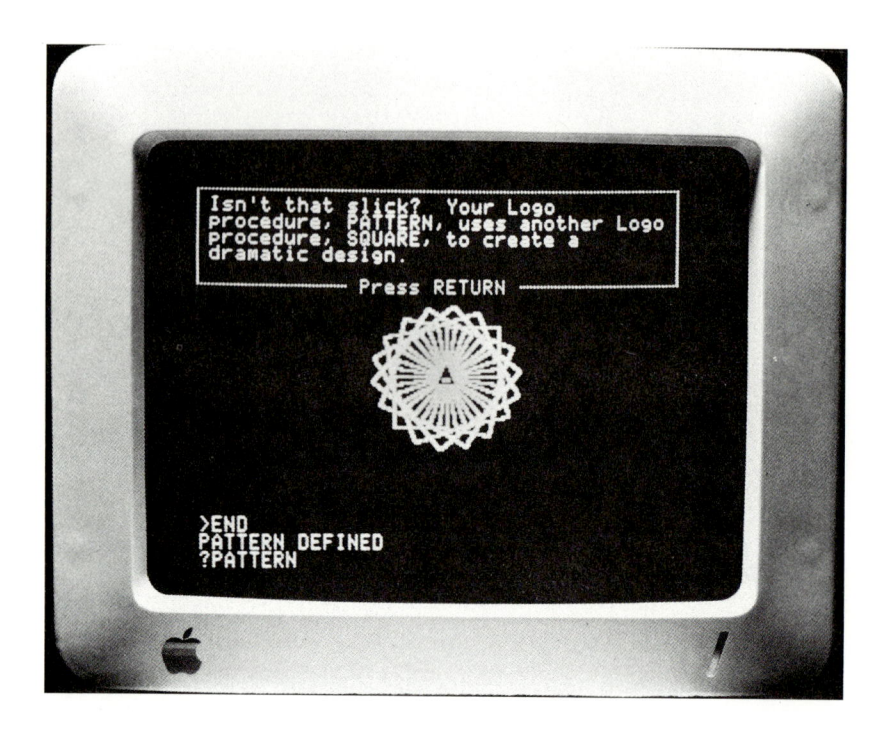

do not realize that they are learning serious programming, but they have fun telling the turtles what to do. Because Logo is a powerful learning tool, it is used in schools, and at different grade levels. There are many different types of Logo available. Logo is a good mix of computer programming and play.

PILOT

Many people such as teachers and home computer users want to write their own programs. Often, they do not have time to learn complicated programming languages. For example, teachers may want to design their own computer-aided instruction (CAI) software even if they do not know how to write programs in BASIC. For these people, authoring languages are a good alternative.

An authoring language is a programming language that helps people who don't know programming write programs. The programs are written in human language and then translated so the computer can understand. One authoring language is PILOT.

PILOT lets people, especially teachers, write their own programs. PILOT asks the user questions. According to the answers, PILOT helps the program writer to write his or her own program. It gives all the help that the writer needs, but it lets the writer use a great deal of creativity in making up the program. Authoring

SOFTWARE AND APPLICATIONS 103

Schools are using computers for instruction, practice, and in many other innovative ways.

languages show that computer programming is becoming possible even for people with nontechnical interests.

Computer software is a dynamic field. It seems to grow and change every day. As more people buy and learn to use computers, they will want to use their computers in as many ways as possible. This means that computer software will become a huge industry in the future. It will offer career opportunities for computer programmers, technical writers, software retailers, and others who help in the designing, writing, and producing of computer software.

CHECK WHAT YOU HAVE LEARNED

1. Why do some programming languages have numbers at the beginning of each line?
2. What is a good programming language to use with preschool children?
3. What does BASIC stand for?
4. What programming languages might be especially useful in business? (Name two.)
5. Before FORTRAN, why couldn't programmers use their programs on many different computers?

WHAT YOU HAVE LEARNED IN CHAPTER THREE

Computer software is the set of instructions that humans write to tell the computer what to do. Another name for these instructions is computer programs. Without proper instructions, or programs, the computer cannot do its work. The programs are written in computer languages that can be translated into numbers the computer can read. Early computer languages were very complicated. Most people did not want to learn them. Now, simpler computer languages are making it possible for many people to write their own programs.

There are two kinds of computer software. The first kind is system software. It is the rules and instructions that help the computer's operating system. For example, it tells the computer how to input or output information. It usually comes with the computer. The computer's operating system controls what the computer does. It controls how information is sent from one part of the computer to another. The supervisor of the computer's operating system tells the computer what order to do its jobs in and when to accept input or send output. It loads instructions from other programs. The operating system also has language translators that translate other programs into machine language and utility programs that help in many ways.

The second type of software is application software. These are programs that tell the computer how to do specific jobs. Without an application program, the computer would not be very useful. Application programs can be written for any job that can be done by a computer. Sometimes people who buy home computers enjoy writing their own application programs. These might include games or programs to help them run their homes.

As new software is developed, programmers are working hard to meet the needs of computer users. One way that they have done this is with integrated programs. Integrated programs are programs that communicate with each other. With integrated programs, the user can use the information from one program while he or she is working with another program.

Writing a computer program is like writing a story or an essay. First, the programmer must decide what the program is supposed to do. Second, he or she must divide this job into a step-by-step outline to tell the computer what to do. Many experts believe that planning is the most important part of computer programming. It can be done by top-down structured programming, writing pseudocode, or drawing a flowchart. Once the program has been planned, the programmer writes the code for the program. The code is the actual instructions that are given to the computer. After the program is written, it must be run to see how well it works. Every new program has bugs. Bugs are mistakes, things that the programmer overlooked in writing the program. When the program is run, the programmer can see what the bugs are and can debug the program. That is, he or she can correct the mistakes.

Several different computing languages have been developed. The newer ones are much simpler to use. In fact, there is a group of programming languages that allows users who do not know programming languages at all to write programs in human language. These are called authoring languages. Some examples of high-level programming languages are FORTRAN, COBOL, BASIC, Pascal, Forth, LISP, and Logo. One authoring language is PILOT.

1. What does the supervisor of the computer's operating system do?
2. What is an integrated program?
3. Name the two kinds of computer software.
4. What is an application program?
5. What type of software usually comes with the computer?
6. What are bugs in a computer program?
7. What is the most important part of writing a computer program?
8. Why didn't many people want to learn early computer languages?
9. What three methods can a programmer use to plan a program?
10. Describe the difference between system software and application software.

USING WORDS YOU HAVE LEARNED

1. _____ software is a set of rules and instructions that help the computer's operating system.
2. The _____ is part of the computer's operating system and tells the computer what order to do the jobs in.
3. An _____ is a step-by-step outline of calculations that a program must perform.
4. A _____ is an electronic ledger.
5. An _____ program tells the computer how to do a specific job.
6. If the programmer finds mistakes in his or her program he or she must _____ it.
7. _____ means false or artificial.
8. An _____ language is one that lets users who do not know programming languages write programs in human languages.
9. _____ programs are programs that can communicate with each other.
10. A _____ is a drawing made up of different symbols. It helps the programmer plan his or her program.

EXERCISING YOUR WRITING SKILLS

Writing a computer program is a little bit like writing a "how-to" paper. The difficult part is in remembering all of the little details that are included in doing a job.

Try writing the outline for a how-to paper. This is like planning a program in pseudocode. You might make your outline on "How to Make Breakfast" or "How to Change a Bicycle Tire." Don't leave out any steps!

Trade your outline with another student. Now act out the other outline. If you get to a spot where a step has been left out, *freeze*. Your partner will have to debug her or his outline before you can continue. You will have to think carefully to be sure you don't miss a step. Remember that you can only do what the outline tells you to do.

Once you and your partner have debugged your outlines, you are ready to write your papers. An outline is an important step in organizing writing, just as it is in programming.

UNDERSTANDING WHAT YOU HAVE LEARNED

MULTIPLE CHOICE

1. The people who write instructions for computers are called:
   a) system analysts
   b) programmers
   c) language translators
   d) supervisors
2. A word processing program would best be used to:
   a) write a report
   b) calculate students' grades
   c) discover natural laws
   d) analyze systems
3. Logo is a computer language that:
   a) is used primarily by engineers
   b) is named for the fourth generation of computers
   c) is an authoring language
   d) moves a turtle around the floor or the CRT screen
4. To debug a program you must:
   a) spray insecticide
   b) use a language translator
   c) correct your mistakes
   d) integrate your software
5. BASIC is:
   a) a very easy language to learn
   b) a very complicated language
   c) used only by expert programmers
   d) not recommended for microcomputers
6. A window is:
   a) a see-through part of the CRT screen
   b) a glass portion of the keyboard
   c) an input device
   d) an area of the CRT that shows information from a specific program
7. A data base is an example of:
   a) system software
   b) application software
   c) an electronic ledger
   d) a business letter
8. Language translators are important because:
   a) they translate other languages into machine language
   b) they do not speak many different languages from other countries
   c) they supervise all the other jobs
   d) they make sure the user has permission to use the system
9. A flowchart is useful for a large project because:
   a) the symbols all have the same meaning to all programmers
   b) it connects the data base to a spreadsheet
   c) it is difficult to use for a small project
   d) the symbols are large
10. To use an authoring language you must:
    a) be an engineer
    b) be a teacher
    c) be interested in writing a program
    d) be a mathematician

TRUE OR FALSE

1. FORTRAN was one of the early computer languages.
2. Pseudocode is written entirely in binary numbers.
3. A word processing program is generally used to plan finances.
4. BASIC only works on one type of computer.
5. System programmers write rules and instructions for the computer's operating system.
6. Software is the instructions that tell the computer how to do its job.
7. PILOT is a program that teaches airline employees how to fly aircraft.
8. Once the programmer has written the code of the program, his or her work is finished.
9. A flowchart is a drawing made up of different symbols.
10. Integrated software was one of the first types of software developed.

SHORT ANSWER

1. What computer language would you use to write a program if you didn't know anything at all about programming?
2. Name three ways you might plan a computer program.
3. Think of one use for a data base program that is not named in this chapter.
4. How can word processing save you time if you are sending one letter to five different friends?
5. Name two things that a supervisor of the computer's operating system does.
6. What is the difference between software and hardware?
7. Describe how integrated software can save time.
8. Why are the lines of BASIC, COBOL, and FORTRAN programs numbered?
9. Why is it important to have a computer language that is the same everywhere?
10. What is application software? Give an example not mentioned in this chapter.

WHAT YOU WILL LEARN IN CHAPTER FOUR

By the end of this chapter, you will be able to:

1. Define word processing.
2. Explain three common uses of word processing.
3. List three advantages of word processing.
4. Name four types of word processors.
5. Describe five tasks that can be performed with a word processor.

Word Processing: Writing Made Easier

WORDS YOU WILL LEARN

cursor
dedicated word processor
font
form letter
function key
graphics
justify
merge
proofread
shared-logic word processor
stand-alone word processor
text
time-shared word processor
word processing

Computers are becoming so popular because of the many ways they help humans to do their work. In a way, computers are like hammers and nails; they are tools that people use to get work done quickly, easily, and well. This is why it is important that people not feel frightened or uneasy about using computers. Computers do not think, feel, and respond the way humans do. They merely follow the instructions people program into them to do the work they are given to do.

One of the most important things people do is write down their ideas. Without the written word, most of the important ideas of our time would be forgotten. Without writing, the works of the greatest scientist or the most learned historian would be lost. Mathematicians, teachers, scientists, doctors, police officers, and many others must use writing in their jobs. Sometimes the task of writing a report, letter, proposal, or paper takes up a great deal of time. Often, the writing and rewriting of documents make it difficult for the professional to work on anything else. The computer is making the task of writing much easier. Through word processing, much of the busywork of writing is eliminated. Writers, whatever their profession, can prepare written documents more quickly, easily, and correctly than ever before.

What Is Word Processing?

Word processing is one of the most popular applications of computer power in use today. It is the process of writing, editing, storing, and copying text by using the computer. **Text** is the written material being prepared. Word processing does not make use of the computer's ability to calculate numbers. Instead, it takes advantage of the computer's ability to store and process information.

When the typist uses a computer to prepare a document, the words that are typed appear on the CRT screen. Another character also appears to show the typist where the next letter, number, or symbol will be. This character is called the **cursor**. The cursor looks different on different computers. It may be a flashing

The cursor helps keep track of where text will appear on the screen. The cursor in this example is at the end of the first paragraph.

```
Dear Principal:
   Thank you for the opportunity to meet
with your teachers and students in
November. The drama group will perform for
approximately one hour.▮
```

square or an underline character. The cursor helps the typist keep track of where text will appear on the screen. As the text becomes longer, it is moved so that the user is always able to look at the middle of the screen to see the line that is being typed. But the words that disappear from the screen are not lost. They are stored in the computer's memory and can be recalled by moving back to them on the screen or by printing the document. After the document is complete, the user simply commands the computer to print the document. The printer types the words onto paper much faster than a typist would be able to do on a typewriter. The document can also be saved on a disk so that it can be used again (or recalled) later. This allows the computer user to use the document again without having to retype it.

The computer understands only numbers. How can it be used to type words and letters? This is an interesting question. The computer can process words because it translates each letter into a binary number. A translation system allows the computer to use numbers to produce words that humans can read and understand.

But the computer helps the typist to do much more than just type. It allows the typist to change the text, insert new text, find words, correct the text, print the text, make copies, and much more. It is difficult to compare word processing to any system used earlier because no system helped the typist to do as much. The system that comes the closest to doing the same job as the word processor is the typewriter. Let us see how closely the typewriter can come to the work done by a word processor.

People and Computers

Samuel W. Soule

Did you ever wonder who decided where the keys should be on a typewriter? Samuel W. Soule designed the typewriter keyboard in 1867. He wanted to make it difficult to type quickly. He was afraid that if the keyboard were easy to use, fast typists would jam the levers and gears in the typewriter. He designed the keyboard for the Remington Type Writer of 1867. Although other, easier keyboards have been designed, none have been very popular. Many people who are touch typists have mastered Soule's keyboard and can type very quickly. They don't want to learn a new keyboard. It is very difficult for a typist to learn to use a new keyboard after becoming accustomed to another one—even if it *is* awkward! Computer keyboards, even with additional keys, can be easy to use.

CHAPTER FOUR

CHECK WHAT YOU HAVE LEARNED

1. What is word processing?
2. What do we call the written material that is being prepared?
3. How does the computer understand words?
4. Explain why writing is important.
5. Where does the computer user see the words he or she has typed on a word processor?

Word Processing and Typewriting

Word processing has made many office jobs much simpler.

In the past, most businesses have hired secretaries and typists to process written material on standard typewriters. If you have used a typewriter, you know that this can be a long, slow process. You must press the keys, change the paper, and correct mistakes. To make copies on a typewriter, you must use carbon paper. This is messy and does not always produce clean copies that are easy to read.

But today more and more businesses are turning from typewriters to word processing. Word processing makes the job of writing, typing, correcting, and copying text much faster and easier. Everything is done on the computer. No paper is used until after the text has been written and corrected and is ready to be printed. Then the text can be stored on disk so that it can be corrected and printed again whenever it is needed. It does not have to be retyped.

You can easily see the advantage of word processing over typing with a typewriter. First, when text is typed on the computer keyboard, it appears on the screen. Typing errors can be seen and corrected quickly. On a typewriter, a typing error takes time to correct. Also, it is almost impossible to correct a document that is being typed on a typewriter without leaving some mark. With a word processor, the typing error is never visible in the finished product because it is corrected before the text is on paper. This means that the finished product looks better when a word processor is used than when a typewriter is used. Sometimes it is very important that the finished document look nice.

Second, commands can be entered into the computer to change the text in any way the typist wants. The typist may decide that the margins should be larger or that a paragraph should be moved. With a word processor, this is not a difficult task. The computer can do these things very quickly. With a typewriter, this task might require the retyping of the entire document. A simple example of this is in the typing of business letters. Many secretaries can tell you about the frustration of arriving at the end of a letter only to find that there is not enough room on the page for the signature! If a typewriter is being used, the typist must take the paper out of the typewriter, get new paper, and begin all over again. This time, the typist can make the margins a little smaller and move the address up on the page. Unless the typist is very practiced, he or she must hope that the guesses about how much smaller the margins should be are correct. If they are not, the letter may appear too small and crowded onto the page. The typist may have to begin again until the letter looks nice enough to send out. And, unfortunately, after the third or fourth try "nice enough" may not mean perfect. But what if the typist is using a word processor? In that case, when the error in spacing is discovered nothing has yet been printed out on the paper. The typist can ask the computer to try out a different margin. This takes only a moment. If the letter does not look perfect, the computer can try another one. When the correct margin is found, the letter can be printed out onto the paper.

Third, the computer prints as many copies of a document as a person needs. This means that the secretary or typist does not have to spend time typing text more than once. The typist also does not have to make carbon copies. Each printing of the letter looks like the original. This can be very important if copies of the document must be given to several people.

Fourth, documents can be stored on disk so that they can be printed again whenever they are needed. Disks are smaller than files and less bulky than paper. As the document is needed again, it can be found on the disk and can be changed or printed again very quickly. Of course, even if a paper document is found in a file, it must be retyped if any changes are to be made or if it is to go to someone else.

The word processor keyboard looks a great deal like a standard typewriter keyboard. The letter and number keys are arranged in the same way. This makes it easier for the typist to switch from the typewriter to the computer. Along with the letters, numbers, and symbols that you find on a typewriter keyboard, the word processor keyboard has other keys as well. There are keys that allow you to insert text or to delete (erase) it. And there are special numbered keys called **function keys**. Function keys perform routine tasks when pressed. For example, the typist might press a specific function key to check spelling in the document.

The computer keyboard looks very much like a typewriter, but has ten function keys on the left-hand side, and additional special number and function keys on the right.

With a typewriter, text is printed directly onto the page.

Typing on a word processor is very similar to typing on a typewriter. But the computer does certain tasks for the typist to save time. If you have used a typewriter, you know that as you press keys letters appear from left to right. When you reach the end of a line, you must return the carriage (or type ball) to the beginning of the next line. This is not necessary in word processing because the printer automatically returns to the beginning of the next line when the computer has measured out a certain number of characters.

CHECK WHAT YOU HAVE LEARNED

1. Name two reasons why typing errors are easier to correct on a word processor.
2. What does the word processor keyboard look like? Tell how it is similar to and different from the typewriter keyboard.
3. What is a cursor?
4. List three advantages of a word processor over a typewriter.
5. Give an example of something you could do more easily on a word processor than on a typewriter. Do not use an example from this book. Why is it easier?

Tasks a Word Processor Can Do

There are many commands that can be given to the computer to cause it to perform certain tasks. For example, the computer can read lines or paragraphs from one piece of text and then copy them into another so that the same text does not have to be typed twice. The computer can search an entire document to find all the places where a certain word or line occurs and replace it with another. It can even check spelling by comparing the words in a document to those in a dictionary stored in its memory! It can also center text on a page, make right and left margins equal and straight, and number pages. This saves the human typist from having to count spaces and lines and look up words in the dictionary to make sure they are spelled correctly. Let's look at how the typist uses the word processor to do some of these things.

```
Dear Principal:
    Thank you for the opportunity to meet
with your teachers and students in
November. The drama group will perform for
approximately one hour.
    We hope that our two-act play will be
amusing and interesting. The cast is
looking forward to a question-and-answer
period with the audience at the end of the
performance.
                           Sincerely,
                           The Actors Workshop
```

This letter written on a word processor to a principal about a visiting drama group is brief and general. But the writer can make some changes easily by substituting specific information.

Correcting or Changing Text

As the typist is typing, the text is shown on the CRT screen in front of him or her. If a mistake is made, the typist has only to move the cursor back to the place where the mistake is and erase the mistake. Sometimes it is necessary to insert more text between two words in the document. With word processing, this is a simple matter. The typist simply goes to where the words should be and types the words in. The computer not only makes room for the new words, it also moves all of the rest of the text down. With a typewriter, a typist would have to retype the entire document in order to insert one or two words.

This revised letter now includes the principal's name, date of the play, the drama group's name, name of the play, and the letter writer's name.

```
Dear Mrs. Ramirez:
    Thank you for the opportunity to meet
with your teachers and students on
Thursday, November 7, 1985. The Actors
Workshop will perform for approximately
one hour.
    We hope that our two-act play, The
Strange Intruder, will be amusing and
interesting. The cast is looking forward
to a question-and-answer period with the
audience at the end of the performance.
                            Sincerely,
                            Joseph Davis
```

After a typist prepares an important document, it is usually necessary to **proofread** the document. Proofreading is simply reading the paper over carefully to be sure that there are no errors in typing, punctuation, or content. Usually, after the document is proofread it must be corrected. If more than one person is proofreading the document, it must be corrected several times before each person thinks it is perfect. If the document is stored on a disk and is to be corrected with a word processor, the process of correcting it can take only a few moments. If the document is prepared on a typewriter, the typist must think of the first effort as a first draft. There may be several additional copies of the document before a final draft is agreed upon. If the document is a long one, the process of proofreading and correcting text can take a very long time. This often means that a document prepared on a word processor is more correct. Proofreaders are unlikely to make minor changes if they know that those changes are going to cost the typist a great deal of time. If they know that the changes can be made quickly, however, they will feel more free to point them out.

Checking Spelling

You might think that the computer helps with the correction of a document, but not with the proofreading. In fact, the computer can help the proofreader check spelling as well. Often, mistakes in typing are made when one or two letters are left out of a word, rather than whole words being left out. For example, a typing error might look like this: *Th box is by the bed*. When such an error is made, one of the words is misspelled. This type of error is difficult to find when proofreading. Most of us read so quickly that our eyes automatically add the *e* in where it is missing. With many word processing systems, however, the computer can check the spelling of the words.

After the typist finishes typing the document, he or she can ask the computer to run a spelling check. This is usually done by pressing a function key. The computer then checks each word in the document against the words in a dictionary in its memory. If the word matches, the computer goes on to the next word. If the word does not match a word in the dictionary, the computer might highlight the word. It might ask the user if the word is correct. The user then has an opportunity to correct the spelling. Or the user can tell the computer that the word is correct and it can proceed to the next word. This is necessary because it is difficult to program the computer to know all of the words a typist might use. For example, the computer probably would not recognize names or slang expressions. With most word processing systems that include a spelling check, the user can expand the computer's dictionary to include words that he or she uses often. The company name or the name of the user are examples of words that might be entered into the computer's memory.

If the proofreader is assured that he or she does not have to look for spelling errors, the job of proofreading is made much simpler. The proofreader can spend more time looking for punctuation or content errors.

Merging Information

It is often necessary to send the same letter to many people. For example, a business might be explaining a new policy or a college might be explaining application procedures. The names and addresses of the people who are getting the letter have to appear in the upper left-hand corner of the letter. This means that a typist must retype each letter separately or that the typist must prepare **form letters**. Form letters are letters that leave blanks where the names should be. The names are filled in by hand after the letter has been copied. You have probably seen form letters at your school. The problem is that form letters do not look very personal. Everyone receiving a form letter is aware that he or she is one of many people who is being told the same thing. This is not always very polite.

With word processing, the typist can avoid retyping the document and can have the computer prepare the letters. This is done by **merging** or putting together the letter with a list of names and

The drama group is on tour for four weeks, performing different plays at different locations. Using a word processor, Joseph Davis can send the same letter to many different schools—only the school names and addresses, dates, and names of the plays need to be changed.

> Charles R. Martin
> South City High School
> Los Angeles, California 90925
>
> Dear Mr. Martin:
>   Thank you for the opportunity to meet with your teachers and students on Friday, November 8, 1985. The Actors Workshop will perform for approximately one hour.
>   We hope that our two-act play, *The Nightingale*, will be amusing and interesting. The cast is looking forward to a question-and-answer period with the audience at the end of the performance.
>   Sincerely,
>   Joseph Davis

addresses. The typist types the letter that will be merged with an address list. But instead of leaving blanks where the name should be, the typist tells the computer to look at a specific item in its mailing list to fill that space. For example, the computer may be asked to look at the name to complete the first line of the letter. After the list has been prepared and the letter has been written, the computer is told to merge the lists. It prepares and prints one letter for each person on the mailing list. Each letter is typed correctly, without blanks.

Once a business has prepared a mailing list, it can be used in producing many different documents. The typist has only to type a letter. The computer merges the letter with the mailing list and prints a final copy for each name on the list. This saves the typist a tremendous amount of time and still makes the final letters more personal.

CHECK WHAT YOU HAVE LEARNED

1. Explain how the computer can check spelling.
2. What is proofreading?
3. What is wrong with a form letter?
4. How can merging files help prepare a letter?
5. How would a typist insert extra text with a word processor? How would a typist insert extra text with a typewriter?

Justifying or Centering Text

When you look at a book, you will see that usually all of the lines of type end at exactly the same place on the right-hand side of the page. The process of adding just enough space between words to make this happen is called **justifying**. Justifying can be very difficult for a typist to do by hand. In order to do this, the typist usually has to count every character in all of the lines. The typist finds an average number of characters and must add in or take away spaces in the lines to make the right side come out even. This can take a great deal of time. Few typists justify text unless it is absolutely necessary.

With word processing, the computer can take care of justifying. The computer, of course, does not mind counting characters or taking averages. It does this work very quickly. In fact, the user simply tells the computer that the text must be justified. The computer can do this automatically.

Similarly, when text must be centered in the middle of a page, the typist must count all of the spaces in the line of text and all of the spaces on the page. The text must be placed so that half of the blank spaces are on its left and half are on its right. This takes a person a very long time and is also very boring work. The computer can center text quickly and easily.

Searching, Finding, and Changing

The search-and-find function in word processing can be very useful. This function allows the user to ask the computer to find any word that has been used and to highlight it on the screen. For example, the user may be looking for a name, *John*, or an adjective, *silly*. He or she can press the function key for find. The computer asks the user what to find, and the user types in a word. The computer then searches the entire document for that particular word. It can do this very quickly, even if the document is long. The same task probably would require the user to spend a long time reading the entire document over again!

The user may be trying to locate a word for a number of reasons. It may be necessary to add, or insert, more information about a particular person or topic. Or it may be necessary to change one word to another throughout an entire document. With word processing, the word can be located and changed. The computer user can be confident that he or she has not missed the word anywhere and that the document has been completely corrected.

Suppose The Actors Workshop planned to send the first letter to ten different schools. A new director decided, however, to present a new one-act play. By using the search-and-find function, the writer can locate the reference to the original two-act play, and change it to the name of the new one-act play.

```
Dear Principal:
    Thank you for the opportunity to meet
with your teachers and students in
November. The drama group will perform for
approximately one hour.
    We hope that our one-act play, Lincoln's
Dilemma, will be amusing and interesting.
The cast is looking forward to a question-
and-answer period with the audience at the
end of the performance.
                        Sincerely,
                        The Actors Workshop
```

Imagine that a personnel clerk has just typed a ten-page memo describing John's job. When the memo is complete, he learns that John has just taken fatherhood leave and that Mary has been hired to do the job during that time. The memo must now describe Mary's job, not John's. Not only is the name wrong, but the personal pronouns are wrong throughout the memo! With a word processor, the personnel clerk can simply ask the computer to find the word *he* and change it to *she*, the word *him* and change it to *her*, and the word *John* and change it to *Mary*. What could have been a major revision on a long document can take a minute or two on the word processor.

Changing Fonts

A **font** is a set of type all of one style or shape of lettering. One font that you are probably familiar with is italics. There are many different fonts that are used for different purposes. A fairly simple and dignified font is usually preferred for business letters, while a more romantic lettering might be desired for a letter to a boyfriend or girlfriend. Silly lettering might be perfect for a letter to a pal, and old-fashioned lettering might be just right for an advertisement for the history club. Or in the preparation of a document, italic lettering might be used to highlight a particular word or phrase and romantic lettering can be used for a heading, title, or dedication. The entire document is made much more beautiful through the use of different styles in its preparation.

Few typewriters even allow the typist to change fonts. Those that do make it necessary for the typist to physically remove the type ball for one font and insert another each time the font must

```
APEX WOGITS, Inc.
To all personnel:

DEAREST LESLIE,

Hi Frank!

OLDTIMER'S Club
```

Here are four examples of different styles of fonts.

be changed. This can take a great deal of time and it is usually not possible at all. With many word processors, the font can be changed at the push of a button. The computer can be directed to change the font for a particular word or phrase or even for the entire document. This means that the finished product is often much more interesting visually. The word processor can be used for advertising, art, and invitations—functions that usually had to be done entirely by hand before.

Changing the Type Size

The size of the lettering can also be changed with many word processors. This means that titles and subtitles can be enlarged, words can be emphasized, and captions can be made more striking. Imagine an invitation to a Halloween costume party. The user has drawn a picture of a ghost and a haunted castle on the page. He or she has chosen old-fashioned Gothic lettering for the text. Beside the ghost, the typist has written *Boo*. The *B* is very large. The next *o* is slightly smaller and the final *o* is even smaller than that. Under the castle is smaller type in which the particulars of the party are given, still in Gothic type. The overall effect is very scary. Now imagine the same invitation using entirely business type. The effect is much less impressive. And if we imagine the *Boo* as the same size as the other lettering, it becomes lost in the picture. The ability of the computer to change the size of the type means that the computer can be used for many applications for which a typewriter cannot be used.

This party invitation was prepared on a computer, using appropriate styles and sizes of type.

Merging Text with Graphics

When the computer user was making the invitation just described, the chances are that he or she did not have to draw the ghost and castle by hand. With many word processing systems, the computer allows the user to use a **graphics** system and to insert the graphics into the text. Graphics is a computer feature that allows a user to make drawings for display or printing (the computer is able to display a drawing because it processes it in mathematical terms). This is not only useful for fun applications like invitations. For example, advertising designers find this to be an important function because ads can be designed completely on the computer. A businessperson preparing a report might also find it important to illustrate the text of the report with graphs or pictures. A schoolteacher can make worksheets and handouts much

New Ideas and Computers

User-Friendly Computers

Computers are becoming more and more user friendly. When computers were first developed, directions or commands were given through the use of punched cards. Now tape drives, disk drives, and the keyboard are ways of inputting data to the computer. Even faster ways are developing. Digitizers, such as the Koala-Pad and light pen, allow us to input information to the computer without writing. The mouse is used with many computers. We can even enter data and make choices just by touching the computer screen. The computer can sense where the screen has been touched in one of two ways: either there is a touch-sensitive membrane on the surface of the monitor, or horizontal and vertical beams of light are broken when your finger nears the screen. Digitizers give the computer information about how far something has moved across a pad or, in the case of the mouse, how far the mouse has been moved across an object. Computer art is improving. The computer can become an artist's easel by allowing the user to draw an image that appears instantly on the computer screen. The user can make a mistake and remove it with a simple point of a finger. Colorful, creative, animated art is now possible. And communicating with the computer is getting easier—computers that can understand and follow voice commands are on the way.

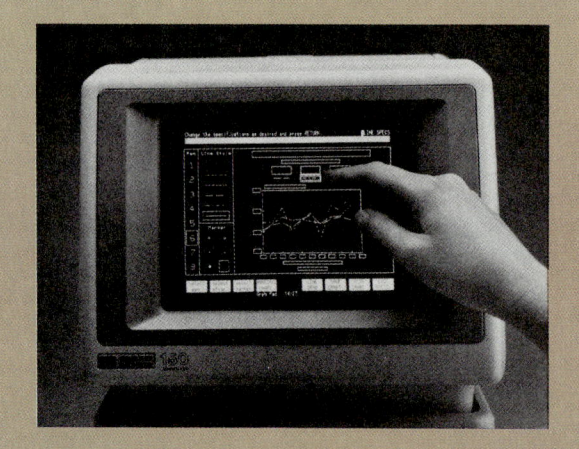

more interesting. An architect might use this function to draw and then describe a particular building. Typing and illustration of any prepared material is not necessarily a two-step process with a computer.

Making Multiple Copies

Once the document has been prepared, the computer user can ask the computer to print one or many copies. Each copy is like the original, of course, because it is printed from the same disk. While this is being done, the typist is free to do other work.

Moving and Copying Text

Sometimes a typist must move a paragraph from one part of a document to another. On a typewriter, of course, this is a major task. The entire document must be retyped because of a few lines. Often, the move is simply not worth the time that would be required, even if it would make the text better. Other times, the typist may spend hours moving the paragraph only to find that it was really better in its original place. The word processor makes this task an easy one. The computer user can simply press a function key, asking the computer to move text. The computer asks which text it must move. The user uses the cursor to highlight the necessary text and shows the computer where it should be inserted. Not only does the computer insert the text in the correct place, it moves all the other text down to make space and the document is complete in seconds.

Similarly, when a paragraph must be repeated in a document, the computer user does not have to spend time retyping the same words. The computer can copy the paragraph automatically into the spot the user chooses. Obviously, this can be a great timesaver.

CHECK WHAT YOU HAVE LEARNED

1. What is a font? How does it affect the way a document looks?
2. What is the search-and-find function of a word processor?
3. How would a typist justify with a typewriter?
4. How would a typist center a phrase with a word processor?
5. Give an example of a place in which you might see a different font than the one you see in this book.

Four Kinds of Word Processors

There are four basic kinds of word processors. The **time-shared** word processor is a microcomputer linked to a larger computer. With time-shared word processing, several people can do word processing at the same time. Even though a number of people are working on the computer at the same time, each typist, sitting at a separate terminal, has the sense of being the only person using the system. This is because the computer can process words so much faster than the typist can type them that the typist is not kept waiting. This is a popular type of word processing for people who cannot afford to buy a large computer. Time-shared word processing is also popular with businesses that have many typists.

Another type of word processor is the **shared-logic** system. This is a computer that is used for word processing and for other tasks. With this system, a computer can be used for several purposes at once. It can be used by one person to keep track of sales while another person uses it to type letters and contracts. This is a good system for small businesses that need to use their computers to do a number of different tasks.

Stand-alone, or **dedicated**, word processors are computers that are specifically designed for use as word processors. This is the only job they are expected to do. These word processors are very powerful and save their users a great deal of time. Dedicated word processors are used in businesses such as publishing and secretarial services, where typing text is a major job.

The fourth type of word processor is a microcomputer that uses word processing software. This software is popular with many users. Small businesses, teachers, and families often use word processing software.

1. What is a shared-logic word processor?
2. Who might use a dedicated word processor?
3. What is word processing software?
4. When is time-shared word processing useful?
5. In which type of system is the computer used for many purposes, including word processing?

Who Uses Word Processing?

Word processing is used in many different environments. It has become quite popular in businesses because it makes the secretary's or typist's job much easier. It also produces more attractive copies of text.

If a letter is word-processed instead of typed, each copy can be error-free and printed automatically.

Think for a moment about all of the writing that must be done by most businesses. They must write letters to other businesses, letters to customers, and letters to their own employees. They must write advertisements that will attract new customers. Often, they must write reports to let other businesses or branches of the same business know what they are doing. They must write instructions for their employees about how to do certain tasks. In fact, businesses have to process millions of words in order to stay in business.

In the past, many businesses hired typists and secretaries to process words. This was done by a person operating an ordinary typewriter. But this is a slow process for several reasons. First, it is easy to make typing mistakes, and these mistakes take time to correct. Second, the typewriter can only produce one copy at at a time. Of course, a typist can make carbon copies while typing, but these copies are of poor quality. Third, when a letter or report must be changed, it is necessary to type the entire letter or report over again even though there may be only minor changes. Fourth, the typewriter has no way of remembering the information that has been typed. Computers that do word processing have solved many of these problems for typists and secretaries.

But businesspersons are not the only ones who recognize the usefulness of word processing. For example, word processing is being used in some schools to help students learn to write. Because correcting mistakes is so fast and easy with a word processor, students are more likely to revise their essays, stories,

Youngsters can learn keyboarding skills in school, and will find that these skills come in handy as they use computers in their work.

With a modem, typed manuscripts can be sent to publishers or other offices by computer.

and poetry. Also, students may decide to revise their writing after seeing the teacher's comments on the rough draft. Word processing makes it easy for them to put paragraphs in a different order, add new sentences to their writing, and correct their spelling. Revising their work makes it better, so students learn to produce better writing.

Professional writers appreciate word processing for the same reason. Instead of having to crumple up paper and throw it in the wastebasket each time the writer wants to start over, he or she can merely edit the writing on the screen. Again, when their editor or publisher suggests changes in the text, the changes are easily made. It is important that writers feel good about making additions or changing the text. But it is difficult for them to feel good about it if those changes will cost hours and hours of time.

Word processing has revolutionized the field of publishing. Many authors who use word processing send their books, articles, and stories to their publishers on disk. In fact, some authors do not even need to mail the disks. Instead, they may connect their computers to the publisher's computer with a modem. In this way, the written material is transferred automatically to the publisher. Before computers were used, publishers had to deal with bulky typed manuscripts. The author of a book had to mail hundreds of pages of typed material to the publisher.

The editor's job is also easier with word processing. Before word processing, the editor had to go over each written page carefully. He or she had to mark changes and corrections by hand.

Careers and Computers

Computer Consultants

Computer consultants are very helpful to businesses that want to learn how to use computers in their work. The computer consultant is a person who knows what kinds of computer hardware and software can be used by a particular business. The computer consultant is hired by a business on a temporary basis. He or she studies the computer needs of the business and then chooses a system of computer hardware and software to meet those needs. This is useful to business people who do not know a great deal about computers and who need assistance from a computer expert.

Computer consultants come from a wide range of backgrounds. They often specialize in helping a specific kind of business. For example, a computer consultant may specialize in helping retail stores choose computer systems for their operations. In this instance, the computer consultant must have some knowledge of retailing as well as a knowledge of which computers are best for use in stores. Usually the computer consultant has worked in the type of business he or she specializes in to get a special understanding of that field. The computer consultant also needs to have education and experience in the field of computers.

Most computer consultants are well paid for their work, but they do not usually have permanent jobs. They are hired for short periods until the business they are helping has installed its computer, and appropriate software and programs have been selected. Then they are hired by other companies. This means that computer consultants often have to travel to different cities where they are needed. This is a good field for people who want to work with computers, and live and work in different places.

Secretarial Services Employees

People who work for secretarial services agencies have become proficient users of computers and software. No longer is quick and accurate typing the only skill needed to meet the needs of businesses looking for contracted help. Many offices have need for people who can work with word processing, data bases, and spreadsheets. Also, office personnel do not want to spend hours training a person who may be needed on a temporary basis for only a few days of work. Many agencies now require prospective employees to pass tests on the use of certain computers or software packages. A business may contract a person to work for a day, a week, or a month at a time. While working in the office this person may need to write and mail several hundred letters using a word processor and a utility program. Another day may be spent mailing out monthly statements using a word processor, or revising a weekly newsletter.

As offices become more and more computerized and efficient, people doing the traditional secretarial type jobs will find that they will rely more and more on job skills related to the use of the computer. It will be valuable to have these important skills.

Then the manuscript had to be typed again so that the changes could be made. This meant that the publishing house was swimming in paper! With word processing, an editor can edit the text by simply inserting the disk into the publisher's computer and making changes on the CRT. With telecommunication (linking of computers in different locations via telephone lines), the computer can read the text from the disk and send it to a typesetting machine. In the past, people had to type text into a typesetting machine before it could be printed. Now this can be done by the computer.

Teachers use word processors to prepare written material for their students. Because many word processors include graphic functions, these handouts can be made very attractive. Even when they do not include graphics, though, handouts prepared on a word processor are less time-consuming and can be more attractive. The teacher can store tests and materials prepared on a disk. As the material changes from year to year, the teacher can make additions or changes in the materials quickly and easily. An example of this might be the teacher who prepares a schedule of activities for his or her class. The teacher presents almost the same material each semester in almost the same order. But each year he or she must retype the schedule simply because the dates of the class change from year to year! With a word processor, the teacher can store the schedule on a disk and change the schedule slightly each year. He or she can then print out many copies of the schedule so that each student has one.

Personal computer users have also found many applications for word processing. They may use it to write personal and business letters that are neat, correct, and attractive. Or they may use it to write resumes and applications for jobs. Students may use word processing to help complete homework assignments and prepare final reports that are neat and correct. In fact, word processing is useful for any work that involves the written word.

CHECK WHAT YOU HAVE LEARNED

1. Name three problems with using a typewriter.
2. How does a word processor help an editor?
3. How can word processing help students learn to write?
4. Try to think of a way in which each member of your family over the age of five can use a word processor.
5. How has word processing changed publishing?

The Future and Computers

Telecommunications

One way that computers function as a powerful tool in offices, schools, homes, and other places is referred to as **telecommunications**. Telecommunications is the sending and receiving of information from one point to another without changing the information as it is sent or received.

As you can imagine, businesses rely on telecommunications to send and receive information from office to office. A branch office in Chicago can send information to a branch office in San Francisco in much less time than it would take to send the same information through the mail. In business, time is money. Telecommunications is one way that businesses use computers to save both. However, telecommunications is not used only to link computers that are located miles apart. It can also be used to enable computers in the same building or even in the same office to communicate with each other.

Telecommunications may bring great changes in the way banks, libraries, stores, and even schools work. For example, students may use their computer terminals as learning tools. They would no longer have to meet in classrooms in order to study academic subjects. Instead, they would enroll in classes given through the computer. Disabled students who are unable to travel to schools to attend classes would be able to study at home. Adult students who may be working fulltime would be able to work around their schedules and take classes at their own pace. Students could take classes from schools in other cities without having to move. A student living in San Diego could study artificial intelligence with a professor at the Massachusetts Institute of Technology.

Telecommunications is done by sending information that has been translated into electronic signals over telephone lines or cables. Signals can also be sent through the air via satellite, like radio signals. Satellite communication links all countries of the world. Businesses that have offices in different countries can transfer information quickly and easily through telecommunications.

By using telecommunications, the unnecessary storage of duplicate information can be avoided. One central location can be chosen to maintain and update needed information. When some of that information is needed in another location (a branch office, a different library, a bank in the next town, or factory in another country, for example), it can be sent via a telecommunications system.

Telecommunications turns the computer into an *electronic mailbox*. People with computers and modems can send messages to each other. This is probably the way we will receive our mail in the future. Letters can be sent this way in much less time than it would take to mail them through the post office. We will also probably use telecommunications to do our shopping by mail. Some newspapers are already being sent electronically.

WHAT YOU HAVE LEARNED IN CHAPTER FOUR

One of the most important things that people do is write down their ideas. Without the written word, the work of the greatest scientist or the most learned historian would be lost. Mathematicians, teachers, scientists, doctors, police officers, and many others must use writing in their jobs. But sometimes writing takes up a great deal of time. The computer is making the task of writing an easier one. Through word processing, much of the busy-work of writing is eliminated.

Word processing is the process of writing, storing, and copying text by using the computer. Text is the written material being prepared. A word processor uses a keyboard similar to the typewriter's, but the word processor also has function keys. These are keys that tell the computer to perform routine tasks such as finding a word or checking the spelling in the document. A word processor is much faster than a typewriter because everything is done on the computer. The text appears on the CRT screen. No paper is used until the document is written and corrected and ready to be printed. This way, typing errors can be eliminated quickly and text can be changed without retyping. The user can print out as many copies as necessary, and the document can be stored on a disk for future use.

With word processing, the typist can do many things not possible on a typewriter. The typist can easily correct or change text. The computer can also check the spelling in the document. The computer can merge a document with a mailing list so that clear, original copies of a letter can be made for each person on the mailing list. It can also center words or phrases on a page, and can make sure that all lines of type end at exactly the same place on the right-hand side of the page. With a word processor, the user can choose different type styles and sizes. This makes it possible to prepare documents that are not only correct but also attractive. The computer can also find particular words in the document and change them. Finally, the computer can move whole paragraphs from one part of the document to another or copy paragraphs in other spots in the text.

There are four kinds of word processors. Time-shared word processors are microcomputers that are linked to larger computers. With this system, many people can do word processing at the same time. The shared-logic word processor can be used for several different purposes at once. It is not used only for word processing. The dedicated word processor is one that is specifically designed for word processing. It is very powerful. And finally, there is word processing software for many types of microcomputers.

Businesses use word processors for many tasks. They must write letters, advertisements, reports, and instructions. Students are also using word processors to learn to write. Because correcting text is so simple with word processing, students are more likely to revise their work to make it better. Professional writers use word processors for the same reason. Publishers and editors use word processors to make changes in texts that have been submitted for publication. They have authors send them their books on several disks rather than on hundreds of pieces of paper. Teachers use word processors to prepare handouts for their class. And personal computer users have also found many applications for word processing. In fact, word processing is useful for any work that involves the written word.

1. What is a time-shared word processor?
2. Describe the keyboard of the word processor.
3. If a typist is working on a document with a word processor, where will the text be showing?
4. Define word processing.
5. How does word processing help professional writers?
6. Name two ways in which word processing can help make a document more attractive.
7. List three things that a business might want a word processor to help it do.
8. Tell why a dedicated word processor would be a good choice for a publishing company.
9. Tell why a dedicated word processor would not be a good choice for an average family.
10. Name five careers in which a person might benefit from having a word processor.

USING WORDS YOU HAVE LEARNED

1. The _____ is a character that shows the typist where the next character typed will appear.
2. _____ word processors are very powerful and are often used by publishers or secretarial services.
3. The writing, editing, storing, and copying of text by using the computer is called _____ _____ .
4. The style of lettering used is called the _____ .
5. To give the computer a specific command, the user presses a _____ key.
6. People do not usually enjoy receiving a _____ letter because it is obvious it was sent to many people.
7. When each line of type ends at the same place on the right, the document has been _____ .

8. When a person reads a text carefully in order to check for errors, he or she is _____ .
9. You _____ two lists when you put them together.
10. With a _____ word processor, the computer can be used for several different purposes at once.

EXERCISING YOUR WRITING SKILLS

John has four girlfriends. Their names are Wanda, Georgette, Fufu, and Helena. He really likes all of them, so he has decided to ask each of them to go to a movie with him this week. Of course, he wants to invite them to different movies on different nights! He wants to send each of them a letter, but he hates the idea of writing four different ones. He thought of sending a form letter but is afraid that the girls will get angry if they find out about each other. Being a rather inventive young man, he has decided to write one letter, use correction fluid to change the names and other specific information, and copy it four times. He would like your help in doing this. Write a letter that can be easily changed to fit each situation. The more changes necessary in each letter, the more his chance of being found out. Remember, the letter should be basically the same for each girl. Then produce four letters, remembering to change all necessary names, times, places, and movie titles. Otherwise poor John could get in a lot of trouble!

Were you able to save John from the wrath of four girls? Your task would have been much simpler if you had been able to use a word processor. If you do have access to a word processor or a computer with word processing software, write the four letters again. How did word processing make your job easier?

UNDERSTANDING WHAT YOU HAVE LEARNED

MULTIPLE CHOICE

1. Word processing is useful for:
    a) computing the radius of a circle
    b) measuring the distance to school
    c) writing and editing text
    d) getting to school on time
2. People likely to use word processors include:
    a) secretaries
    b) police officers
    c) students
    d) all of the above
3. The cursor is:
    a) an angry computer operator
    b) a character that keeps your place on the CRT screen
    c) a character at the end of each page
    d) a key that gives the computer a command
4. When someone reads text carefully to check for mistakes, he or she is:
    a) computing
    b) word processing
    c) proofreading
    d) spelling
5. When a typist changes fonts, he or she is interested in:
    a) making the document attractive
    b) checking the spelling
    c) correcting the text
    d) proofreading
6. Dedicated word processors are:
    a) not very efficient
    b) used by everyone
    c) good for people who want to use them for many different types of tasks
    d) only designed to do word processing
7. With a typewriter, a paragraph can be moved only if:
    a) it is not very long
    b) it is retyped
    c) it is not essential
    d) a function key is pressed

8. With a typewriter, it is:
   a) impossible to justify text
   b) easy to justify text
   c) necessary to justify text
   d) very difficult to justify text
9. The word processor checks spelling by:
   a) referring to a dictionary in its memory
   b) highlighting every word
   c) working very slowly
   d) proofreading for punctuation errors
10. A professional writer can often send his or her manuscript into the publisher's office by using a:
    a) data base
    b) function key
    c) modem
    d) font

TRUE OR FALSE

1. While a word processor can be fun for many, it is really only used professionally by secretaries.
2. The computer always knows how to spell every word in a document.
3. A proofreader reads a text carefully for errors.
4. A computer can help an editor but not a proofreader.
5. It is possible to move whole paragraphs in seconds using a word processor.
6. The computer can print out many copies of a document.
7. With a typewriter, it is possible to merge a mailing list and another document automatically.
8. Text can be changed on the CRT before it is printed onto the paper.
9. Margin errors are easily corrected on a typewriter.
10. To justify text, the computer must convince itself that the text is correct.

SHORT ANSWER

1. How might a word processor be useful to a police officer?
2. Describe how you would check for spelling errors with a word processor.
3. How does a typist justify text using a typewriter? A word processor?
4. How does changing the font affect the appearance of a manuscript?
5. Why is it useful to be able to merge text with graphics?
6. When would a businessperson be likely to merge a mailing list with a document?
7. Describe time-shared word processing.
8. How does the word processor help an editor?
9. Tell one reason why documents prepared on a word processor are likely to be more correct than those prepared on a typewriter.
10. What does the cursor do?

INSIDE A COMPUTER FACTORY

As computers become more and more a part of everyday life, computer companies must plan for efficient production of their products at the lowest possible cost to meet consumer demands. Some companies are making use of advanced technology and research to manufacture great quantities of computers every year.

Apple Computer, Inc. opened a factory in California in 1984 to exclusively produce its Macintosh computer. A year later, the factory's employees and a fully-automated (and partially robotized) system were turning out one million Macintosh computers a year—or one computer every fourteen seconds!

One reason for the factory's efficiency is receiving needed parts daily from only a few suppliers. These parts are already tested before they arrive, with the exact number of parts being delivered for assembly over a two-week period. And they are delivered to the exact location in the factory where they are assembled.

Much of the plant is fully automated. For example, some components (or parts) are automatically inserted on finished circuit boards (**1**). It is necessary, however, for some parts to be inserted by hand (**2**), and for the assembled part to be visually inspected (**3**). When a circuit board is assembled, it is possible to use a computer to test that assembly. Here, then, is a computer being used to test a partially-built computer!

INSIDE A COMPUTER FACTORY 135

Some tasks require the careful attention of factory workers. The chassis assembly, the cathode-ray tube (CRT), and the disk drive are all added by hand (**4**), (**5**), and (**6**). Alignment and focus of the display screen is another step that relies on the careful placement by a factory worker (**7**).

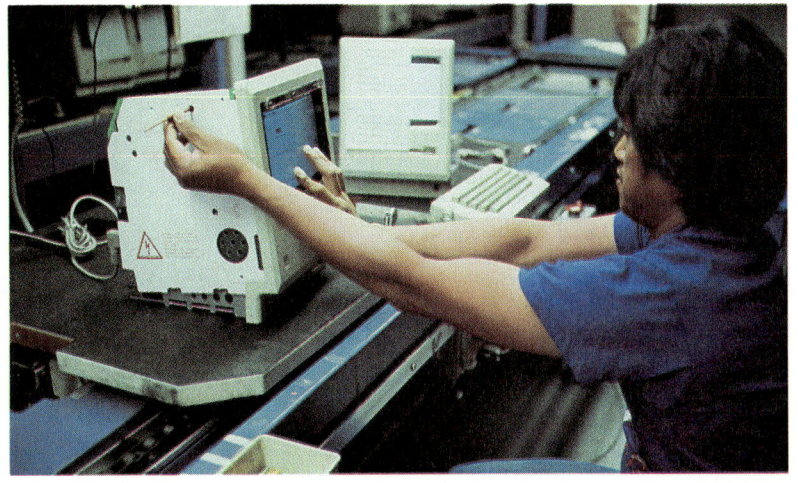

136 PHOTO ESSAY

8

9

After the computer has been assembled, it automatically travels to an area within the factory for a twenty-four hour test (**8**). The machines run continuously for that time period, and are then given a final test (**9**), again with the aid of another computer and operator.

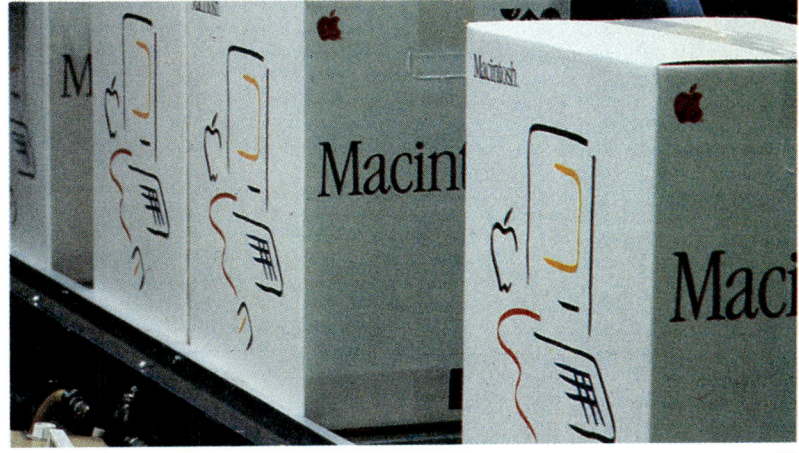

INSIDE A COMPUTER FACTORY

Packaging of a brand-new computer is very important—a company wants its customer to receive the product in the best possible condition. This means it must be packaged in plastic to keep it as dust-free as possible (**10**), and carefully boxed (**11**) to protect the delicate mechanisms within the computer itself from being damaged in shipping. Twelve cartons of computers are lifted gently by an industrial robot and placed on a pallet (or wooden platform) that is easy to transport from place to place (**12**).

With this last step, the finished computer is ready for transport to distribution centers, stores, etc., to fill customer orders. The manufacturing process of the hardware has been completed in a short length of time, saving manufacturing, warehousing, and labor costs. But another process is just beginning: that of using the computer as a helpful tool in today's world.

WHAT YOU WILL LEARN IN CHAPTER FIVE

By the end of this chapter, you will be able to:

1. Define data base.
2. List three advantages of using a computerized data base.
3. Describe briefly how a small data base system might be used.
4. Explain how keys help the computer to find useful information.
5. Name several uses of data bases in different areas of personal and professional life.

Data Bases: Finding Information Fast

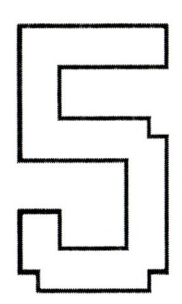

5

WORDS YOU WILL LEARN

accountant
accounts payable
accounts receivable
data base
data item
display
field
file
key
menu
payroll
record
relational data base
update

Handling information has become very important in today's world. Each day we find ourselves trying to learn more, store more, keep more information about the things that go on around us. Families usually have information stored about the health of the members of the family, the insurance on the house, cars or appliances, bills that they must pay, taxes that they have paid or will pay, recipes that they use to cook, and so on. Professionally, they may keep information about customers that they serve or jobs that they have done. Students usually keep some kind of record of the classes that they take and the homework that they do.

One of the ways that computers help us is in handling all of the information that we must deal with. This information used to be kept in paper filing systems, but now computers have allowed us to store it in different ways. The computer makes keeping and using information much easier than it was when it was all written on pieces of paper.

What Is a Data Base?

We already know that computers are especially useful in situations where people need to use and keep large amounts of information. Think of the federal government, for example. The government keeps many records for all of its citizens. These records may be tax records, health records, employment records, or many other types of records. All these records add up to mountains of information that the government keeps.

But all of this information would be useless unless it were stored or kept in an organized and logical way. The people who need the records must know where or how to find them. Otherwise, there is no reason to keep them. This is one way that computers have made life simpler. They store large amounts of information and make it easy for us to find the information we need.

In the late 1960s and early 1970s, businesses began storing more and more information in computers. People began to see a need for better and more effective ways of storing large numbers of records. During the third generation of computer development, the concept of the **data base** was developed.

Actually, a data base is not really a new concept. If you have a recipe file, a checking account, or a list of homework assignments, you already have a data base. A data base is just a collection of data that is organized into a system that makes it usable.

This organization can be very difficult, however. The method you use to organize the information may make a big difference in the way it is used. For example, the cook who organizes a recipe file in alphabetical order may have difficulty finding a dessert recipe that uses a specific ingredient. The person who organizes checks according to the amount spent may have difficulty finding a check written on a certain date. The cook would probably have more success if recipes were organized according to type. For example, main categories might include desserts, breakfasts, casseroles, and so on. The person organizing checks should consider filing them according to the date on which they were written.

On a computer, the data base is a tool for storing information. A data base is a way of storing many files that contain information needed for different jobs. For example, consider a company that stores employee records in a data base. It can use the same records for payroll, for health insurance, and for personnel purposes. This is a more effective way of storing information than to store payroll, insurance, and personnel records for each individual in several different files. Instead of storing three different but related records for each employee, the computer can store one record in a data base that contains all of the information it needs to do different tasks.

When fewer files are stored, less space is taken up. Information is easier to get to because there are fewer records to read through. This means that retrieving information from a data base is faster than having to look through different records to find the one that contains the information needed.

The computer can search its memory very quickly. There are some things that can be done with a computer electronically that cannot be done with paper files. One difference is that the computer can organize the same information in many different ways. For example, let's go back to the cook who wants a dessert that uses a specific ingredient. The cook can ask the computer to find all recipes that use that ingredient. Or he can look up all desserts. He can even become very specific and ask the computer to look for two or three things: all desserts that use that ingredient and require less than three hours to make.

The person who has her checking account in a data base has little problem finding the check she wants. She may ask for a list of the checks in which a certain amount was spent. Or she may ask for a list of all checks written to a certain person. Or she may ask for a list of all checks written on a certain day. She might even ask the computer to find all checks for $6.50 written between February and June to John Doe. The data base can organize the information

"I know you struck out the first 26 batters, Fernando, but the computer says we have to take you out."

Computers are helping everyone to make decisions!

This engineer is using a data base to find important information about materials used in his design.

in one or many different ways, depending on what she needs to find out.

A data base does not process any data. That is, the data base does not change the data or give the user new information. It is just a place to store data. Some data base systems are organized in a way that makes it unnecessary to repeat any information at all. These systems are called **relational data bases**, and they are fairly complex. They look up information by searching a series of files that lead the computer to find the right file. By not repeating information in different files, they save a great deal of room and allow the user to get information more quickly.

CHECK WHAT YOU HAVE LEARNED

1. What is a data base?
2. What is a relational data base?
3. Briefly explain how the way you organize your data may make a difference in how you use it.
4. When was the concept of a computerized data base developed?
5. Why is it especially useful for the government to have a computerized data base?

How a Data Base Is Organized

There are several terms that you should be familiar with so that you can understand how a data base is organized. Each space where specific information is stored is called a **field**. For example,

Last Name: _____

is a field where a last name can be stored. In each field is a **data item**. A data item is a piece of information that is filled in for each field. For example, in

Name: *T.J. Smith*

T.J. Smith is a data item stored in the name field.

```
Thelma Jane Smith
1800 E. Madison Drive
Charlottesville, Virginia 20522
202-555-1897
202-555-3024
```

A simple data base can include several *fields* such as ones for name, address, work phone number, and home phone number. The specific information in each field is a *data item*.

It is probable that the user will want to have more fields about T.J. Smith. He or she may want to keep a record of T.J. Smith's address, phone number, occupation, purchases, special interests, and so on. All of the information about Ms. Smith, taken together, is called a **record**. A record does not have to be about people, of course. Some users may want to have a record of a certain piece of merchandise, a historic event, or a class at a school. A record is simply a collection of several fields that are about the same thing.

A data base stores many **files**. A file is a collection of records. For example, one file might have records containing the names, addresses, and purchases of *all* clients. Each file is made up of several records.

Let us imagine a data base that is kept in a small office. The office has five employees: Hilda, John, Jill, Steven, and Maria. Information on each employee is kept in the data base. All of the fields filled with data items that tell about Maria make up Maria's record. There are several fields in Maria's record. There is a field for her name, address, phone number, salary, position, and so on. But there are also records on the other employees. All of the records on all of the employees might be called the employee file.

All the information about Ms. Smith is called a *record*. When different records are stored together, they are called a *file*.

```
Thelma Jane Smith
1800 E. Madison Drive
Charlottesville, Virginia 20522
202-555-1897
202-555-3024

Ray Kealoha
1445 Ala Moana Boulevard
Honolulu, Hawaii 96601
808-555-1135
808-555-6205

Samuel Watenabe
348 Princeton Way
Newark, New Jersey 10172
296-555-8400
296-555-8149
```

Data base information should be updated periodically so that the information is always correct and complete.

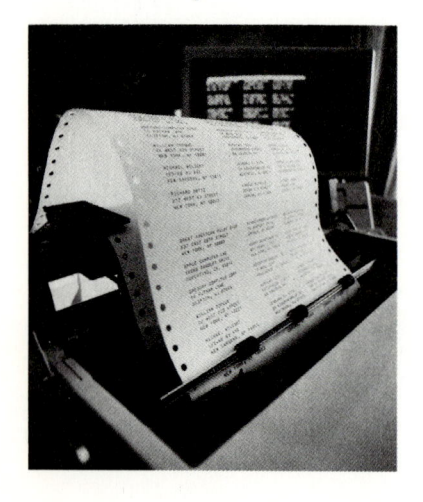

The computer must have some way of organizing files so that it can find and display them when someone needs to read them. Think about a filing cabinet for a moment. Paper files must be kept in some logical order. They may be arranged in a certain way within a manila folder. They are usually arranged alphabetically or numerically. And the folder may be identified by a name, a policy number, a date, a color, etc. This way, they can be found quickly and easily when they are needed. This is also the case with files stored in a data base on the computer. Information that is stored in the computer in an organized manner is much easier to find when the time comes to use that information.

The computer organizes and stores files by looking for **key** information. The person creating the data base must choose certain fields as keys. For instance, the last name field might be designated as a key. Then the computer puts the files in alphabetical order by last name. *T.J. Smith* appears after *O.W. Roberts* and before *C.X. Taylor*. When someone requests to see the file for T.J. Smith, the computer reads through the names in its files until it reaches the correct file. The user might name two or three keys for the computer to look for. Instead of asking for the entire file for T.J. Smith, he or she might ask the computer to look for T.J. Smith, purchases, and amount owed. Then it will display the fields that show T.J. Smith's purchases and the amount she owes on the screen or print a paper copy of this information if it is so commanded.

DATA BASES

CHECK WHAT YOU HAVE LEARNED

1. What is a field?
2. How does the computer organize and store files?
3. Explain the difference between a file and a record.
4. How do keys help the user to find the information he or she needs?
5. Where are data items entered?

Why Data Bases Are Better than Paper Files

You have probably seen a business office that uses filing cabinets to store all kinds of information. The files may contain information about customers, other businesses, or matters within the business itself. All of this information is important. Without it, the business could not run as it should. Imagine what would happen, for example, if a business lost all of its files of customers who owed money to the business. A great deal of money would be lost if the business did not know who was supposed to be making payments to the company.

Until recently when computers became popular, most businesses used file folders and filing cabinets to keep track of the information they needed to stay in business. But there were several problems with this method. First, human workers had to spend a lot of time filing papers in a logical way so that the information contained in the files could be found again when it was needed. This was usually done by organizing the information according to one important aspect of the file. For example, a file of all clients might be organized according to the clients' last names. The problem, of course, is that sometimes people need the information organized in a different way. Suppose, for example, that a manufacturer wished to have a list of all the clients who had bought a particular item. In order to find those clients in a paper filing system, someone would have to go through all of the files to check the purchases of each client. This would take a great deal of time. The manufacturer might decide that the files should be organized according to purchases. But then if he or she needed to know all of the purchases Mr. Jones had made, someone would have to check each file again to see if Mr. Jones had bought each item. In other words, with a paper filing system the user is locked into a system of organization that is not always useful.

Finding specific information in a bulky, paper filing system can be time-consuming and frustrating.

An advantage of storing information on computers is that it is easier to find the information when it is needed. Instead of having to sort through file drawers that contain thousands of sheets of paper, the person who needs information only has to enter a few simple commands into the terminal. In a matter of seconds, the computer searches its memory for the information needed and displays the information on the screen or prints out a copy of it. In this way, businesses keep all the information they need at their fingertips.

Second, workers sometimes make mistakes while they are filing and put papers into files where they do not belong. This makes it nearly impossible to locate the information in the future. It is difficult to make this mistake with a computer system. Because the computer does the actual filing, items can always be found by looking up related information.

Third, the files and filing cabinets required to store the large amounts of information needed by a big company take up a great deal of space. The more files a business has, the longer it takes to find information from the files. Sometimes whole libraries are needed to house the information used by a business. With a computerized data base system, this information can be stored on small disks and kept close to the person who is likely to be using it.

The Future and Computers

Satellite Telecommunications

With the continued expansion of satellite communications, it will soon be commonplace to access data banks and communicate with other computers directly through satellite relays. As access to data banks becomes easier, the size of the data banks will increase astronomically. Large amounts of information will be available for all who seek it. Information will be constantly updated and added to the data banks, allowing computer users to get the very latest information concerning anything from the history of aeronautics to zoology. Magazines and newspapers may become completely electronic: you will ask your computer to "fetch" the newspaper, and then it will find the parts you want and read them to you! People will be able to take their small computers with them almost anywhere and still be able to access their homes, banks, and offices. Many business transactions will be done via satellite. Access to information will become simple. Information will literally be at arm's length!

Fourth, paper can be damaged or destroyed easily. This means that valuable information could be lost in a fire or flood. Or it could be destroyed by someone who did not wish for the information to be seen or used by other people. Because extra copies of paper information take up a great deal of space, it is usually not practical to make copies of all important documents. The computer can make copies of information kept on disks very quickly and easily. Disks are much smaller than paper files, so it is less difficult to store copies.

Computers have changed the way many businesses store their information. Instead of using the traditional paper files and filing cabinets, businesses now use cassettes, tapes, and disks to store the same amount of information in a much smaller space. Also, it is very easy to make backup copies of information stored by computer. With backup copies, business are sure to have extra copies of information, even if files are destroyed. Data bases store huge amounts of information for businesses of all sizes and types.

Today's "filing cabinet" can store a great deal of information right on the user's desk.

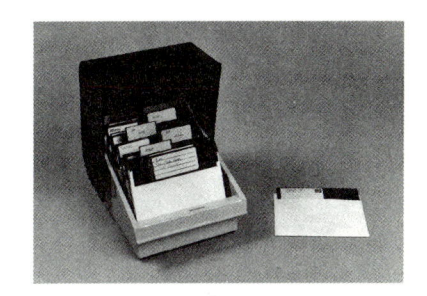

CHECK WHAT YOU HAVE LEARNED

1. Describe briefly why a user is locked into one system of organization with a paper filing system.
2. How do data bases save space?
3. How do data bases save time?
4. Why is it easier to keep copies of computerized files?
5. Why is it difficult to file something in the wrong place with a data base?

Setting Up and Using a Data Base

There are many different types of data base packages, and each one is a little bit different. Some are very complicated. Larger relational data base systems might take quite a while to learn to use. Some data base filing systems are very simple, however. The next few sections outline how to create a file, how to enter data into that file, and how to display the data. It is really not as difficult to set up and use some data base systems as you might think.

Creating a File

The computer, using data base software, will probably first give you a list of choices (called a **menu**) from which you can choose your task. Since you cannot enter any data items until you have a file set up, your first job in using a data base system is in creating a file. You choose the option on the screen that allows you to create a file. What type of information do you want to keep? You may, for example, decide to keep a file of homework assignments. The computer will ask you what the name for your file will be. You type in *Homework*.

But once you have decided that you will keep a file on homework, you must make a decision about what you will want to know about that homework. For example, you might want to know when it was assigned, what class it is for, and when it is due. These are pieces of information that can be filled in later, as your work is

A menu gives the user a choice of activities or tasks.

assigned. But you cannot fill in information unless you have created a field for it to go into. Part of creating a file is choosing the fields that will be important later on. You decide on five important fields that belong in a file on homework: class, date assigned, homework description, date due, grade.

The computer may ask you how big to make each field—that is, how many character spaces you will need to fill in information. For the dates you need only five characters or spaces, because you can put in numbers for the month and day like this: 10/21. The class name that contains the most letters will help you decide how many characters to allow for that field. The description of homework can take some space, so you allow fifty characters for that field. For grade you probably only need two or three spaces.

Entering Data

Once your fields have been created, you are ready to enter the data items. To do this, you return to the menu and choose the option that allows you to enter data. The first field that you are to fill in appears on the screen. After you type in the data item for each field and press a key to enter that information, the screen shows you the next field. You continue until you have filled in all of the information you can. Using the homework example, your first record might look like this:

   Class: <u>English</u>
Date Assigned: <u>12/04</u>
Homework Description: <u>Descriptive essay</u>
Date Due: <u>12/14</u>
Grade:

You can leave the grade blank until after the homework is corrected and returned. That will be a good time to **update** your record. Update means to change, correct, or add to data that has been entered before. Sometimes information (mailing addresses, telephone numbers, employee salaries, or scientific data, for example) can change over time. The computer cannot know if the information you have stored is still correct. If your information has been updated, it will also probably be much more useful. In this case, for example, it would be possible to ask the computer to show all of your homework grades (for homework that had been returned) in English. This might give you an indication of your final grade in that course.

CHAPTER FIVE

Displaying Data

Information from a data base can be shown in a number of different ways.

Now that you have created a file and entered the data into it, you can use your file to get general or specific information. From the main menu, you choose the option that allows the computer to **display** or show the data in the data base.

You may ask the computer to sort the homework according to class and then to display all the homework for the semester. It would probably be more useful, however, to ask the computer to display all those assignments with a specific due date. You might do this each night to be sure that you have completed all homework assignments due on the next day. Or you may decide that you would like to see all English assignments for the semester. You may even want to become very specific and ask the computer for the English assignment due on a certain date.

The commands that you give the computer depend on the data base program you are using. But any data base program allows you to arrange the file in several different ways. You can decide which way the information will be useful to you as you are using

People and Computers

George Tate and Hal Lashlee

George Tate was born in 1943 and became interested in computers as a young man. Like many people in the early 1970s, Tate bought a computer kit and built his own microcomputer. He also joined the Southern California Computer Society. He and a friend, Hal Lashlee, an accountant, were sure that microcomputer software would become an important industry in years to come. In August of 1980, they formed a software mail-order business.

It was not long before their company began receiving requests for a software called Vulcan. This software was designed by Wayne Ratcliff, a systems designer at Jet Propulsion Laboratory. Ratcliff had developed the software, but had been unable to sell it. Ratcliff, Tate, and Lashlee made a deal, and Tate and Lashlee began to advertise the software. They renamed it dBase II.

By 1981, dBase II had become a very popular data-base management system. It is designed for microcomputers. By predicting that microcomputer software would be a major industry, and by locating and marketing a data-base management system for microcomputers, Tate and Lashlee became leaders in the field of computer software.

it. You may make a different decision later. With a data base, you are not locked into seeing the information in only one way and searching through it to find the information you need. The computer will do the searching for you.

CHECK WHAT YOU HAVE LEARNED

1. What must you do before you enter data into your data base?
2. What must you decide in order to create a file?
3. Why is it important to update a file?
4. What should you consider when you ask the computer to display the data?
5. Give an example of some information you might file in a data base.

Where Are Data Bases Used?

Data bases are used in many different ways and in many different situations. Businesses may design their own data bases to store customer records, employee records, and other types of records that must be stored in large numbers. This gives them fast access to the information they need to keep a business operating smoothly.

Data bases are also useful when there is too much information for people to keep track of by other means or where information changes on a regular basis. Lawyers use data bases to keep on top of changes in laws that affect their clients. They can tap into a data base, ask for information on a certain law or legal situation, and receive immediate answers. They can also determine if any new legal information has been added to the data base that might make a difference. This saves them costly hours of research. Law libraries have needed to store volumes and volumes of legal records and books. By finding necessary information in a data base, less storage space for records is needed.

People in many professions use data bases when they want to research the latest developments in their professions. Students may even use data bases to help them gather information for research papers on a particular subject. The data base can save hours of time in the library by guiding the user to specific sources of information on a wide range of topics.

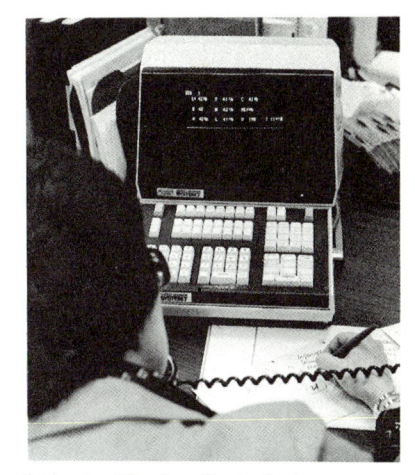

This stockbroker finds that information is at her fingertips through a data base.

In Government

The U.S. government uses data bases to streamline the process of storing vast amounts of information on more than 200 million U.S. citizens. Instead of separate government agencies having to store their own sets of files, they can share a common data base that maintains the information they need. Remember that one of the first major data processing systems used was designed by Herman Hollerith for the tabulation of the 1890 census. Formerly, the census had been a very time-consuming process that took years of work to complete. To do the same procedure manually today with the increased population would require an even greater amount of time to complete.

The census is taken every ten years. The information is collected and entered into a large computer data base. It is used for many applications by state and federal government and by private business as well. State and federal monies are allocated to counties and cities according to their population, as counted by the census. People are classified and put into categories, such as single or married or living in urban or rural areas, by the computer. Growth in population is calculated for cities and counties also by the computer. Areas of the cities and counties are rated by the income average of the persons living there. The census has become a more useful tool because the data base allows the information to be presented in many different forms.

Computers have also become an important part of the election process. Voters are now listed on a printout and their names are verified before they are allowed to vote. Mailing lists are one of the simplest applications of computers. Political candidates can buy complete lists of voters on mailing labels to use when they send their political literature. There are also many other special lists for mailings to organizations or specific groups. The computer can be used to generate a personalized letter from the candidate to potential voters. The data base can also keep track of the funds raised in support of a candidate. The computer can maintain a list of all the contributors.

The Bureau of Vital Statistics keeps records on every citizen. It keeps records regarding births and deaths. Each person's birth is recorded. The record includes the time, date, and place of birth as well as the mother's and father's name. This information is used throughout a person's life. It is first used to provide proof of age when a person is ready to begin school. It is also used to obtain a social security number and a passport. The Bureau of Vital Statistics maintains an enormous data base.

Careers and Computers

Data Base Specialists

Because businesses today use and store great amounts of information on their computers, a new specialization has developed in the field of programming: that of the data base expert. Data base specialists write programs that organize and set up data bases and allow the information stored in the data base to be used with other programs that the business runs.

The data base specialist must know several programming languages and have some special training or experience in data bases. Along with this, the data base specialist must possess good personal communication skills. This is because the job requires the data base specialist to deal with other people in the company to determine what the business's information needs are.

Given the vast amount of data that is stored in data bases, the data base specialist is a valuable member of the data processing team.

Media Specialists/Librarians

The media specialist or librarian is responsible for organizing all of the disks or tapes that a company uses to store its data and programs. In large companies, media specialists must keep track of thousands of disks or tapes. This requires the ability to organize media logically. The media specialist must keep close tabs on disks and tapes so that valuable information is not lost or accessed by unauthorized personnel. In addition to maintaining the disk or tape library, the media specialist may order blank disks and tapes so that the company always has supplies for recording information.

Like other operations personnel, the media specialist is usually trained by his or her company. Data entry operators sometimes move into this job. This job can give a person the experience necessary to learn new jobs in the field of computers.

Airline Reservation Clerks

One industry that uses a great deal of information that is constantly changing is the airline industry. In order to keep track of planes, plane fares, schedules, and other information, the airline reservation clerk must have a great deal of information available to provide customers. Can you imagine how difficult it would be to answer questions about flights if all the information had to be typed, copied, and stored in paper files?

The airline reservation clerk has access to a large data base in which information about flights is stored. This way, the clerk can quickly find out specific information. He or she can compare fares, find out arrival and departure times, and even tell you what meals or movies are available on a particular flight in a matter of seconds. If you decide to make a reservation on a flight, the airline reservation clerk can enter your name into the data base. That way, other clerks throughout the country know immediately that that seat is taken. Because of computerized data bases, choosing and booking airline flights has become a much easier and quicker process.

The Department of Motor Vehicles is another place where a data base is used. This is where all drivers are registered and issued licenses to drive their cars. Their driving records are kept in a large data base. Drivers use these records when they apply to purchase insurance for their automobiles. If they receive tickets while driving, these violations are recorded for a certain period of time. Many states communicate with each other to keep track of drivers with violations that have not been resolved.

Another government agency that uses a data base is the Internal Revenue Service. This is the agency that keeps track of the taxes that must be paid to the government. Here, records are kept of all earnings of people who live in a particular state. Records of the amounts of taxes these people have paid are also kept in this office. These records are organized according to social security numbers.

Data base information can be used to help make decisions.

Police agencies use data bases to store information about crimes that occur throughout the country. A police officer in California can quickly check to see whether a person has committed a crime in New York, for example. This helps police officers to capture criminals who travel from city to city.

Data bases are also used to locate missing persons and runaway children. Information about people who have disappeared helps to identify these people when they are located. Families have been reunited thanks to the effective information storage of data bases.

In Business and Banking

Businesses use computers to keep track of their financial matters. This is called **accounting**. Accounting includes keeping records of how much money a business is making, how much money it is spending, how much it pays its employees, and many other types of information that have to do with money.

Offices that do not use computers to do accounting must have human workers who keep accounting records. These workers are called **accountants**. Many accountants now use computers to simplify their work. Accountants have to keep track of many different processes necessary to keep the business running. One of these processes is **accounts payable**. Accounts payable means all the money that a business owes to other businesses, organizations, and people. For example, stores have to buy from other businesses the items they sell. Often, stores buy items from the factories that manufacture them. The amount that the store owes to the factory is an account payable.

The bigger the business, the larger the number of accounts payable it has to handle. Think of a large department store with thousands of different items. That kind of store has to keep track

A business can keep track of many different types of information with a data base, from a customer's address to its factory inventory.

New Ideas and Computers

Computer Graphics in the Movies

Computers have entered the movie business. Computer-generated graphics have become an important type of animation or special effects in some movies. Scenes that otherwise would have to be filmed many times with different lighting or camera speeds can be done on the computer in a short amount of time. Models of spaceships, stars, or laser effects can be created, moved, and repeated quickly and easily. The entire sequence of a scene can be shown on a computer monitor before it ever needs to be filmed.

People working in this field have been able to simulate photographic effects with a sharpness and color that is equal or superior to the original pictures. Some experts who have seen computer-generated animation or special effects on video-tape have been astounded when informed that the tape's contents were done with a computer and not a camera. The use of this type of computer-generated animation has greatly reduced the overall cost and time involved in making special effects for movies. Soon a common cry in Hollywood may be "Lights! Computer! Action!"

A simple data base display for an invoice used in accounting. The fields have been chosen—only the data items need to be inserted.

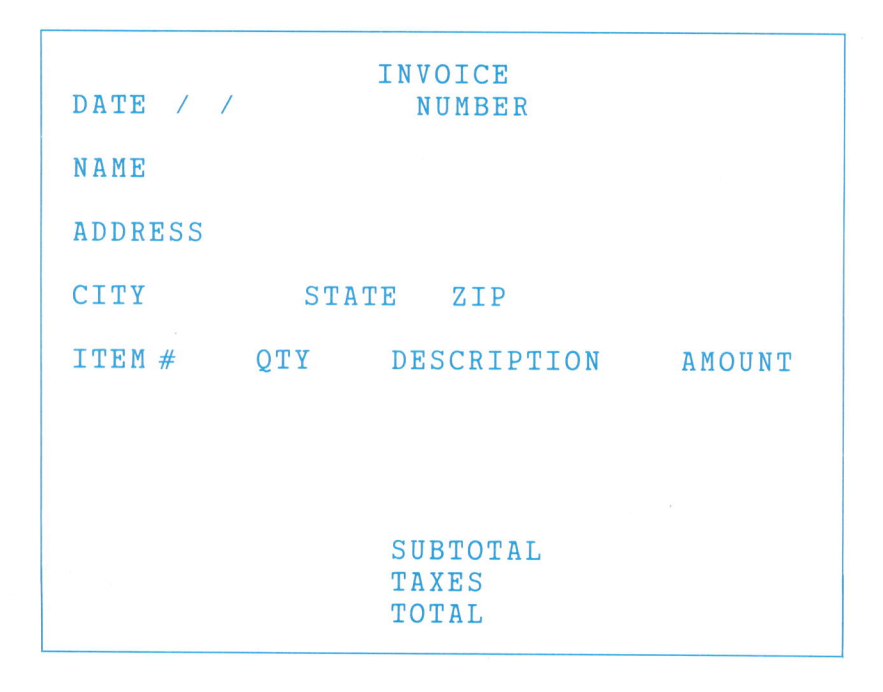

```
                        INVOICE
DATE  /  /              NUMBER

NAME

ADDRESS

CITY            STATE     ZIP

ITEM #    QTY      DESCRIPTION       AMOUNT




                        SUBTOTAL
                        TAXES
                        TOTAL
```

of how much money it must pay for all of the items it stocks. It must also keep track of when the money must be paid. A large number of accounts payable can be very complicated to process.

Computers simplify the process. They store all the information a business needs about who it pays money to. This is better than the manual procedure of keeping files.

In a way, accounts payable is the opposite of **accounts receivable**. Accounts receivable is another job that computers do in the business world today. The term *accounts receivable* refers to all of the money that the customers of a business owe to the business. Of course, a business must keep track of how much money it is owed so that it can make a profit. Imagine what would happen if businesses did not know who owed them money or how much money people owed.

Processing accounts receivable is similar to processing accounts payable. The business must maintain complete and accurate records of which customers owe it money and how much money they owe. This used to be done by keeping paper records of accounts, which had to be filed. Also, the business needs to keep track of when customers pay their bills because not all of the accounts are due on the same day. The business should be able to remind customers when their bills are overdue.

Before computers were used widely in business, accounts re-

DATA BASES

```
                    INVOICE
     DATE 04/15/86       NUMBER 2510

     NAME James Peterson

     ADDRESS 126 Elmwood Drive

     CITY Ames         STATE Iowa   ZIP 20522

     ITEM #    QTY   DESCRIPTION        AMOUNT
     2510       1    Tekgraph 380       1300.00
     3200       1    Dual disk drive     750.00
     1820       1    Disks (10 pkgs)      50.00


                     SUBTOTAL           2100.00
                     TAXES               126.00
                     TOTAL              2226.00
```

The same invoice with data items.

ceivable was a large task that required the efforts of many people. The computer has streamlined the process. First, it stores records of customer accounts. Second, it keeps track of how much money the customer owes to the business. Third, the computer keeps records of when each customer must pay a bill.

Another important computer job that makes use of a data base is **payroll**. The term *payroll* refers to the amount of wages that each employee has earned. Payroll must be paid on a regular basis. In many businesses, payroll is done once each week or once every two weeks. It is important that employees be paid accurately and on time.

Businesses that do not use computers must do payroll manually. This means that someone must keep track of how many hours each employee has worked, what wage each employee is paid, how much tax should be deducted from each employee's earnings, and other information that affects the amount of each paycheck. This is a great deal of information, and it is different for each employee. The data base assists in the payroll. It stores information about employees' hours, wages, taxes, insurance, and other factors.

Most businesses also have large numbers of items to keep track of. Remember the large department store that needed to keep records of how much money it owed to the factories that

Small businesses find data bases useful to keep track of orders, items to process, and operating equipment.

Data bases are useful in banks, where complete information can be kept on each customer.

made the items sold in the store. This is one example of a business that needs to know how many items it has. Another example is a grocery store. A grocery store must keep track of how many cans of tuna it has, for example, so that it will not run out. When the store has a small supply of tuna, it must order a new supply before it runs out. If it does not, customers will be angry that the store does not have the items they want. The store must keep a record of orders, and the names and addresses of their suppliers.

Banks also use data bases to keep track of deposits, withdrawals, and other bank business. With computers, banks can keep their customers' accounts up to date all the time. The computer terminals in the bank can be connected by a modem to other branches of the same bank. Networks of computers keep the branches in touch with each other so that they all have current information.

CHECK WHAT YOU HAVE LEARNED

1. How do data bases help the police?
2. What are accounts receivable?
3. What kind of information does the Bureau of Vital Statistics keep?
4. Name three ways that a business might use a data base.
5. How do data bases help political candidates?

In Insurance and Real Estate

Data bases are very useful in insurance offices. Data entry personnel can enter all sorts of information into customer records. In an auto insurance agency, for example, records must be kept about driving records, age, accidents, models of cars, and many other factors that affect how much the customer's insurance premium (or bill) will be. Storing information on the computer helps the insurance agency maintain accurate customer records. For example, when a customer moves, it is simple to enter the new address into the computer. The computer then changes the address on all of the records for that customer. This is easier than a human having to change an address several times on all the papers that include a customer address.

Real estate is the business of buying and selling land and buildings such as offices and houses. The data base concept makes

DATA BASES

```
Owners Name  Juanita Johnson

Address  10245 Lindsay Court

City St. Louis   Zip 63125   location code E4

Date Listed 05/06/85
Period Listed (months) 6

Asking Price  87900

Square ft.  2250          Lot Size  1 Acre

# Bedrooms  3             # Baths  2

Misc (Y/N)

Family room     Y    Garage(s)     Y
Fireplace       Y    Carport       N
Pool            N    Carpeting     N
Sauna           N
```

Real estate offices find the data base concept useful in matching houses to buyers.

computers especially useful in real estate because it is important to match houses or offices to people. A family with eight children, for example, probably does not want to buy a house with only one bedroom! People may want to live near where they work or near schools or far away from a crowded area. All of this information must be taken into account when matching people to houses. By entering this information into the computer, the real estate agent can keep detailed records of what the customer wants. Then the agent can look for a house that matches the description given by the customer.

Along with keeping customer records, many real estate offices also need to keep records of the properties (land and buildings) that are available for sale. The computer makes this simple. The real estate agent enters all of the information about a property into the computer. The information might include address, size, location, special features, distance from other buildings, and other factors that are important to customers. Once this information is stored, it is easy to print a list of all properties available. The customer can look at this list to decide which properties he or she wants to visit. This way, the agent and customer do not waste time looking at properties that do not meet the needs of the customer.

Insurance companies must keep a file of information on each customer and policy.

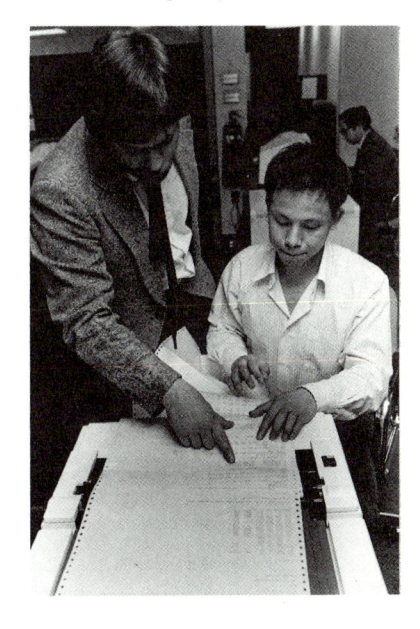

This radio telescope operator can use his data base to help him track objects in space.

In Science

Data bases are a very valuable tool for the scientist. In order to prove a scientific hypothesis or theory, a scientist must first gather a great deal of data. A small amount of data is not enough to show that a certain condition always exists or that an action always occurs in a certain way. After gathering plenty of data, the scientist must carefully examine it. In order to do this, the data must be organized in a meaningful way. With a data base, the scientist can look at one type of data or another. He or she can enter new information or add new entries easily.

Data bases are also useful in medicine and in medical research. Doctors use data bases to make sure that they have current and complete information so that they can provide the best possible treatment for their patients. Doctors contact data bases to learn about diseases they may not have treated before or to learn about new methods of treating diseases. This way they can be sure they are up to date without having to rely on books and articles to provide information. It is also possible for a doctor to diagnose illness by entering a patient's symptoms into the computer. The doctor then uses the data base to learn about diseases that include these symptoms. The data base can be a lifesaver!

In Schools

Teachers can use data bases to keep track of each individual student. Computer-managed instruction, or CMI, can make a teacher's life much easier. Think of a gradebook a teacher uses with all of its columns and rows of numbers and letters. The computer replaces the old-fashioned gradebook by keeping records of grades for teachers. The teacher simply enters the grade information into the computer, and the computer records the grade in its data base. The record on each student might also include previous grades, parents' names, addresses, age, and so on.

The computer can keep all kinds of school records. It can keep track of attendance, for example. This is a time-consuming task that someone in every school must do. But when attendance information is fed into the computer, it takes over the job of processing and storing information. School libraries have found CMI software to be very useful in keeping their book collections organized. The card catalog that contains a card for each book in the library will soon be a thing of the past. Computerized data bases of library information make it easier and faster to locate a book that is needed.

Teachers use data bases to keep track of students, projects, and special subjects.

At Home

Personal computer users also have a variety of data bases available to them. Through the use of a modem, users can tap into data bases that provide them with information about business, health, hobbies, and other areas of everyday life. The user subscribes to the data base service by paying a fee for the use of the data base. By subscribing to data bases, users can monitor the stock market, research almost any subject, learn about new ways to stay healthy, share ideas with people who enjoy the same hobbies they enjoy, and have access to a great deal of other information that they might not be able to locate otherwise.

Users can develop their own data base systems to help organize or record information that most people store in some way in their own homes. Recipes, for example, can be organized and updated. Yearly tax records can be stored easily and used as reference in future years.

The data base is vital to the Age of Information that we are entering. There is so much information available that storing it in printed form in libraries is no longer practical. The computer puts all of this information at our fingertips.

CHAPTER FIVE

CHECK WHAT YOU HAVE LEARNED

1. How can a data base help me to find just the house I want?
2. Use your imagination to describe three changes that a data base might make to our lives at home.
3. Name two ways that a data base can help schools.
4. How can a data base be a lifesaver?
5. Describe briefly how data bases can help scientists.

WHAT YOU HAVE LEARNED IN CHAPTER FIVE

Handling information has become very important in today's world. We already know that computers are especially useful when people need to use and keep large amounts of information. They store large amounts of information and make it easy to find the information we need. A data base is a collection of data organized into a system that makes it usable. It is a tool for storing information.

The computer can store one record in a data base that contains all of the information it needs to do different tasks. It can search its memory very quickly to find specific information. It can organize the same information in many different ways. For example, it may organize a file according to last names of customers or according to type of purchase the customer has made.

Each space where specific information is stored is called a field. The user types a data item into each field. For example, the user might type the data item *Jane* into the field *Name*. All of the fields that are about a specific person or subject are called a record of that person or subject. Many records put together make a file. For example, all of the information about Jane makes up Jane's record, but all of the information about Jane, John, and Fred might make up a file. The computer organizes and stores files by looking for key information. The person creating the file chooses certain fields as keys.

There are several advantages to data bases. First, it takes much less time to organize information in a logical way. With paper filing systems, workers have to file the information and are locked into whatever system of organization they use. Second, with a data base it is more difficult to make mistakes in filing information because the computer does the actual filing. Third, the information can be stored in a much smaller space. Fourth, it is easy to make backup copies of computer disks and to store them in a separate area. This way, the information is less likely to be lost or damaged.

In order to create a file, the user must decide what fields are necessary for each record. After deciding on the fields, he or she can enter the data and can then look up data according to whatever key or keys are needed. The information contained in the data base can be organized in a number of different ways. The way it is displayed depends upon the user's goal.

Data bases are used in many different ways and in many different situations. The U.S. government uses them to manage the vast amount of information it stores about every citizen. Businesses and banks use them to keep track of money that is owed to them and money that they owe. They also keep mailing addresses, customer lists, employee records, and so on. Data bases are useful in insurance and real estate because they enable their users to look up very specific information. For example, a real estate agent can look up only those houses that fit the specifications of a prospective buyer. In science, data bases are used to store huge amounts of data gathered in experiments and to organize them in a meaningful way. Schools use data bases to keep track of students, grades, and even books. Computer users at home can even tap into data bases that provide them with information about business, health, hobbies, the stock market, and other things that might be of interest.

1. What is a data base?
2. Name three advantages of data bases over paper filing systems.
3. What must a person do in order to create a file?
4. What is a field?
5. How does a record differ from a file?
6. How are data bases used by the government?
7. How do data bases help scientists?
8. How does the computer organize and store data?
9. How do data bases help protect information from damage?
10. How might a business use a data base?

USING WORDS YOU HAVE LEARNED

1. A _____ data base does not repeat any information.
2. Each space where information is stored is called a _____ .
3. A _____ is a collection of information about one person or thing.
4. A collection of records that contain information is a _____ .
5. The computer organizes and stores files by looking for _____ information.
6. A specific piece of information that the user types into a field is called a _____ _____ .
7. All the money that a business owes is called _____ _____ .
8. A collection of data organized into a system that makes it usable is called a data _____ .
9. It is a good idea to _____ , or correct, your file from time to time.
10. Your computer screen will _____ , or show, the items corresponding to the information you want.

EXERCISING YOUR MATH SKILLS

The following is a timed activity that you can do with your classmates or by yourself. Use all the numbers between 1 and 100. Work quickly but accurately. Write your answers on a separate sheet of paper.

1. List all numbers whose digits add up to 7.
2. List all numbers divisible by 4.
3. List all numbers that when divided by 3 leave a remainder of 1.
4. List all the numbers that appear in all three of the above lists.
5. Write the larger of the remaining numbers.

   Check your time with those of your classmates. Did anyone correctly finish this in under a minute? Two minutes? How many correctly finished in under five minutes?

Each of the activity lines above could represent a field in a data base. Many numbers belong in several of the fields. Using a computer and data base with the above fields, we could obtain the final number in a fraction of the time it took you to do it by hand. (And not end up with writer's cramp!) We could also tell easily which numbers occurred only in fields one and two. Imagine what it would be like if we had started with ten thousand numbers instead of one hundred. A data base would be essential.

UNDERSTANDING WHAT YOU HAVE LEARNED

MULTIPLE CHOICE

1. A data base does not:
   a) store information
   b) save space
   c) process information
   d) organize information
2. A field is:
   a) a space for specific information
   b) a collection of records
   c) a collection of data items
   d) a space for files
3. Businesses use a data base for:
   a) payroll
   b) accounts payable
   c) accounts receivable
   d) all of the above
4. Data bases are useful in science primarily because they:
   a) are good for mailing lists
   b) can store and organize vast amounts of data
   c) can help with accounts payable
   d) can help with the payroll
5. The computer organizes and stores files:
   a) in alphabetical order
   b) in numeric order
   c) randomly
   d) by looking for key information

6. A relational data base:
   a) is one owned by your uncle
   b) does not repeat information
   c) does not store data
   d) is only used with microcomputers
7. It is sometimes difficult to find specific information in a paper filing system because:
   a) the user is locked into one system of organization
   b) the information is incorrect
   c) the information is on file
   d) the filing system is incorrect
8. Before you enter data into your data base you must first:
   a) make a record
   b) display the data
   c) create a file
   d) create a display
9. It is important to update a file so that:
   a) it forms a relational data base
   b) it displays the data
   c) it makes data entries
   d) the data is always correct
10. An office that would keep a file on different houses and clients might be a(n):
    a) real estate office
    b) insurance office
    c) police station
    d) school office

TRUE OR FALSE

1. A relational data base does not repeat information.
2. A collection of fields is a data item.
3. It is not important to update files in a data base.
4. A paper filing system takes up more space than a data base.
5. A mailing list should not be put on a data base.
6. A data base can sort information in several different ways.
7. Files should never be sorted in alphabetical order.
8. Police agencies use data bases to store information about crimes across the country.
9. A record is a collection of information about a particular person or thing.
10. It is impossible to organize information in more than one way.

SHORT ANSWER

1. How do data bases save time? Space?
2. Name one thing that you must consider when you are creating a file.
3. Name three different professions that use data bases.
4. Explain how data bases make it easier to find specific information.
5. Why is it difficult to file something in the wrong place with a data base?
6. How can a data base save lives?
7. Name three ways that data bases are used by the U.S. government.
8. What is a relational data base?
9. How is a record different from a file?
10. How is a field different from a data item?

WHAT YOU WILL LEARN IN CHAPTER SIX

By the end of this chapter, you will be able to:

1. Explain what a spreadsheet is.
2. Tell how to set up a spreadsheet.
3. Name three ways that a spreadsheet is used in various professions.
4. Explain what a formula is and why it is used.
5. List two ways in which you might use a spreadsheet.

Spreadsheets: Tools for Decision Making

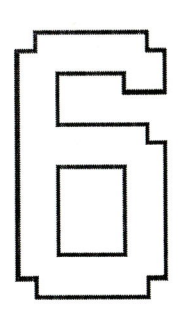

6

WORDS YOU WILL LEARN

cell
column
formula
ledger
row
spreadsheet

One of the most important things that humans do is make decisions. What we decide can determine our success or failure in a number of ways. It can determine whether we make or lose money or whether our product works or not. In some cases it can determine whether we live or die. For these reasons, a decision should be based on the best possible information. It must be based on present conditions and on possible future conditions. Most computers cannot yet make decisions. But they can help humans to make decisions by providing and analyzing information quickly. The electronic spreadsheet is a computer tool that helps humans to make good, informed decisions.

What Is a Spreadsheet?

We already know that computers are extremely useful for work that involves numbers. This is the main reason why they are so widely used in business. A feature of the computer that has contributed to its value as a tool is its ability to process and compute numbers. The electronic spreadsheet is one way that computers do this.

There is a paper alternative to the electronic spreadsheet, just as there is for a data base. For hundreds of years, businesspersons have kept records of their sales, income, and payments on a large sheet in a special book called a **ledger**. The ledger page has vertical lines that separate it into many **columns**. Each of these columns might be for a different kind of entry. For example, there might be a column called "Paper Goods" where the clerk would write an expenditure for paper, and one called "Utilities" where the clerk would write an expenditure for electricity. The ledger page also has horizontal lines dividing it into **rows**. Each row might be for a different kind of entry, too. A row might be labeled with a date, for example. If an expenditure for paper were made on July 12th, for example, the clerk would note the amount in the "Paper Goods" column and the "July 12" row. So the ledger page is really divided into many little squares, each of which is a place for a specific piece of information.

At the end of each column and row on the ledger page, a total is kept. This way, the clerk can look at the ledger page at the end of the month and see how much money was spent on paper goods that month (by looking at the total at the bottom of the column for "Paper Goods"). Or he or she can look at the end of the row

Accountants spent many hours pouring over ledger pages that kept records of sales and expenditures.

SPREADSHEETS

Ledger

July	Paper Goods	Rent	Utilities	Total
1-6		100.00		100.00
7-12	25.00			25.00
13-18	10.00		37.00	47.00
19-24	50.00			50.00
25-31	4.00		6.00	10.00
TOTAL	89.00	100.00	43.00	232.00

Ledgers include columns and rows—modern-day computer spreadsheets are ledgers, too.

for July 12th to see how much money was spent on that day. If all the columns and rows are totaled at the end of the month, the total amount spent that month can be seen in the lower right corner.

An electronic spreadsheet is very much like a ledger page. It is a format for information. It has columns and rows that can contain important information. The outline of a spreadsheet might look like this:

Spreadsheet

	Column 1	Column 2	Column 3	Column 4
Row 1				
Row 2				
Row 3				
Row 4				

The spreadsheet can contain as many rows and columns as are needed to display whatever information is to be included. Spreadsheets are used by businesses to keep track of accounting information. Figures such as number and amount of sales, percentage of profits, amount spent for payroll or travel or raw materials, and so on, are entered into the spreadsheet.

An electronic spreadsheet is different in some ways from a ledger page, however. Information is typed into the computer, rather than written down. The computer is given formulas to calculate totals. What used to take people a great deal of time now takes the computer only an instant.

After the operator enters data into the spreadsheet, the computer will make the necessary calculations.

CHAPTER SIX

Spreadsheets aren't only useful for business. The spreadsheet can also be used by teachers to keep track of grades, by households to keep track of budgets and expenditures, by scientists to keep track of experimental data, and by many other professionals.

Youngsters enjoy computer games, but they can also use computers for practical purposes, such as using a spreadsheet to figure out how to spend allowance money.

CHECK WHAT YOU HAVE LEARNED

1. What is a ledger?
2. Describe how a spreadsheet is divided into little squares.
3. How would you find the total amount of money spent on paper goods in the spreadsheet example we used?
4. How many rows and columns does a spreadsheet have?
5. How might a business use a spreadsheet?

New Ideas and Computers

Computer Simulations

You are probably familiar with computer **simulation** if you have ever played games on a computer. Simulation is the ability of the computer to present different situations in realistic ways. For example, you may pretend to fly a spaceship and be asked to make decisions about burning fuel or firing rockets. This is computer simulation. Simulation is used for many purposes—entertainment, learning, research, and more.

Simulation can help in the testing of new engineering designs, for example. This is much less difficult, expensive, and time-consuming than making a model of the product to be tested. In some cases, it is also less dangerous. Testing new cars or airplanes can be a hazardous job. With simulation, engineers are able to analyze the potential stresses and danger points of new products. As the computer simulates the performance of the product, the engineers can look at any part of the product to see the amount of stress that it receives and whether or not it is strong enough. This means that each tiny piece of airplanes, artificial limbs, machinery, cars, and even shoes can be designed to withstand the pressures it might undergo.

Simulation is also being used in education. For example, we might imagine a science project in which students are learning about outer space. With computer simulation, the students can pretend to be astronauts, flying through space at incredible speeds on their way to a distant planet. The computer can tell them what conditions are on the planet they have chosen, and they must decide whether or not to land there. Can they survive under the conditions on this planet? Will they be able to breathe? Will they find water to drink? What kind of life is likely to inhabit this planet? The computer can help them explore questions like these as it teaches them about outer space. Simulation allows students to learn new skills and to test those skills under realistic conditions.

The military also uses simulation for basic and advanced training. It is much less dangerous and more productive to teach a new pilot how to control a $24 million aircraft through the use of a simulator rather than in the actual aircraft. The user can have the computer simulate many different weather conditions for flying just by pushing a few buttons. Pilots learn to apply their training techniques without the danger of an actual crash. There are also training programs that train senior officers to make fast decisions in emergency situations.

Research scientists use simulation in many ways. They may use the computer to simulate the responses of humans or animals in experiments. This saves time and does not really place humans or animals in danger. Another way that scientists use computer simulation in medical research is in looking for new chemical and drug compounds to treat disease. The scientists can use three-dimensional graphics to create pictures of atoms. Then they can combine these atoms into molecules that represent different chemicals and drugs. They can combine the atoms in many different arrangements on the computer without ever having to mix actual elements and chemicals. This saves time and reduces the chance of human error.

In space research, computer simulation is used for many things. NASA scientists use it to test every system and activity of space travel, to simulate different conditions that could occur in space, and to train astronauts. The computer can simulate any condition that may occur during a flight into space. It can help determine what will happen if any system fails. This helps NASA ensure that every precaution has been taken to protect the safety of the astronauts. The astronauts themselves are trained with computer simulation. This allows them to experience and react to emergency situations while they are still safely on the ground.

Simulation is also used by astronomers to "see" stars that cannot be seen from Earth. This is done by feeding information from NASA's Orbiting Astronomical Observatory into computer terminals. The computer then has a map of the universe in its memory. Astronomers use this method to observe and study stars that are thousands of light years away from the Earth. With this technology, astronomers hope to discover whether there is life in outer space.

As you can see, simulation is an extremely useful and important development.

Advantages of Using a Spreadsheet

Traditionally, the accountant or bookkeeper in an office must keep track of business information by writing it down in a ledger. Then the numbers written on the ledger page must be computed and total amounts recorded. This way a business can see where it is spending money, how much it is spending or earning, and where it can cut expenses so that its profits will be higher. Accountants and bookkeepers can use calculators or adding machines to compute the numbers on a ledger page, but there is a high chance of human error with this method. It also takes a great deal of time to compute totals and percentages, even with a calculator or adding machine.

The electronic spreadsheet has reduced the chance of human error since all of the calculations are done by the computer. Instead of writing numbers on a ledger page, the bookkeeper or accountant enters the numbers into the computer by way of the keyboard. He or she then instructs the computer to perform the

A spreadsheet can be very helpful for keeping records of a family's expenditures, income, and investments.

calculations necessary to arrive at the totals. Assuming that it is given the correct numbers to work with, the computer produces accurate totals at a much faster rate than a human can.

The speed with which the electronic spreadsheet works makes many other things possible. With an electronic spreadsheet, it is possible to look at many different possibilities very quickly. For example, imagine that you have entered all of your grades into an electronic spreadsheet. You want to know what your final grade will be in English, but there is one assignment you have not gotten back yet: an essay that counts for 10 percent of your final grade. With the spreadsheet, you can look at the possibilities. You may think that you did very well on the essay, so you enter a 90 for the essay grade and see how that affects your total. But you are not sure you got a 90. What will happen if you got an 80? How about a 95? In another class, you know what your grades have been, but want to see if extra credit work will change your final grade. By entering the extra credit work into the formula for computing your grade, you can see if the final result will change a little bit or a great deal.

Without an electronic spreadsheet, the calculations that you would have to make to find out how different possibilities would affect your grade would take you a long time. In fact, you might even decide that figuring out all of the possibilities would not be worth the work involved. But sometimes knowing all of the possibilities can be very important, especially in business.

Using a spreadsheet, a business can easily look at possibilities when it is considering making an investment or changing a billing procedure. Perhaps a utility company follows a certain billing process for one year. Then a rate increase and new equipment means every one of its thousands of customers must receive a revised bill. The rate increase will be charged all year long, but the new equipment charge will be billed for only six months. In business, planning is extremely important! The company that is able to plan ahead will be able to make decisions based on what will happen, not just on what is happening right now. The company can use a spreadsheet to help it make these decisions. For example, a company might wonder what would happen to the monthly budget if the company bought a new computer and paid $500 per month for thirty-six months. How much interest would have to be paid over thirty-six months? Would it be better to pay for it all at once? What else might change if that investment were made? Is it affordable at all? If not, by how much would the company need to increase its income in order to afford it? In looking at all of the possibilities, the company can make a more informed decision about new investments.

Sometimes computer spreadsheets are useful for billing procedures.

CHECK WHAT YOU HAVE LEARNED

1. Explain how the speed of an electronic spreadsheet helps people to make decisions.
2. How might a student use an electronic spreadsheet to determine his or her grade in a class?
3. How does an electronic spreadsheet eliminate human error?
4. Name two advantages of using an electronic spreadsheet instead of a ledger page.
5. Why is planning important for a business?

Setting Up a Spreadsheet

We can set up an electronic spreadsheet for our own needs by naming the columns and rows. For example, let us assume that we want to calculate the total sales of a business during a six-month period from January through June. To begin with, we must name, or define, the columns and rows of our spreadsheet:

SPREADSHEETS 175

	Number of Sales	$ Amount of Sales
January		
February		
March		
April		
May		
June		
Totals		

We have defined our columns as the "Number of Sales" and the "$ Amount of Sales." The rows will show which months the sales figures correspond to. We have also added a row that will display the total number and dollar amount of sales.

The next step in using our spreadsheet is to enter the data that the computer will need to calculate our totals for us. The place for each specific piece of information is called a **cell**. For example, in the following spreadsheet we have placed the number 43 in the cell in the row "February" and the column "Number of Sales." When each of the cells is filled with the correct information, our spreadsheet might look like this:

	Number of Sales	$ Amount of Sales
January	50	500
February	43	430
March	55	550
April	101	1010
May	26	260
June	75	750
Totals		

The computer does not yet know what to put into the cells in the row "Totals." Of course, the addition is not very difficult and it would be possible for us to simply add up the columns and enter the totals into that row. But if we did that, we would not really be using the spreadsheet. After all, we want the computer to do the addition for us! How can we do that?

We can teach the computer how to calculate the total by giving it a **formula**. We must think about how we would do this work by ourselves. With a computer we must think out every step because the computer will only do what we tell it to do.

If we were going to calculate the total number of sales, for example, the first thing we would do would be to find out how many sales there were in January. To do this, we would look at the first cell in the column "Number of Sales." This is the first thing we direct the computer to do. We tell it to look at the first cell in the column. Next, we would add the next number in the column to the first number. We direct the computer to do the same. We continue down the column, telling the computer what to add, until we have added all of the things that we want in our total. Now that the computer knows where to look to find the addends, we can tell it to execute the formula. The correct answer, in this case 350, appears in the cell in the "Totals" row and the "Number of Sales" column.

We may decide to change one of the numbers in our column. We may find, for example, that in June we made 80 sales instead of 75. Now we can be very glad that we entered a formula instead of a number in the "Total" row. When we change the June entry to 80, the total automatically changes: the computer almost instantly adds the numbers again and changes the total to 355. If we had just entered a number, of course, the number would have remained the same. The computer would not have known that the total depended on the other entries.

Often, the formulas we use to calculate numbers can be very complicated. In order to arrive at a final calculation, it might be necessary to take 2 times the entry in row one, the entry in row three plus 5, and 10 percent of the entry in row two, total them,

People and Computers

Clive Sinclair

Clive Sinclair has been an inventor ever since he was a young boy. When he was only twelve years old, he built a small mechanical calculator! By the time he was forty, he had invented digital wristwatches, tiny television sets, and pocket calculators that could do sophisticated mathematics.

In the early 1980s, he introduced a personal computer that sold for well under $100. The computer was manufactured with very little memory. But it could do many of the things that people want to do at home: it could serve as an entertainment unit or it could calculate a home budget.

Sinclair is still inventing today. His work so far has made computers available to many people who otherwise would not be able to afford them. His future inventions may change the industry even more.

and divide by 4. As long as the correct formula is entered into the cell in which the calculated answer is to appear, the computer will do all of the calculations. If one cell is changed, all of the other cells that depend on that cell will change also, throughout the spreadsheet. You can see that in some cases that can be very useful.

Of course, our sample spreadsheet is a very simple one with only two columns and six rows. Spreadsheets often are much more complicated. In fact, they often have dozens of rows and columns. With complex spreadsheets, the computer saves a great deal of time and frustration by calculating figures for the user.

CHECK WHAT YOU HAVE LEARNED

1. What is a cell?
2. Explain why it is important to enter a formula instead of a number in some cells.
3. What must one do in order to find out what formula to enter?
4. If we have used the spreadsheet correctly, what will happen if we change one of the cells?
5. Why don't we enter formulas into all of the cells?

Uses of Spreadsheets

Now you know what a spreadsheet is, why it is better than a ledger page, and how to get started using one. Spreadsheet programs have been available for only a very few years, but already many different uses have been found for them in many different fields. We've already seen how spreadsheets are used for accounting in business. Now let's look at a sample of other uses.

In Business

Electronic spreadsheets are used in business for other purposes besides accounting and bookkeeping. They are also used to provide businesspersons with important information they need to make decisions about how to run their businesses. For example, when a businessperson looks at the information on a spreadsheet

Careers and Computers

Programmer/Analysts

The programmer/analyst is a person who combines the skills of the programmer and the system analyst. Programmer/analysts are usually experienced programmers who are in the process of moving to a position as a system analyst. Along with writing programs, the programmer/analyst performs other tasks that have some bearing on the computer's operating system.

The programmer/analyst possesses valuable and flexible job skills. In a small company that does not have a large programming staff, the programmer/analyst is especially important to the data processing department. Programmer/analysts often receive higher salaries than programmers, and there are many career opportunities open to them.

Athletes

Computers are being used more and more in the world of sports. Simulation programs are used by managers and coaches to simulate plays, and spreadsheets are used to calculate averages. Computers are used by players to improve reaction time and reflexes. They are even being used in very complicated ways to train Olympic athletes!

Some American athletes in training for the 1984 Olympics were the first to work with biomechanics to help them improve their techniques. Biomechanics is a way of measuring movements and body position, analyzing them, and sometimes comparing them to a computer-made "best" movement. The athletes can look at computer-generated stick figures that are placed upon movies of their own movements. As they watch, they can see the ways in which the movement of their body differed from that of the stick figure. Then they know what to concentrate on as they practice. Stick figures can also be made from the films of the athletes as they perform. The computer can then be told what to look for (for example, a knee turned in) and to highlight it as the film progresses. The computer cannot create a great athlete, of course. But one small improvement in technique can sometimes add up over long distances. Among great athletes, sometimes a tiny improvement can decide who will win the race or the game.

he or she may note that sales were higher in one month than in another. Why did this happen? The businessperson can look back at other records to try to understand why sales were so high in one month and not in another. Did the business have a special sale or promotion? Perhaps another sale would help boost profits. Why did the sales fall off in another month? What can be done to prevent this from happening again?

Wise planning is important to any professional. The electronic spreadsheet is one way that the computer aids in planning and decision making to help businesses make money and continue to grow.

In Education

Think of a gradebook with all of its columns and rows of numbers and letters. The computer spreadsheet replaces the old-fashioned gradebook. It keeps records of grades for teachers. The teacher simply enters the grade information into the computer, and the computer records the grade on the spreadsheet. When report card time arrives, the teacher can instruct the computer to calculate grades and even print out paper records of the grades. This saves hours of adding, subtracting, and averaging grades. It also means that grades are figured more accurately than a human could do. And each student can have a computer printout that explains the grades in detail.

NAME	G1	G2	G3	G4	AVERAGE
ARLINGTON D	90	88	95	82	88.75
FOSTER S	80	85	90	100	89.25
IWAMOTO R	90	100	85	82	89.25
JOHNSON A	79	100	80	90	87.25
JONSON G	90	92	99	90	92.75
LOPEZ H	82	89	92	85	87
MARSHALL G	80	70	75	82	76.75
TURNER K	90	84	92	99	91.25
				CLASS AVE	88.5

A computer spreadsheet gives a teacher an easy record of class grades. Students can figure their own grade averages using a spreadsheet.

In Government

One place where spreadsheets may be extremely useful to the government is in the Internal Revenue Service. This office collects the taxes on each tax-paying citizen in the United States. That is quite a task! An electronic spreadsheet can simplify the process of collecting and checking taxes. A citizen's income, number of dependents, and deductions can be entered into the spreadsheet, where formulas automatically calculate and verify the amount of tax owed.

Spreadsheets also help the government to keep records of

Spreadsheets are useful for calculating income tax. This spreadsheet program has searched, listed, and totalled all medical expenditures, which can then be taken as an income tax deduction.

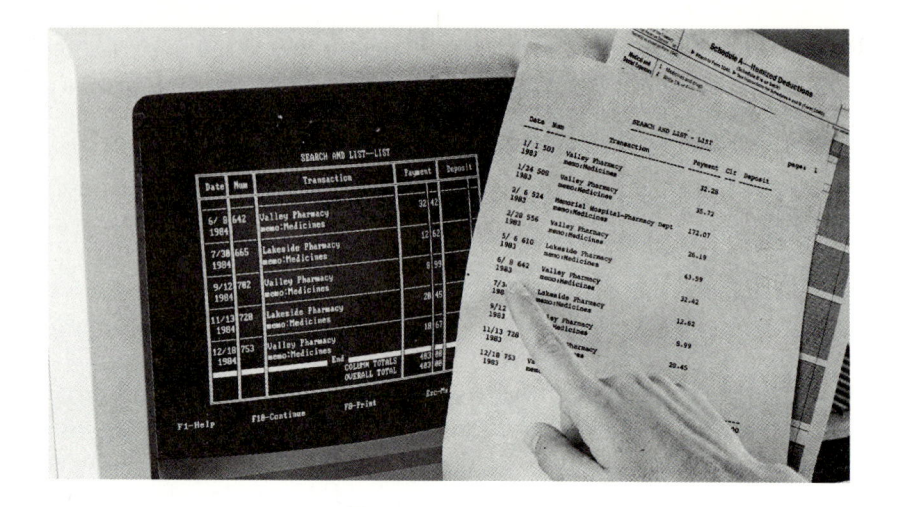

other important information. Using the information from the census, for example, they can help calculate average incomes, total population, and more. Spreadsheets are used to make governments budgets, keep track of expenditures, and plan for the future.

In Banking

One of the banking industry's most important jobs is making loans to its customers. The bank charges a certain amount of interest for each loan. The amount of interest charged may depend on the size of the loan and the time it takes the customer to pay

Bank statements are spreadsheets that show deposit and withdrawal activity in a checking account.

CHECK #	DATE	PAY TO	CHECK AMT	DEPOSIT	BALANCE
		BALANCE			2145.00
201	10/20	PHOENIX P & W	145.00		2000.00
	10/21	DEPOSIT		300.00	2300.00
202	10/23	VIDEO CRAFT INC.	45.00		2255.00
203	10/23	BUSI- NESS FORMS INC.	200.00		2055.00

the money back to the bank. The bank must calculate the total amount of the loan, the amount still owed at any particular time, and so on. All of these calculations take time.

The spreadsheet can help by providing a quick and easy program for calculating the possibilities on the loan. What if the loan is paid off in three years instead of ten? What if the bank charges 11 percent interest instead of 15 percent? The spreadsheet can help the bank decide if the loan is a good investment and can help the customer decide if the loan is possible or profitable in the long run.

The bank also pays interest on the money that clients have placed in savings and other accounts. This interest can be complicated to keep track of. The spreadsheet can simplify working with all of this data.

In Real Estate

Most people take out loans to buy a house or property. These loans are usually long-term loans and may involve a large amount of money paid in interest, property taxes, and insurance. Actual payments for the property cannot be figured out simply by dividing the cost of the property by the number of months of payment! Because the calculations are complicated and involve several variables, spreadsheets can help the real estate agent to explain payments to possible buyers. The buyers may want to explore

A computer spreadsheet can help to plan family finances and to budget money to pay bills.

several possibilities. What if they put $20,000 down on the house instead of $10,000? What will happen if they take out a 20-year mortgage on the house instead of a 30-year mortgage? The real estate agent needs to be able to give them answers quickly, and the spreadsheet helps to do that.

The Future and Computers

The Political Spreadsheet

Each year, a great deal of money is spent by political candidates who need to estimate how many votes they will get. One important thing that they must look at is the impact that different things might have on the election. For example, what will happen if there is an increase in unemployment? Will that increase change the results of an election? What if the price of oil goes up? What if it is found that a major official accepted a bribe? What if the President supports an issue that is unpopular with one group of people but is popular with another? Each of these things might make a difference in the way people vote.

To find out how important the difference may be, professional pollsters interview some people to try to estimate how most people will react. Once they have found this out, they must make mathematical calculations to estimate how these reactions would affect the election. For example, they might find out that 3 percent of the men in the country and 4 percent of the women will simply not vote if a politician supports a particular issue, and that 2 percent of the men and 4 percent of the women will vote for the other party's candidate. With these figures, they can mathematically compute the probable election results. This may help a politician to decide whether or not to support that issue. In the U.S., this is one way that the people can be sure that politicians represent them. If politicians don't keep a close eye on what the people would like them to do, the politicians may not be elected again.

But it can take pollsters a very long time to calculate the effects of certain events. This means that many things are often simply not analyzed and that others may be analyzed too slowly for the results to be useful. As it has in many other types of number analysis, the spreadsheet is becoming a useful tool for the political pollster. Formulas can be written into the spreadsheet that will help to predict election results. In the future, we may see political analysis spreadsheet programs become common. The politician may want to see spreadsheet analyses before committing himself or herself to an issue. By allowing the politician to closely analyze the effects of his or her decisions, the spreadsheet may help government officials to represent their constituents more closely.

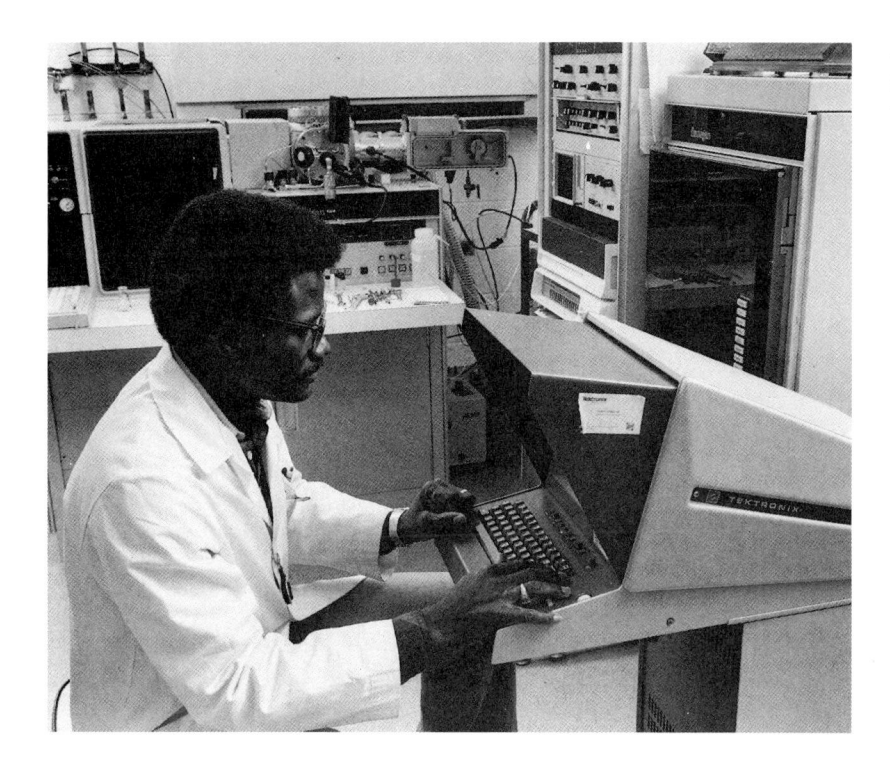

Spreadsheets can be used by research scientists to analyze vast amounts of data.

In Science

Spreadsheets help research scientists keep track of huge amounts of information, organize it, and analyze it. Research scientists might use the columns in a spreadsheet to indicate test conditions (for example, plants with light, plants without light) and the rows to indicate another variable (for example, the date or the type of plant). They might fill the cells with the experimental results (for example, the amount the plant has grown). With a spreadsheet, the research scientist can look at the results and analyze them according to several formulas (for example, total amount of growth for each condition, difference in growth, average growth, and so on).

In Space

Like other scientists, space scientists rely heavily on spreadsheets to help them analyze the possible results of any change in conditions. Because the scientists can change one cell and see how the change affects other cells, spreadsheets can be used to make decisions about the design and cost of many projects.

In Industry and Design

Anyone interested in designing new products may find the spreadsheet extremely useful. The designer, engineer, or architect must attempt to find a happy medium between the strength, durability, and effectiveness of the product on the one hand, and the price on the other. The engineer who designs a perfect bicycle that no one can afford will not make a great deal of money. Spreadsheets help by allowing the designer to enter different variables into the cells and to calculate the possibilities.

An architect who designs a bridge may find out by using a spreadsheet that if he or she builds it out of one material the city will have to charge a toll to drivers wanting to cross it, but if it is built from another material no charge will be necessary. A designer may find that the same blouse made out of silk will cost twice as much as if it were made from polyester, and cannot be sold to as many people. The spreadsheet can help determine which blouse will be most profitable. In this way, spreadsheets help both the consumer and the producer by keeping costs as low as possible.

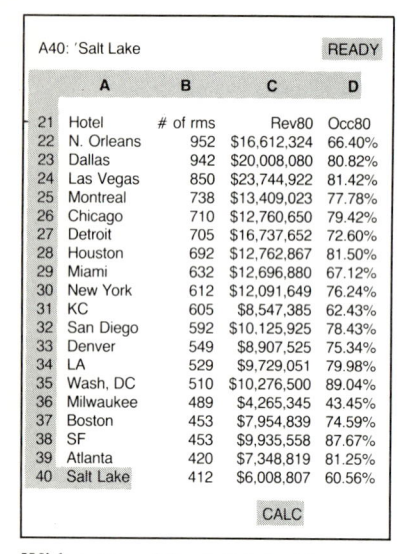

	A	B	C	D
			Rev80	Occ80
21	Hotel	# of rms		
22	N. Orleans	952	$16,612,324	66.40%
23	Dallas	942	$20,008,080	80.82%
24	Las Vegas	850	$23,744,922	81.42%
25	Montreal	738	$13,409,023	77.78%
26	Chicago	710	$12,760,650	79.42%
27	Detroit	705	$16,737,652	72.60%
28	Houston	692	$12,762,867	81.50%
29	Miami	632	$12,696,880	67.12%
30	New York	612	$12,091,649	76.24%
31	KC	605	$8,547,385	62.43%
32	San Diego	592	$10,125,925	78.43%
33	Denver	549	$8,907,525	75.34%
34	LA	529	$9,729,051	79.98%
35	Wash, DC	510	$10,276,500	89.04%
36	Milwaukee	489	$4,265,345	43.45%
37	Boston	453	$7,954,839	74.59%
38	SF	453	$9,935,558	87.67%
39	Atlanta	420	$7,348,819	81.25%
40	Salt Lake	412	$6,008,807	60.56%

With a spreadsheet, this hotel chain is able to calculate approximate income and can make good decisions in planning for future years.

CHECK WHAT YOU HAVE LEARNED

1. How might a teacher use a spreadsheet?
2. How do spreadsheets help the Internal Revenue Service?
3. Why are spreadsheets important to scientists?
4. What type of information might a scientist place in the columns and rows of a spreadsheet?
5. How can spreadsheets help architects and engineers to design low-cost products?

WHAT YOU HAVE LEARNED IN CHAPTER SIX

One of the most important things that humans do is make decisions. These decisions must be based on the best possible information and must plan for the future as well as for the present. The electronic spreadsheet is a tool that can help us to make informed decisions.

SPREADSHEETS

The spreadsheet is a way to organize numbers. It is divided into columns by vertical lines and into rows by horizontal lines. Each row and column is labeled for specific information. The rows and columns can be totaled, or other mathematical formulas can be entered that use the information in the rows and columns. The electronic spreadsheet can contain as many rows and columns as are needed to display whatever information is to be included.

The electronic spreadsheet is much faster and more accurate than a human would be in calculating and keeping track of numbers. One advantage of this is that the user can try several different possibilities and see their effects on the total very quickly. This way, people can make decisions based on which outcome would be the best.

We can make a spreadsheet that fits our needs by giving names to, or defining, the rows and columns. The place for each specific piece of information is called a cell. Each cell contains a piece of information that corresponds to its row and column. We can enter formulas into some cells. Formulas tell the computer to look at other cells to find out which numbers to work with. For example, we can tell the computer to look at all of the numbers in the row and add them to find a total for the row. By entering a formula, we make sure that if we change one of the cells in the row, the total will automatically change, too.

Spreadsheets are used by businesses to keep track of accounting and bookkeeping figures. They are also used by many other professionals like teachers or researchers. Spreadsheets can be used by teachers to calculate grades for students. The government uses spreadsheets in the calculation of taxes, census information, and the budget. Spreadsheets are extremely useful to research scientists who must collect, organize, and analyze huge amounts of information.

1. Name three professionals who might use computer spreadsheets to help them make decisions.
2. Explain how a spreadsheet is divided into little squares or cells.
3. What does a formula do?
4. How might a research scientist use a spreadsheet?
5. How does the speed of a spreadsheet help people to make better plans?
6. How many columns and rows does an electronic spreadsheet have?
7. For what might a teacher use a spreadsheet?
8. Name two types of information that can be entered into a spreadsheet.
9. Explain what would happen if you changed one of the cells in a spreadsheet.
10. How does the government use spreadsheets?

USING WORDS YOU HAVE LEARNED

1. On a spreadsheet, the place for each specific piece of information is called a _____ .
2. Businesspersons have traditionally kept records on a large sheet in a special book called a _____ .
3. A spreadsheet is divided into _____ by vertical lines.
4. A _____ is a format for information.
5. We can enter a _____ instead of a number into a cell to get the computer to calculate the entry.
6. A spreadsheet is divided into _____ by horizontal lines.

EXERCISING YOUR MATH SKILLS

Teachers and students can calculate grades using electronic spreadsheet programs. In order to do this activity, divide a piece of paper into columns and rows just as they would appear on a spreadsheet or in a ledger. Then, enter the names of each of your classes as titles for the columns. You can use the first row of cells to enter titles. Next, enter the grades you have received for each course in the rows below. Use number grades like 80 or 90, or 1, 2, 3, 4, 5, not letters. For example, a 1 can equal an A, a 2 can equal a B, and so on. Enter five grades in each column. (You can make up grades if you don't remember your grades or if you have not yet received enough grades for this project.)

In the row following your grades, make a row for totals. Write the formula for the total in the cell where the total would go. To do this, write down where you would look in order to calculate the total. In a cell below the total, enter a formula that will tell you to divide the "total" cell by 5. This will give you an average grade for that class.

Now you can pretend that you are the computer. On a separate paper, calculate the totals and averages for your class. See if changing one of the grades will change the total and the average. See if you can use your "spreadsheet" to find out what would happen if you forgot to do one assignment. What if you got 100 on four assignments and then got only a 20 on the last? A spreadsheet is a tool that you can use to help you understand your grades.

UNDERSTANDING WHAT YOU HAVE LEARNED

MULTIPLE CHOICE

1. Using an electronic spreadsheet is faster than using a ledger page because:
    a) nobody has to enter the figures
    b) the computer does all the calculations
    c) the computer doesn't forget the entries
    d) it is important to make formulas
2. The number of rows and columns in an electronic spreadsheet is usually:
    a) twelve
    b) four
    c) eighteen
    d) as many as are needed
3. It is important to enter formulas in some cells because:
    a) the entry may depend on other cell entries
    b) formulas use letters of the alphabet
    c) the spreadsheet only records formulas
    d) it is impossible to enter numbers
4. Spreadsheets are used:
    a) in education
    b) in industry
    c) in science
    d) all of the above
5. Scientists use spreadsheets to:
    a) write formulas
    b) teach classes
    c) analyze and record information
    d) keep track of grades
6. A cell is:
    a) divided into columns
    b) a space for a specific piece of information
    c) divided into rows
    d) a place to keep a computer

SPREADSHEETS

7. If you change a cell entry on a spreadsheet:
   a) you have to enter new formulas
   b) other cells that depend on that entry will change automatically
   c) other cells that depend on that entry will change if you request it
   d) nothing happens
8. Spreadsheets are important to a business because:
   a) without a spreadsheet it won't make sales
   b) with a spreadsheet it can hire more people
   c) with a spreadsheet it can make better plans
   d) without a spreadsheet it cannot make plans at all
9. To write a formula it is important to:
   a) think about how we would do the work ourselves
   b) look in a book
   c) calculate the total number of sales
   d) change one of the numbers in our columns
10. Teachers would probably use a spreadsheet to:
    a) compute grades
    b) invent and test new products
    c) invent new exam questions
    d) introduce their students to imaginary but realistic situations

TRUE OR FALSE

1. A spreadsheet is divided into columns and rows.
2. The spreadsheet contains less than twelve columns.
3. Spreadsheets can only be used in large mainframe computers.
4. The spreadsheet calculates some entries according to formulas.
5. Astronauts often train using spreadsheets.
6. Formulas in spreadsheets can be very complicated.
7. Spreadsheets can help to work with large amounts of data.
8. Scientists use spreadsheets to help them work with dangerous substances.
9. The Internal Revenue Service uses spreadsheets to calculate taxes.
10. Spreadsheets work best when formulas are entered into every cell.

SHORT ANSWER

1. In what way can a spreadsheet help in decision making?
2. How does an architect use a spreadsheet?
3. How might a teacher use an electronic spreadsheet?
4. Why is it important to enter formulas in some cells even if you can add the numbers yourself?
5. What is a cell?
6. Name two ways that a business can use a spreadsheet.
7. How can spreadsheets help control costs of materials?
8. How might a spreadsheet help you decide if you want to take out a loan?
9. What kinds of formulas can be used with a spreadsheet?
10. How does a research scientist use a spreadsheet?

THE MANY USES OF COMPUTERS

1

2

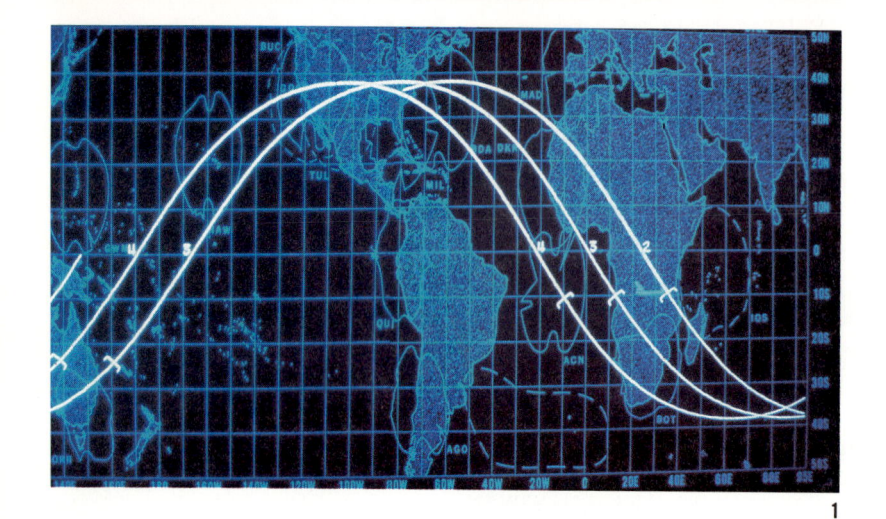

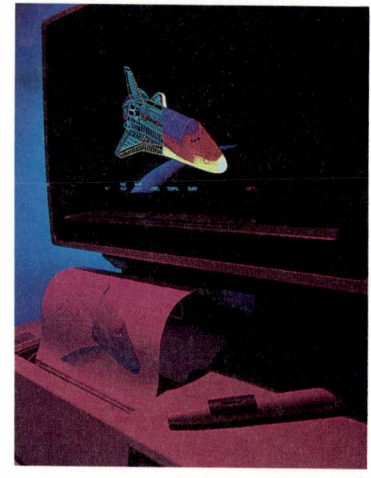

Computers these days are used in so many different ways that we need a computer to help us list all of them! A few examples are shown here to give you a taste of how computers are already affecting life today. Think about your own hobbies and interests, or new subjects that you are learning about—have computers made an impact? What about art, geology, music, navigation, and athletics? Computers are helping in the enrichment of our lives.

NASA Space Center in Houston, Texas provides tracking data for earth-orbiting satellites and space vehicles (**1**). With each pass over designated ground stations, an on-board computer stores and relays data. Some data is graphically displayed to show the paths of the space vehicle over different parts of the world.

(**2**) Aeronautics and space research have advanced rapidly with the use of computers. The storing and processing of vast amounts of information, and computer-aided design (CAD) and computer-aided manufacturing (CAM) have led to new discoveries and exciting exploration possibilities.

Schools are keeping in step with the Age of Information. Computer use in the classroom, library (**3**), and administrative offices is increasing awareness of just how valuable computers can be in the school environment.

3

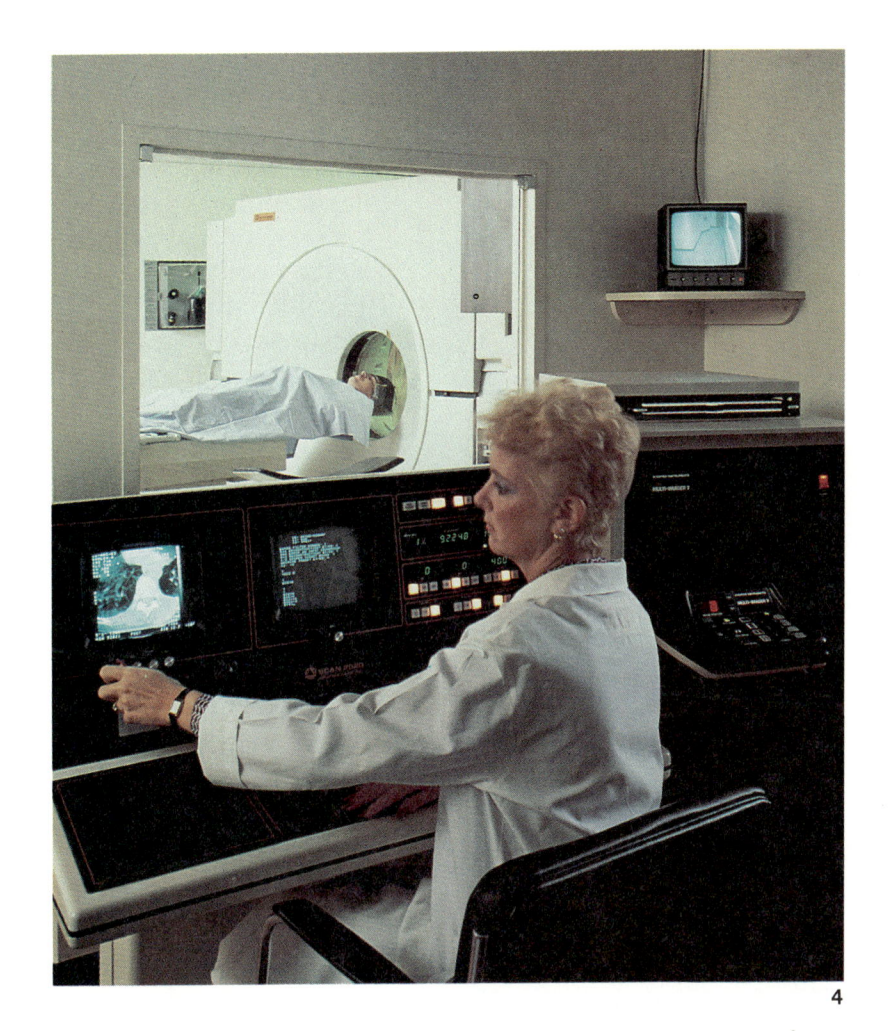

THE MANY USES OF COMPUTERS   189

Electronic image recorders (**4**) are components of medical diagnostic equipment. Diagnosis of disease is easier for the patient if a technique is painless and doesn't involve surgery. When a tissue sample is needed for study—such as a section of heart muscle (**5**)—a computer display of tiny pieces can make a big difference. Graphically displayed and enlarged, the representation of tissue plus medical data bases make the diagnostic process fast and more accurate.

One type of computer output is hard copy (**6**). Government agencies, education centers, etc., store lots of information about many people. The same information is sometimes stored on hard copy as a back-up if original computer-stored data is accidently tampered with, or lost.

4

5

6

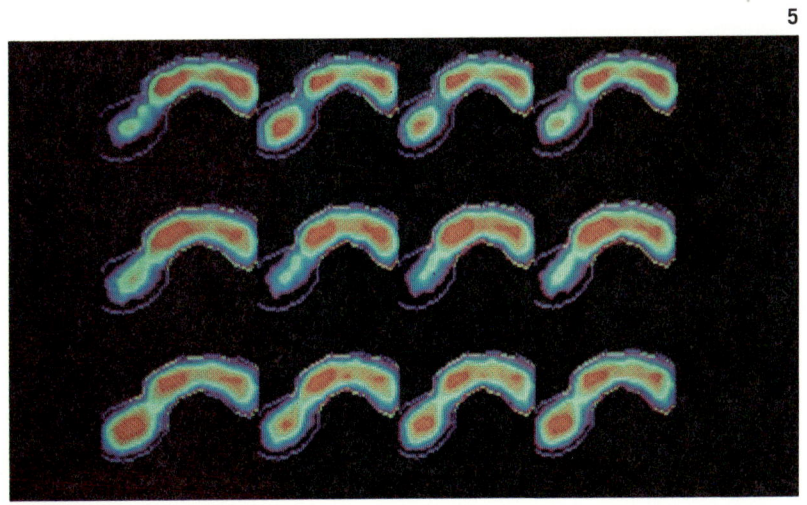

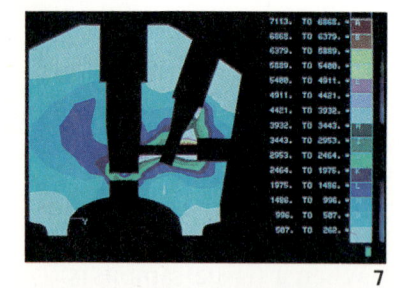

The field of engineering is expanded with the help of computer-aided design and analysis. A solid metal component can be tested for stress under simulated operating conditions (**7**). The color variations indicate points of greater or lesser strength in the metal.

A computer provides an engineer with opportunities to review stages of systems development, to refine entire equipment installations, or trouble-shoot a defect that might otherwise go unnoticed. Here a graphics tablet makes inputting of changes very easy (**8**).

When a solid model is assembled, it can be displayed on a computer screen, graphically increased in size, turned slightly, and viewed from any angle (**9**).

Architects plan and design buildings and living or working spaces for all of us. Part of the total design includes, of course, interiors as well as exteriors. With the help of a computer, the architect can input the shape of various furniture, duplicate the same desk and chair over and over (to show many in the same room), and move them or change the angle of view until the arrangement is just right (**10**). This makes moving day a lot simpler!

THE MANY USES OF COMPUTERS   191

10

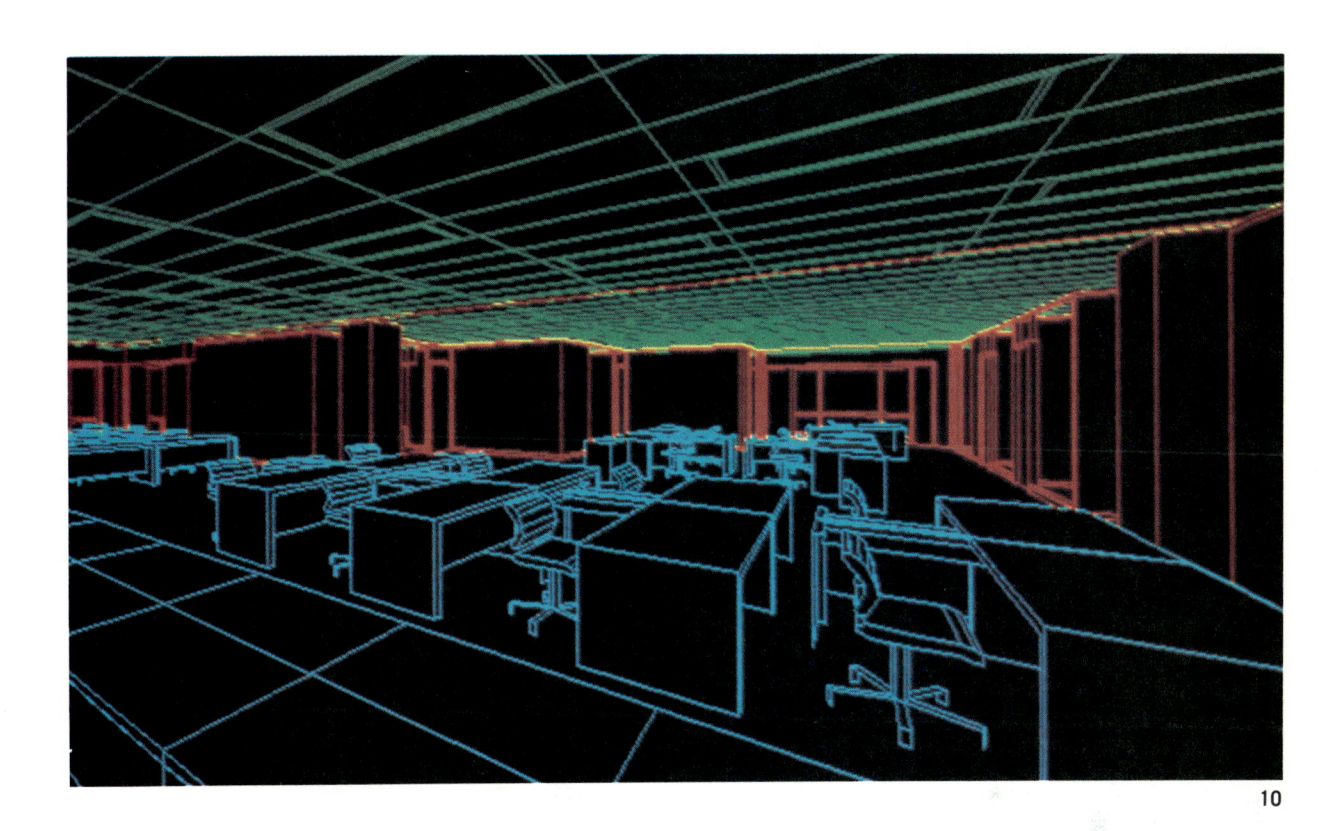

The farms of today make use of computers to store, process, and retrieve data (**11**). As data bases and spreadsheets store information about crops, livestock, weather patterns, equipment expense, etc., more and more people in farming share the fact that the computer is a useful tool in their lives, too.

Robots perform jobs that are often too dangerous for humans to do. For large welding, a robotic arm withstands intense heat and sparks (**12**).

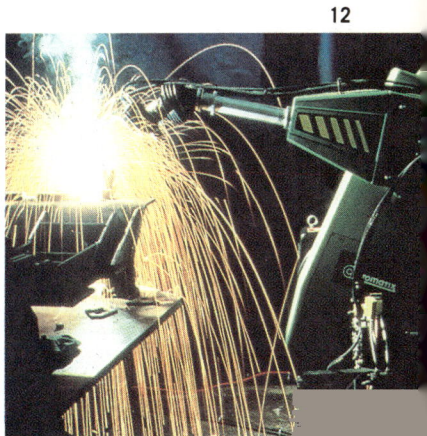

11

12

WHAT YOU WILL LEARN IN CHAPTER SEVEN

By the end of this chapter, you will be able to:

1. Tell how programming relates to problem solving.
2. List the steps in writing a computer program.
3. Identify three methods used in outlining a computer program.
4. Flowchart a program.
5. Write a simple program in BASIC.

Programming: Taking Steps to Solve Problems

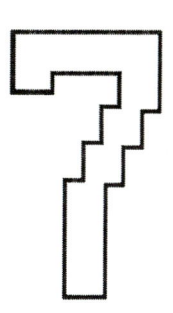

WORDS YOU WILL LEARN

bottom-up programming
code
counter
decision symbol
documentation
flowchart
input/output symbol
loop
main routine
process symbol
pseudocode
routine
statement
subroutine
syntax
terminal symbol
top-down structured programming
variable

In science fiction books, there sometimes are computers that can be asked many questions and can solve many problems automatically. For example, the heroine of the book has a crime to solve. She types the names of criminals into a computer and the name of the person who committed the crime is typed out on the computer's printer. But computers cannot yet really do things like that. In fact, computers have to have very thorough instructions for solving even the simplest problems. Remember that they can only do what they are told to do. They cannot even add 2 plus 2 without directions. In this chapter you will learn a little bit about how the orders (or programs) computers need to do their work are written.

Problems and the Steps to Solve Them

A problem is any task that requires a solution. We face problems in everything we do. Some problems are simple. For example, a simple problem is the addition of 2 plus 2. In fact, a problem such as 2 plus 2 doesn't seem like a problem, because through experience we have come to know the answer. We don't even have to think about it. But some problems are very complicated. A complicated problem might be designing the budget for a factory. Whether the problem is simple or complex, the problem must be defined and analyzed before it can be solved. This is especially true in computer programming.

Defining the Problem

Have you ever stopped in the middle of doing a problem and thought, "Oh, no! What am I doing?" Most people have. When we fail to define the problem before we begin, we often find ourselves doing too much work, too little work, or the wrong work in trying to solve our problem. When we write a computer program, it is important to decide exactly what the problem is before we begin. This way, we can be sure that we are always working toward the goal that we have set.

Problems must be stated in specific terms. You must decide what you want the computer to do. Here are a few examples of specific statements of problems that might be solved by a computer:

PROGRAMMING 195

1. Find the area of a square given the length of a side.
2. Find the average number of points scored in ten basketball games.
3. Compute how much you can earn on a paper route in ten weeks.

Once the problem has been defined, you can begin to ask yourself how to solve it. This can be done in a number of ways.

Analyzing the Problem

When you analyze a problem, you probably automatically use many techniques or strategies that you have already learned. First, you may look at the problem and try to divide it into steps. You may want to look for patterns in the problem or for similarities and differences. You automatically rule out some answers as inappropriate or impossible. (For example, you know that the sum of 250, 195, and 430 is not Pittsburgh.) You may make diagrams or charts to help you eliminate possibilities and find the correct answer to your problem. Or you may need to work out your problem mathematically. Sometimes, the only way to arrive at a correct answer is to guess and check. This is the strategy you use when you play the game Twenty Questions.

There is no correct way to analyze all problems. Different

People and Computers

Jean Sammet and Grace Murray Hopper

Both Jean Sammet and Grace Hopper have been great innovators in the field of computer programming. Grace Hopper developed the first compiler in 1952, and the first English language data compiler in 1957. The compilers translate high-level programs into machine language instructions. She also is considered the "grandmother" of Cobol.

Jean Sammet helped develop the programming language Cobol in 1959. Later, she and her colleagues at IBM developed the computer language FORMAC, which stands for FORmula MAnipulation compiler, in 1964. This was the first language to be used on a practical basis for mathematical problems. Jean Sammet was the president of the Association of Computing Machinery from 1974 to 1976. She continues to be recognized as a leader in computer science and engineering.

problems require different techniques or combinations of techniques. Some problems are easier to work out on a computer. Some problems are impossible to work out on a computer. For example, the computer can easily help you to compute your average grade for your math class, but it cannot very well help you decide which math teacher you like best. The problems that the computer is best at solving are those that require the manipulation of numbers. Ways to solve these problems can usually be planned out step by step, so that the computer can be told exactly what to do. To compute your average grade for your math class, you can first plan and explain how to do each step. The advantage of using the computer is that although you have to do the planning, the computer can do all of the mathematical calculations for you.

What Is Programming?

When you tell the computer exactly what to do to arrive at an answer, you are programming the computer. But you cannot just type the instructions into the computer in English. You must use a

After a problem has been analyzed, a programmer will use a programming language to communicate the problem to the computer.

language the computer can understand. Many programming languages have been developed to help computer-users communicate with their computers. But programming in any language relies on step-by-step instructions and planning, just as problem solving does.

You might stop and think about how you have arrived at the answers to some of the problems you have faced over the last few days. How did you decide if you would have time to do your homework after dinner? How did you decide what the answer was to that social studies question? Could you explain to a computer how you arrived at your decision?

Most of us do not analyze the steps we take to arrive at our decisions. One of the most difficult things to do is to tell *how* we know what we know. But when you are programming a computer it is necessary to consider how to arrive at a decision. If you cannot describe it, you cannot tell the computer how to do it.

But sometimes we know exactly how to arrive at an answer, and the difficult part is getting there. When there are large numbers to manipulate or things to be repeated many times, it may take us a long time to arrive at the correct answer. When we do, we may feel that we need to check our answer two or three times because the possibility of having made a minor mistake is so great. Many people can describe how to do long division, but most people would groan if asked to divide 5,476,523,976 by 345. When the problem is one in which calculations must be repeated many times, the task is boring even if you know exactly how to do it. When you are calculating averages to find out your grade in each class, for example, adding in another history test grade is more annoying than difficult. You know how to add and divide, but you hate to have to do it again!

Problems that you know how to solve but that are difficult or boring are problems that you might program a computer to solve. The computer can usually perform these tasks very quickly and easily. Instead of taking another fifteen minutes to calculate your history grade *again*, you can simply type the additional grade into your computer and run the averaging program. The corrected average appears on the CRT screen almost immediately!

CHECK WHAT YOU HAVE LEARNED

1. Why is defining a problem important?
2. Name one problem that a computer might be able to help you solve. Do not use one mentioned previously.

3. Name one problem that a computer would not be able to help you solve. Do not use one mentioned previously. Why wouldn't the computer be able to help you?
4. Name three strategies that you might use to solve a problem.
5. Suppose that you have three math grades (85, 80, and 84) for the semester. How would you determine your average semester grade?

Planning a Problem Solution

The most important part of programming is done before you sit down at the computer at all! You must first identify the problem that you need to solve. Then you must work out a plan to solve the problem. Planning helps you to organize your thoughts. It helps you to list the steps that need to be done to solve the problem. It also helps you to avoid forgetting important steps. The plan must then be changed into step-by-step instructions. These instructions must be run and tested to make sure that the program runs the way you expect it to run.

After the first planning stages, programs may be written for many purposes. This man is working with computerized designs on knitting machines.

New Ideas and Computers

Talking with a Computer

You can buy equipment that will let you talk to your computer! It will do certain things that you tell it to do. And you can use software that reads aloud what you type in on the keyboard. However, it will be quite a while before the computer can intelligently talk back to you. Why is this so?

The computer can do computation with numbers very easily. But getting the computer to deal with language is quite another matter. When you talk with a friend, you know what you mean by the words you use. The problem is that the same word may not have the same meaning to different people. For example, you might say that you live in a big city. If you had just moved from a rural area to a town of 100,000 people, the city would be a big city to you. But a friend of yours who lives in New York (with millions of people) would say you live in a small town. If people have a problem interpreting the meaning of words, imagine the problem computer scientists are facing to get the computer to understand and interpret the meaning of words.

There are also other problems. The computer has to deal with voice dialects. Dialects are simply variations of how we speak the same language. For example, people who live in Georgia might have a different dialect from people who live in New York, Wisconsin, or California. Another problem is the structure of language. People sometimes speak in incomplete sentences. That would really confuse a computer. If you said "How you feeling?" instead of "How are you feeling?," the computer would need to know that the verb had been left out. But we understand the question. Another problem deals with specific requests. If you said to a salesperson, "Please show me that one over there," the request would be honored. The computer needs to know what "that one" is referring to. Although it may be some time before computers are able to carry on a conversation with you, computer scientists are working on these problems, and may have solutions soon.

Short programs to do one specific task can be written without any planning. This type of programming to solve a problem is called **bottom-up programming**. But almost all programs involve more than one set of instructions or one task to be performed.

Because planning is so important, several programming tools are used to plan programs. One tool is **flowcharting**. Flowcharting is showing the logical steps of a program using pictorial symbols. Instructions are written inside the symbols. **Pseudocode** is another tool used to plan a program. It is a sentence outline of the programming steps. The programmer describes each step of the program in a separate sentence. In addition to using these tools, most programmers plan their programs using a **top-down structured** approach. Such an approach makes a program easier to write and debug. It is also easier to change at a later time. Let's look at flowcharting, pseudocode, and top-down structured programming more closely.

CHECK WHAT YOU HAVE LEARNED

1. What is pseudocode?
2. How is pseudocode different from flowcharting?
3. Why is planning important?
4. What kind of program can be written with bottom-up programming?
5. Why is it easier to write very complex programs with top-down programming?

Flowcharting

Although today many programmers consider flowcharting to be somewhat complicated, flowcharts were at one time a very popular way to plan programs. Using symbols, flowcharts show us a "picture" of how a problem is to be solved. The most common symbols are shown and described in the next paragraphs.

The **terminal symbol** is oval-shaped: ⬭. This symbol indicates the beginning and ending points of a program or a part of a program, called a **routine**. The **input/output symbol** is shaped like a parallelogram: ▱. It indicates places in the program where data is either entered or printed out. The **process symbol** is shaped like a rectangle: ▭. It indicates places in the program where the computer must do a calculation.

PROGRAMMING

The **decision symbol** is diamond-shaped: ◇. It indicates a place in the program where the computer needs to decide, based on tests to see what conditions exist, which of two branching routes to take. Because the computer can't think for itself, we must tell it what conditions are to be tested. If the condition is true, the computer goes to one place in the program. If the condition is not true, the computer jumps to another place. The flowchart's decision-making symbol shows where the program will go based on the conditions.

Lines connect the flowchart symbols together. Arrows on the lines show the direction in which you read the flowchart.

The following flowchart uses these symbols to show how to solve a grade averaging problem. Remember that we mentioned earlier that in a flowchart, instructions are written inside the symbols.

```
        ( Find the Average )
                 ↓
         / Read next number / ←──────┐
                 ↓                    │
         | Sum = sum + number |       │
                 ↓                    │
         | Total entries =    |       │
         | total entries + 1  |       │
                 ↓                    │
              < Last number? > ───────┘
                 ↓            no
               yes
                 ↓
         | Average = sum      |
         | divided by total   |
         | entries            |
                 ↓
         / Print average /
                 ↓
              ( End )
```

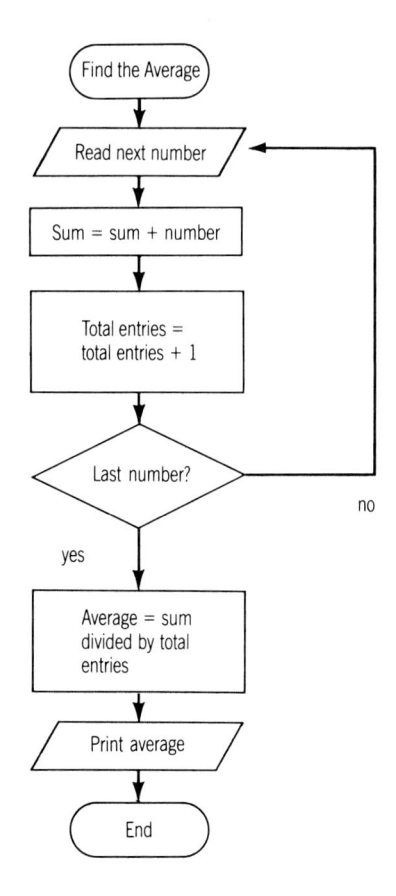

The flowchart has terminal symbols at the beginning and end of the program. The input/output symbol is used when the computer reads the numbers from a list of numbers, and when it prints the average. The process symbol is used at the point where the computer calculates total entries, sum, and average. The decision-making symbol is used where the computer must decide whether the last number has been read. Based on its decision, the computer must jump to a different part of the program. If there are more numbers to be read, the computer will go back and get another number. If there are no more numbers, the computer finds and prints the average and then goes to the ending terminal symbol. The flowchart is complete.

Pseudocode

Planning the steps to be taken in a program can also be done using pseudocode. Pseudocode is an outline in sentence form of the program. Many programmers like pseudocode because they can write the program outline using everyday words. Here is a pseudocode outline of the averaging problem:

Averaging the Numbers

1. Read the next number
2. Add number to sum
3. Add 1 to total entries
4. If there are more numbers, go back to 1; if not, go to 5
5. Find the average by dividing the sum by total entries
6. Print the average

End

The program has six steps, numbered 1–6. Step 1 is to select the next number. Step 2 adds that number to the sum. Step 3 adds 1 to the number that counts the total entries, called the **counter**. Step 4 checks to see if there are more numbers to be read. If so, the computer goes back to Step 1 to get another number. If not, it goes on to Step 5 where it calculates the average. Step 6 prints the average. This ends the program.

CHECK WHAT YOU HAVE LEARNED

1. Why are different symbols used in flowcharting?
2. Explain why you might prefer flowcharting or pseudocode.
3. What is a counter?
4. What do the lines and arrows in a flowchart show us?
5. What does a decision symbol mean in flowcharting?

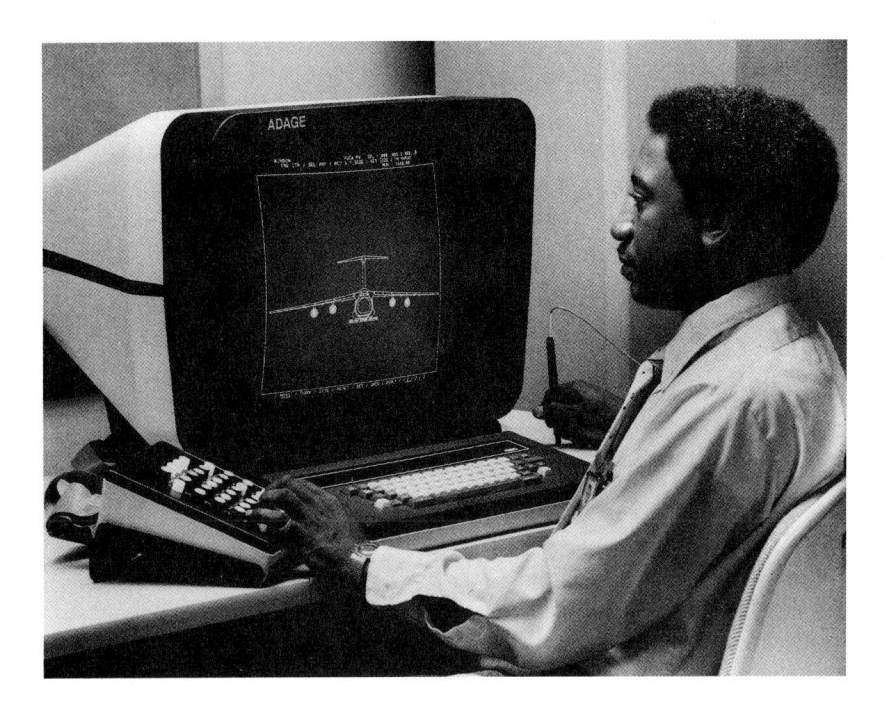

Computer-aided design (CAD) is helping airplane designers solve problems while still on the "drawing board."

Top-Down Structured Programming

As programs become more complex, they become more difficult to plan. The easiest way to work with a larger program is to break it up into smaller parts called **subroutines**. Subroutines are small "programs" within the larger program. Each subroutine should do only one major task. For example, in a program to find the average income of three newspaper carriers during a certain week, one subroutine might compute the amount of money one of them earned during the week. When the subroutine is finished, the program returns to the step following the one that sent the program to the subroutine.

Here is the pseudocode for a large program that computes the final grade in a science class:

Final Grade

1. Print instructions
2. Enter grades for each assignment
3. Count total number of grades
4. Compute total grades
5. Divide total by total number of grades
6. Print average

End

These six steps make up the **main routine**. Each step can be written as a separate subroutine. Step 1 might be written like this:

Print Instructions

1. Instruct user to enter grades for each assignment

Return

The word *Return* means that the computer is to return to the main routine once it has finished this subroutine. This subroutine has only one numbered step. How much detail needs to be listed in a subroutine depends on the experience of the programmer, who else is likely to look at the outline, and the complexity of the program.

The second subroutine's purpose is to enter grades for each assignment. It might look like this in pseudocode:

Enter Grades for Assignments

1. Enter the grade for each assignment

Return

This subroutine is similar to the first one. It is short and it does one task. The task is to enter a grade for each assignment.

The third, fourth, fifth, and sixth subroutines count the total number of grades entered, compute the total of the grades for each assignment, divide them by the total number, and print the average. They might look like this:

Count Grades Entered

1. Count number of grades

Return

Compute Total Grades
1. Total grade = sum of grades

Return

Compute Average
1. Divide total grade by number of grades

Return

Print Average
1. Print average

Return

End

Each of these subroutines has only one step to be done, but most subroutines have several steps. However, there should never be so many steps that the subroutine appears cluttered.

PROGRAMMING

A top-down structured program can also be flowcharted. For the averaging problem, the main flowchart would look like this:

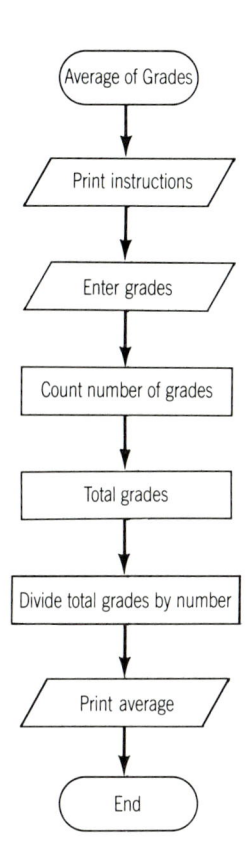

```
        ( Average of Grades )
                 │
                 ▼
          / Print instructions /
                 │
                 ▼
            / Enter grades /
                 │
                 ▼
         [ Count number of grades ]
                 │
                 ▼
            [ Total grades ]
                 │
                 ▼
     [ Divide total grades by number ]
                 │
                 ▼
           / Print average /
                 │
                 ▼
               ( End )
```

Each of the subroutines could also be flowcharted. Flowchart lines should never cross each other. If they are crossed, it means a subroutine is too complicated. The programmer should consider rewriting the subroutine to have it call for another subroutine.

CHECK WHAT YOU HAVE LEARNED

1. What is a subroutine?
2. How many tasks does each subroutine perform?
3. Can top-down structured programming be written in pseudocode, flowcharting, or both?
4. How many steps should each subroutine have?
5. What does the word *Return* indicate at the end of a subroutine?

Careers and Computers

Application Programmers

Like system programmers, application programmers write instructions for the computer to follow in performing its work. But the application programmer writes instructions that tell the computer how to perform a specific task, while the system programmer writes instructions for the computer's operating system.

In many respects, the application programmer's job is similar to the system analyst's job. Both require a knowledge of programming and computer languages. Both demand someone who gives attention to detail and who works well as a problem-solver. It is also important for application programmers to be able to communicate well with other people since they must work with other personnel in a company to determine the work that needs to be done by the computer.

Once their programs are written, application programmers must follow through by testing and debugging the programs until they are correct. This can be a long and slow process. In fact, programmers may spend as much or more time in testing and debugging as they spend writing their programs. The application programmer must be willing to see a project through until the program is working as it was intended to.

Many application programmers have degrees in computer science or programming, either from a four-year university program or from a technical school or junior college. Most know several programming languages such as BASIC and COBOL.

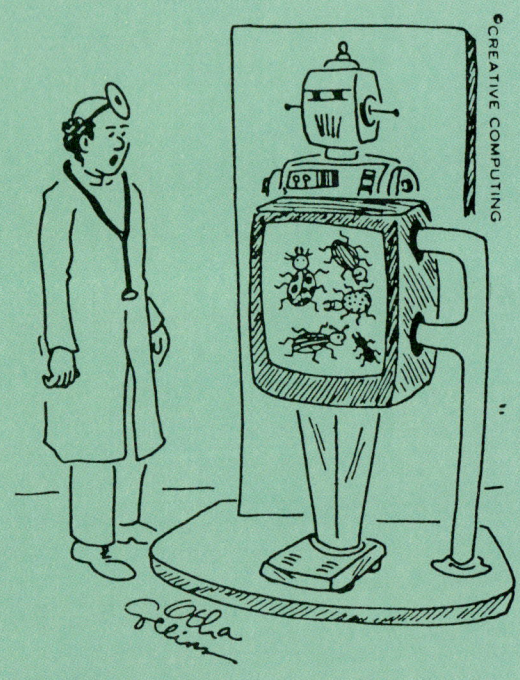

"You'll be fine once we get the bugs out."

As we turn to computers to do more and more of the work we have previously done by hand, our need for application programmers will increase. Application programming is a good starting point for those interested in system programming or system analysis as well.

Engineers

Engineers invent and design computer equipment. They study the problems that users have with systems that are currently available, and then try to design computers that do not cause these problems. In recent years, electrical engineers have concentrated on building computers that are smaller, faster, and have more memory than computers built in the past.

The work of electrical engineers is exciting and interesting because they are involved in creating state-of-the-art computer technology. In a sense, they are creating the future. While we use the computers of today, the electrical engineer is busy inventing the computers we will use in the future.

Electrical engineers must be problem-solvers. They understand what types of computers need to be designed, and they discover ways to design them. These computer professionals must have a high level of technical knowledge. Engineers have college degrees, and many choose to expand their knowledge by enrolling in graduate programs. They must also have a good deal of hands-on experience with computers.

Because of their high level of technical knowledge and experience, engineers command high salaries. They are among the most sought-after professionals in the field of computers, and they are able to choose from many job opportunities.

Scientists and Laboratory Technicians

We often think of scientists and laboratory technicians as people who wear glasses and white coats and pour mysterious liquids into glass beakers on complicated machines. But of course most scientists are not really like that at all. Scientists are people who make guesses about what might happen under certain circumstances and then test those guesses. Usually, their guesses are based upon a theory or idea about the circumstances they are testing. For example, if a scientist believed that a certain amount of practice in running mazes affects our ability to run a new maze, he or she might give different animals practice running mazes, and then allow them to try a new maze. The theory is that a given amount of practice makes perfect. Therefore, the scientist would expect that animals with *less* practice would not be able to run the new maze, but those with *more* would be able to run it.

The scientist must consider all of the things being measured and all of the other factors that may affect the experimental results. For example, it may be important to be sure that all the animals are equally hungry so that the scientist can be sure that one animal is not running faster than another simply because it is hungrier. It is a scientist's job to design the experiment, to decide how the data will be analyzed, and to interpret the results of the experiment.

But the scientist does not necessarily run the experiment. The laboratory technician is a very valuable assistant to the scientist. He or she may have the job of actually running the experiment and recording and analyzing the results according to the scientist's specifications.

The computer has become extremely important to both the scientist and the laboratory technician. The computer is able to keep track of and work with huge amounts of data that may be recorded and analyzed. But it is also useful for many other things. It is often necessary in experiments to be sure that what is being tested is assigned to experimental groups at random. The computer can do this. The computer can also be used to give cues to subjects and can measure responses in periods of time much smaller than those that can be recorded by humans. And with computer simulation, often the entire experiment is run on the computer! For example, the computer can be given information about a particular disease, and can simulate the disease's response if a certain drug is administered.

Because the computer has become so important in scientific research, it is often necessary for scientists or laboratory technicians, or both, to be able programmers. It is important to the scientist to know and understand the capabilities of the computer, and to be able to design an experiment that will make good use of those capabilities. It is also important for the laboratory technician to be able to use the computer to run the experiment and, sometimes, to write the program that will test what the scientist would like to test.

Programming in BASIC

BASIC is one of the easiest programming languages to learn. You can do simple programming after you learn just a little bit of the vocabulary and syntax of BASIC. Vocabulary, of course, means the words that the computer understands as part of a language. **Syntax** is the order and arrangement of those words in a specific language.

You can understand syntax if you realize that different human languages also differ in vocabulary and syntax. The Spanish words *el caballo bueno* could be translated directly into English as *the horse good* if we didn't change the syntax. But *the horse good* would not be correct English. In English the phrase should read *the good horse*. Both syntax and vocabulary are important in computer languages as well.

A program consists of a number of lines, called **statements**, that tell the computer what to do. In most forms of BASIC, each line is numbered. We could start numbering with 1 and name the next line 2 and the next line 3 and so on, but this is not a good idea. The problem with using consecutive numbers is that if we find we have left something out or if we change the program, we have no numbers to give new statements. For this reason, it is usual to number each line with a multiple of 10. If we find when we are debugging the program that we would like to add another statement between line 10 and line 20, we can add a line number 15 and the computer will automatically put it in the right place.

PROGRAMMING

Many youngsters are enjoying computer camps where they learn programming skills.

but powerful statements in BASIC. Each statement begins with a key word. In the following paragraphs, these key words are written all in capital letters. Here are some of the key words you will learn:

REM	RETURN	IF...THEN	GOSUB
PRINT	LET	GOTO	END
			INPUT

Documentation

Documentation is the method of supplying information about a program within the program lines to the programmer or user. One way is to have notes accompany a program, telling the user how the program works. Another way is to build into the program special remarks at various lines to describe what is going on.

REM statements are used as documentation in a BASIC program to remind the programmer of what is happening at that point. (REM is short for "remark.") For example, you might write "REM this program will calculate the average" or "REM this program is for my algebra class." REM statements can be written in normal English and are not printed or used in calculations by the computer when the program is run. REM statements are only for the programmmer to notice, not for the computer to do anything with. But they help a lot when the program is complicated and the programmer needs to be reminded of what happens next.

GOTO statements tell the computer to go to another line. You might write a program like this:

```
10  PRINT "I love computers."
20  GOTO 10
```

Because a GOTO statement can branch to any location in the program, it is often difficult to find program errors. Therefore, GOTO statements are discouraged.

A PRINT statement tells the computer to print out some information. When the computer ran this program it would first do what it was told to do in line 10—that is, it would print "I love computers" or display it on the screen. But almost instantaneously it would proceed to the next line, 20, and be told to go back to 10. It would repeat 10, go to 20, repeat 10, go to 20, and so on endlessly until the program was interrupted.

A GOSUB statement is like a GOTO statement, except that it tells the computer to go to a subroutine instead of to just one line. A program might have a main routine and several subroutines. If the main routine told the computer to GOSUB 200, for example, the computer would go to line 200 and would read the lines which followed until it was told to RETURN. Then it would go back to the next line of the main routine and see what was next. It would finally stop when it reached an END statement.

In BASIC, variables must be named. A **variable** is something that can change in the program. For example, a variable might be the cost of an item or the number of times the program has been run. Each variable might be given a letter name. The LET statement assigns a value to a variable. For example, a BASIC statement might read LET T = 0: REM TOTAL. This tells the computer that T equals 0 for now. The REM statement reminds the programmer that T stands for total. The variable might change during the program. Later, a statement might say LET T = T + 1. How can T equal T + 1? The computer is being told that T now equals a new number. Instead of standing for 0 now, it stands for 0 + 1, or 1. If it comes back to the statement LET T = T + 1 again, then T will equal 2, and so on. Sometimes the key word LET is left out of this statement. If so, it still means the same thing.

An INPUT statement tells the computer to wait and allow the

The Future and Computers

True BASIC

The original version of BASIC was developed at Dartmouth College in 1964 by John Kemeny and Thomas Kurtz. Changes were made at the university during the later 1960s to make BASIC a structured programming language. When microcomputers were developed, the manufacturers chose to use the original 1964 version or one similar to it. This made BASIC a simple, but not very powerful, language.

All that is about to change. For the past ten years, about thirty volunteers from universities, schools, and computer companies have worked on a committee to recommend changes that should be made in BASIC. This committee is part of the American National Standards Institute (ANSI for short). Partly because of the recommendations presented by ANSI, Kemeny and Kurtz have developed a new language called True BASIC.

True BASIC is still as easy to learn and to use as the original BASIC, but is more powerful and allows its users to work faster and correct errors more easily. More powerful and sophisticated graphics are also available.

The best part about True BASIC is that it is transportable. This means that users can run the same programs on different types of microcomputers. This is very important because it allows programmers to make programs for several different types of machines. Until now, programs had to be written for a specific machine, and rewritten if they were to be run on a different computer.

---

person using the program to type in a variable in the form of a number or letters. If the variable is to be letters, we tell the computer to expect letters by typing a $ sign after the name of the variable. For example, you might write a program like this:

```
10   PRINT "What is your name?"
20   INPUT N$
30   PRINT "Hello, " N$ ". How old are you?"
40   INPUT A
50   PRINT N$ " is " A " years old."
60   END
```

This program asks the user's name and waits for the user to type it in at the keyboard. Then the computer prints "Hello," and calls the person by name. So if Betty were using the program, the computer would print "Hello, Betty. How old are you?" It would wait for Betty to type in her age. If Betty were twelve, it would then print "Betty is 12 years old."

An IF...THEN statement tells the computer to look at some information it has and then make a decision based on that information. For instance, you might tell the computer that IF the value of a certain variable is less than 10, THEN it should go back to a certain line and continue calculating. Calculations are indicated in BASIC programs with the math symbols you are already familiar with, such as * for multiply and / for divide.

With this vocabulary of BASIC words and phrases, you could already write a simple program. In the next section, we will write a program to solve a problem.

CHECK WHAT YOU HAVE LEARNED

1. Why are REM statements important?
2. Why don't programmers number each line in BASIC with consecutive numbers?
3. What sign is used in BASIC to tell the computer to expect letters instead of numbers?
4. What is a variable?
5. What is the difference between a GOTO statement and a GOSUB statement?

Solving a Problem by Programming

Now we are ready to complete a programming problem. We will follow the steps in solving a problem to write a computer program. Identifying the problem is a must no matter what programming language is used. The specific instructions (called **code**) will vary for each language. After writing code, you must run the program to test it for all possible errors.

Here is our problem: to write a program that will compute the total cost of purchases, including a 6 percent sales tax, when there are an unknown number of items to be purchased.

Writing the Pseudocode

We will write the pseudocode first, using top-down structured programming. We will write subroutines to enter the values for the purchases, compute the total with the taxes, and request to rerun the program if there are more purchases to enter. Also, at the beginning of the program we need to tell the computer to start counting the number of purchases and doing its calculations at 0. Here is one example of **initializing** the variables to 0.

The pseudocode might look like this:

Purchase Program

1. Initialize variables
2. Enter purchase values
3. Compute total + taxes
4. Restart program request

End

The first subroutine initializes all of the variables used in the program. Remember that the number that counts the total entries is called the counter. Counters must always be initialized. It is a good idea to initialize other variables, too. The first subroutine might look like this:

Initialize Variables

1. Set total to 0
2. Set price to 0
3. Set tax to 0
4. Set request to 0

Return

The second subroutine will allow you to type in the prices of the items being purchased. It will continue repeating itself, or **looping**, until you enter a 0 to stop the loop. You don't know beforehand when you will want to quit because the number of items purchased is unknown. The pseudocode is:

Enter purchases

1. Enter purchase amount
2. If purchase amount is 0 then return
3. Let total = total + purchase
4. Go to 1

The third subroutine adds the amount of taxes to the total amount of purchases. The pseudocode might look like this:

Total Purchases + Taxes

1. Let taxes = total $\times$ .06
2. Let total = total + taxes
3. Print total

Return

The final subroutine is to determine if you wish to restart the program. The pseudocode looks like this:

Restart Program Request

1. Enter request Y or N (Y stands for yes, N stands for no.)

Return

College students use terminal rooms at their universities to learn advanced programming skills.

Drawing Flowcharts

The flowchart of the program begins with the main routine. It looks like this:

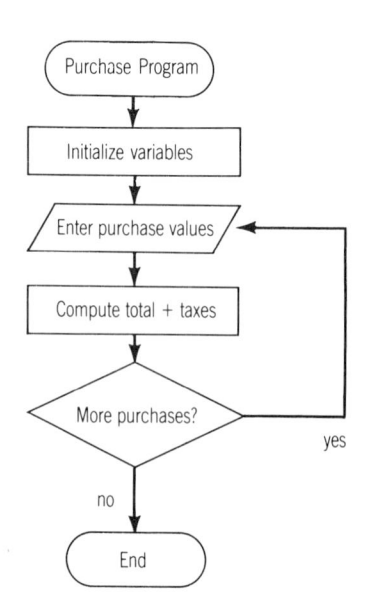

```
       ( Purchase Program )
                │
                ▼
       [ Initialize variables ]
                │
                ▼
       / Enter purchase values / ◄──────┐
                │                        │
                ▼                        │
       [ Compute total + taxes ]         │
                │                        │
                ▼                        │
         < More purchases? >─── yes ─────┘
                │
                no
                ▼
            ( End )
```

The flowchart for the second subroutine must show that looping will continue until a 0 is entered. It looks like this:

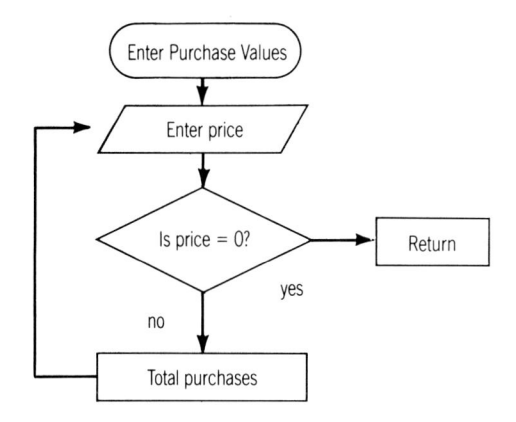

```
        ( Enter Purchase Values )
                   ↓
        ┌──→  / Enter price /
        │          ↓
        │     < Is price = 0? > ──yes──→ [ Return ]
        │          │
        │          no
        │          ↓
        └──── [ Total purchases ]
```

The flowchart for the third subroutine looks like this:

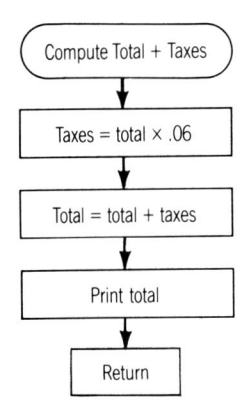

```
        ( Compute Total + Taxes )
                   ↓
          [ Taxes = total × .06 ]
                   ↓
          [ Total = total + taxes ]
                   ↓
              [ Print total ]
                   ↓
               [ Return ]
```

The final subroutine consists of a single input to request a restart. The flowchart looks like this:

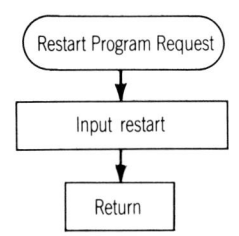

```
        ( Restart Program Request )
                   ↓
             [ Input restart ]
                   ↓
               [ Return ]
```

Writing the BASIC Code

The next step is to translate the program into BASIC instruction codes. (If you have a computer, you can test the program after each section. You will get error messages until you have a completely entered program.)

We can write the code for the main program routine by translating from either the pseudocode or the flowchart. The code looks like this:

```
100    REM PURCHASES PROGRAM
110    GOSUB 200: REM INITIALIZE VALUES
120    GOSUB 300: REM ENTER PURCHASE VALUES
130    GOSUB 400: REM COMPUTE TOTAL + TAXES
140    GOSUB 500: REM RESTART PROGRAM
150    IF A$ = "Y" THEN 100
160    END
```

The subroutines are translated next. Each is translated from the pseudocode using correct variable names. They look like this:

```
200    REM INITIALIZE VALUES
210    TTAL = 0: REM TOTAL
220    PRICE = 0: REM PURCHASE PRICE
230    TAX = 0: REM TAX
240    RETURN: REM TO LINE 120

300    REM ENTER PURCHASES
310    INPUT "ENTER PURCHASE PRICE OR 0 TO
315    QUIT "; PRICE
320    IF PRICE = 0 THEN RETURN: REM TO LINE 130
330    TTAL = TTAL + PRICE
340    GOTO 310

400    REM COMPUTE TOTAL + TAXES
410    TAX = TTAL * .06
420    TTAL = TTAL + TAX
430    PRINT "TOTAL = "; TTAL
440    RETURN: REM TO LINE 140

500    REM MORE PURCHASES
510    INPUT " MORE PURCHASES (Y/N)"; A$
520    RETURN: REM TO LINE 150
```

Running the Program

Let's imagine what the computer does as the program is run. The computer does not print the REM statements, as they are only to remind the programmer what each routine or subroutine does. The first thing the computer does is to go to line 200, as it is told to do in line 110. As it goes from line 200 to line 230, each counter is set at 0. When it reaches line 240, it is told to return to line 120. Line 120 sends the computer to line 300.

When the computer gets to line 310, it asks the user to input a purchase price or to enter 0 to quit. The program names this purchase price PRICE. Line 320 tells the computer that if the user has typed in 0 it should return to line 130. If the user has not typed in 0, the computer will continue to line 330, where it is told to add the new purchase price to the total of purchase prices. Line 340 tells it to return to line 310 so that the user can type in another purchase price. The computer will continue to go around in this loop until the user types in 0 as a purchase price. In other words, typing in a 0 tells the computer there are no more purchases. Then it will go back to line 130.

Line 130 sends the computer to line 400. Line 410 tells the computer to compute the tax (TAX) by multiplying .06 times the total of the purchase prices (TAX = .06 * TTAL). Line 420 changes the total (TTAL) so that it equals the total of the prices plus the tax. Line 430 tells the computer to print this total. Line 440 tells the computer to return to line 140.

Line 140 sends the computer to line 500. Line 510 simply tells the computer to ask the user if there are more purchases. The user types Y or N. The computer names this answer A$. The computer is then sent back to line 150. Line 150 tells the computer to make a decision. If the user has typed Y in answer to its question, then the computer goes back to line 100 to start all over again. If the user has not typed Y, then the computer goes to line 160 where the program ends.

If we were running this program, this is what we would see:

Computer Would Print:	User Might Type:
ENTER PURCHASE PRICE OR 0 TO QUIT	85
ENTER PURCHASE PRICE OR 0 TO QUIT	15
ENTER PURCHASE PRICE OR 0 TO QUIT	0
TOTAL = 106	

Programming Steps
- Define the problem
- Analyze the problem
- Plan a solution
- Write the pseudocode or flowchart
- Write the code
- Run the program
- Document the program

Writing Code in Other Languages

Our program could also be written in other languages with few changes to the outline. Let's look at some of the parts of the program as it would be written in Logo and Pascal.

Logo routines are called **procedures**. The main procedure or routine can be placed anywhere in the program. To run any procedure, you simply enter the procedure name. In Logo, the program would look like this:

```
TO ENTER.PURCHASE.PRICE
  CLEARTEXT
  PRINT [ENTER PURCHASE AMOUNT]
  MAKE "PURCHASE.PRICE FIRST REQUEST
  MAKE "TOTAL :TOTAL + :PURCHASE.PRICE
  PRINT [ ]
  PRINT [ANOTHER VALUE (Y/N)?]
  MAKE "ANSWER READLIST
  IF :ANSWER = [N] [STOP]
  ENTER.PURCHASE.PRICE
END

TO RESTART
  PRINT [DO MORE TOTALS (Y/N)?]
  MAKE "ANSWER READLIST
END

TO COMPUTE.TOTAL.TAXES
  PRINT1 [TOTAL =]
  PRINT :TOTAL *1.06
  PRINT [ ]
END

TO INITIALIZE
  MAKE "PURCHASE.PRICE 0
  MAKE "TOTAL 0
END

TO BUY
  INITIALIZE
  ENTER.PURCHASE.PRICE
  COMPUTE.TOTAL.TAXES
  RESTART
  IF :ANSWER = [N] [STOP]
  BUY
END

ENTER PURCHASE AMOUNT
37.56

ANOTHER VALUE (Y/N)?
Y

(new screen)
ENTER PURCHASE AMOUNT
73.97

ANOTHER VALUE (Y/N)?
Y
```

```
(new screen)
ENTER PURCHASE AMOUNT
864.23

ANOTHER VALUE (Y/N)?
Y

(new screen)
ENTER PURCHASE AMOUNT
1.20

ANOTHER VALUE (Y/N)?
N

TOTAL = 1035.58
DO MORE TOTALS (Y/N)?
N
```

The problem and logic of the BASIC and Logo programs are the same. The vocabulary is different. In Logo, there are no line numbers. And you might notice that all versions of Logo use meaningful variable names. Each Logo procedure begins with TO followed by a procedure name. Each procedure is also terminated with an END statement. Other differences include replacing the LET statement with MAKE, changing syntax rules with equations and quotation marks ('') in different statements, and using brackets ([ ]) in the PRINT statements.

Pascal is a programming language that is used in many schools. Some universities and colleges require new programming students to learn Pascal as their first language. Like Logo, Pascal encourages structured programming. Look at the Pascal version of the purchases program:

```
PROGRAM BUY;
(*Variables must be listed *)
VAR PURCHASE, TOTAL, TAX : REAL;
    ANSWER : STRING[1];

PROCEDURE INITIALIZE_VALUES;
  BEGIN
    PURCHASE := 0;
    TOTAL := 0;
    TAX := 0;
  END;

PROCEDURE ENTER_PURCHASES;
  VAR REPLY : STRING[1];
  BEGIN
    REPLY := 'Y';
  WHILE REPLY = 'Y' DO
    BEGIN
```

```
            WRITE ('ENTER PURCHASE PRICE ');
            READLN (PURCHASE);
            TOTAL := TOTAL + PURCHASE;
            WRITE ('ANOTHER PURCHASE (Y/N) ');
            READLN (REPLY);
            WRITELN;
          END;
      END;
  PROCEDURE COMPUTE_TOTAL;
    BEGIN
      TAX := TOTAL *0.06;
      TOTAL := TOTAL + TAX;
      WRITELN ('TOTAL FOR PURCHASES INCLUDING
      TAX ', TOTAL:10:2);
    END;
  PROCEDURE RESTART_PROGRAM;
    BEGIN
      WRITE ('RESTART PROGRAM (Y/N) ');
      READLN(ANSWER);
    END;
  BEGIN
      ANSWER := 'Y';
        WHILE ANSWER = 'Y' DO
          BEGIN
            INITIALIZE_VALUES;
            ENTER_PURCHASES;
            COMPUTE_TOTAL;
            RESTART_PROGRAM;
          END;
  END.
  ENTER PURCHASE PRICE 37.56
  ANOTHER PURCHASE (Y/N) Y

  ENTER PURCHASE PRICE 73.97
  ANOTHER PURCHASE (Y/N) Y

  ENTER PURCHASE PRICE 864.23
  ANOTHER PURCHASE (Y/N) Y

  ENTER PURCHASE PRICE 1.20
  ANOTHER PURCHASE (Y/N) N

  TOTAL FOR PURCHASES INCLUDING TAX     1035.58
  RESTART PROGRAM (Y/N) N
```

Again, the problem is the same. Much of the planning is the same. The major differences are in syntax and in the free-form way the program is written.

CHECK WHAT YOU HAVE LEARNED

1. Why is it important to initialize the variables?
2. How is Logo different from BASIC?
3. What does the computer do when it encounters a REM statement?
4. Why is it necessary to use pseudocode and flowcharts before writing the program in code?
5. Explain briefly why subroutines are useful.

WHAT YOU HAVE LEARNED IN CHAPTER SEVEN

Computers can only do what we tell them to do. Programmers give computers the instructions they need to do their work. But before a programmer can solve a problem with a computer, he or she must be able to explain in step-by-step instructions exactly how to arrive at the solution to the problem. Programming steps include carefully defining the problem, analyzing the problem, planning a solution, writing a pseudocode or flowchart, writing the code, running the program, and documenting the program.

If you are writing a computer program, you must carefully plan out the program before you ever sit down at the computer. Some programmers prefer to use a flowchart. Flowcharting is showing the logical steps of a program using pictorial symbols. Pseudocode is another choice—it is a sentence outline of the programming logic in simple words. These two techniques are the most commonly used ones in planning computer programs.

Flowcharts employ a number of different symbols. The terminal symbol is oval-shaped. It marks the beginning and ending points of a routine or program. The input/output symbol is shaped like a parallelogram. The process symbol is shaped like a rectangle. The decision symbol is diamond-shaped and marks places at which the computer must make a decision about what to do next. Lines connect the flowchart symbols together and arrows show the direction in which the flowchart is read.

It is best to write complicated programs using top-down structured programming. The programmer breaks the program up into smaller parts called subroutines. When each subroutine is finished, the program goes back to the main routine and the main routine tells the computer what to do next. Top-down structured programming can be flowcharted or written in pseudocode.

Once the main routine and subroutines have been flowcharted or written in pseudocode, they can be translated into programming language. Each language has its own vocabulary and syntax. We can translate the program into BASIC, Logo, or Pascal with few changes to the original outline.

1. What is top-down structured programming?
2. What shapes are used in flowcharting?
3. Name two methods used to plan programs.
4. What must a programmer be able to do before he or she can solve a problem with a computer?
5. What is the difference between pseudocode and flowcharting?
6. Does pseudocode only apply to programs to be written in BASIC? Why or why not?
7. What are the major differences between BASIC, Logo, and Pascal?
8. What must be done after the program has been carefully planned?
9. What does the terminal symbol mark?
10. What is a subroutine?

USING WORDS YOU HAVE LEARNED

1. In flowcharting, the _____ symbol is diamond-shaped.
2. _____ _____ programming separates the program into several subroutines.
3. A _____ shows us a "picture" of how the problem is to be solved.
4. _____ statements remind the programmer what each routine or subroutine does.
5. Each _____ is a small "program" within the larger program.
6. _____ show us in which direction to read the flowchart.
7. A step-by-step outline of the program using everyday words is called _____ .
8. The _____ routine tells the computer to go to certain subroutines.
9. In flowcharts, the _____ symbol is oval-shaped.
10. In flowcharts, the symbols are connected by _____ .

EXERCISING YOUR MATH SKILLS

Carla was a very bright twelve-year-old, but she just hated to work out long problems on paper. Her math teacher was asking her to do twenty-five long division problems every day! Carla told her teacher that she knew exactly how to do the problems, but that she was bored with working them out. Her teacher told her that if she could write a computer program explaining exactly how to do long division, she would not have to do any more long division problems for homework. Carla decided that she would plan the program in pseudocode. Can you show what her plan would look like?

UNDERSTANDING WHAT YOU HAVE LEARNED

MULTIPLE CHOICE

1. Pseudocode can be written:
    a) in programming languages only
    b) in BASIC only
    c) in simple words
    d) in BASIC or Logo only

2. The most important part of programming is:
   a) translating
   b) planning
   c) debugging
   d) the subroutine
3. Flowcharting and pseudocode are both:
   a) ways to plan a program
   b) computer languages
   c) made only for BASIC programming
   d) done only with simple programs
4. Each subroutine in a program does:
   a) the work for the main routine
   b) the initializing of the variables
   c) one major task
   d) two or three major tasks
5. A GOSUB statement tells the computer:
   a) to go to a subroutine
   b) to return to the main routine
   c) to end the subroutine
   d) to end the main routine
6. The computer can solve:
   a) all problems
   b) problems the programmer does not know how to solve
   c) only simple problems
   d) only problems the programmer knows how to solve
7. The input/output symbol in a flowchart is:
   a) at the beginning
   b) at the end
   c) shaped like a parallelogram
   d) only for REM statements
8. Flowchart lines should:
   a) always cross each other
   b) never cross each other
   c) only go in one direction
   d) always be vertical
9. When you initialize the variables, you:
   a) set the counters to 0
   b) set the tax at 0
   c) add the total of the numbers
   d) count all numbers
10. Logo is different from BASIC in its:
    a) vocabulary
    b) syntax
    c) punctuation
    d) all of the above

TRUE OR FALSE

1. Top-down structured programming is only used with very simple programs.
2. Pseudocode can be written in simple words.
3. A subroutine performs one major task in a program.
4. When planning a Logo program, you can only use a flowchart.
5. It is never important to define the problem you want to solve with a computer.
6. A programmer must plan his or her program with step-by-step instructions.
7. Bottom-up programming is best done with very complex programs.
8. A GOSUB statement tells the computer to go to a subroutine.
9. Each Logo statement is preceded by a number.
10. REM statements are not printed by the computer.

SHORT ANSWER

1. What is the first step in computer programming? Why is this important?
2. What does a REM statement do?
3. How does pseudocode differ from a flowchart?
4. What is a subroutine?
5. Describe top-down structured programming.
6. Name two differences between a Logo program and a BASIC program.
7. In a flowchart, what type of command might be in an input/output symbol?
8. What does a loop in a program make the computer do?
9. In a flowchart, what is a terminal symbol?
10. Name three strategies you might use to solve a problem without a computer.

WHAT YOU WILL LEARN IN CHAPTER EIGHT

By the end of this chapter, you will be able to:

1. Identify three major periods of our society's history.
2. List several applications of the computer in the Age of Information.
3. Define *robot* and describe current uses of robots.
4. Discuss the importance of computer skills during the Age of Information.
5. State several problems that we face at the entry of the Age of Information.

Computers in Our Society

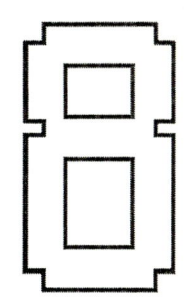

WORDS YOU WILL LEARN

Age of Information
agricultural period
computer literacy
electronic cottage
electronic mail
industrial period
Industrial Revolution
robot

The "horseless carriage" changed the way our society works and lives, but many people were once afraid of it.

Cars have changed a great deal. Will computers do the same?

We are living in an exciting age. In our lifetimes, computers have already become almost as common as typewriters and television sets. Computers are helping businesses, schools, the government, and private citizens. They are used by many different people in many different ways.

We must keep in mind that computers themselves are very young. They have only been in existence since the 1940s. Most computer scientists believe that we cannot even imagine today what computers will be able to do in the years ahead. But new advances are being made every day.

In fact, some experts have compared computers today to the first cars of the early 1900s. In their day, these cars were thought to be very sophisticated. People thought they were comfortable and fast—at fifteen or twenty miles per hour! Some people were afraid of these "horseless carriages"—they refused to ride in them. But when we compare these early cars to the cars we see today, we might be tempted to laugh at how slow and awkward they were.

This story is almost the same for computers. In the early days of computers, people thought the first big, clumsy computers were scientific miracles. They did not operate fast. The first models had to be completely rewired each time a program was changed. (Today, we can change programs just by changing diskettes.) Many people were afraid of computers because they did not understand them. Only large organizations with a great deal of money could afford to buy and use computers.

But computers have evolved rapidly since then. They are faster, more powerful, smaller, and less expensive than ever before. It is not unusual to find a computer being used in a home. It has become rare *not* to see a computer in an office. More and more people find themselves working with computers at school, at home, and at work. And as they work with computers, they find many more ways in which computers can make their lives better.

But will we live happily ever after with computers? Some experts tell us that we must begin to look at the ways that computers are changing our lives. No one doubts that computers have become a very valuable tool for us. They process the vast amount of information that we need to keep track of in a large and complex society. But some of the changes that computers have brought may not be so good for us.

In this chapter, we will explore some of the ways that computers are changing our society. But before we look at what society is changing into, let's first discuss what kind of society we live in today.

COMPUTERS IN OUR SOCIETY

CHECK WHAT YOU HAVE LEARNED

1. How did a computer user change programs with the first computers?
2. In what ways were the first computers like the first cars?
3. Name three ways that computers have evolved since the 1940s.
4. Who uses computers today?
5. Who used the first computers?

The Roots of Our Present Society

Several years ago, a writer named Alvin Toffler published a book called *Future Shock*. This book painted a very dark picture of what the future would be like. Many people who read the book became frightened of the future. They were also afraid of the computer. They believed that the computer would cause terrible changes.

Ten years later, Alvin Toffler wrote another book called *The Third Wave*. This book told a very different story from *Future Shock*. *The Third Wave* talks about some of the good changes that computers will bring. The title of this book refers to a very important concept. There have been three basic periods in our society's history. They have to do with the way people make their livings during a particular time. The three periods society has experienced so far are the **agricultural period**, the **industrial period**, and the **Age of Information**.

During the agricultural period, most people lived in small communities where they worked and lived close to each other all of their lives.

The Agricultural Period

Agriculture means farming. Society really began in the agricultural period. When people began to grow their own food, they began to live in one place. Before people farmed, they had to kill wild animals for meat and skins. They had to eat plants that they found growing in the wild. This meant that people were always moving, following the animals and moving to places where they could find the right plants. People did not stay in one place long enough to form societies as we know them.

Agriculture changed that way of life. Farming means settling on one piece of land and taking care of it. It means living on that land and growing crops. Farmers stay in one place long enough to form friendships with their neighbors. These friendships lead to the building of schools, places of worship, homes, and town halls. Society formed and people began to depend on one another.

During the agricultural period, most people lived in small communities. Most of the people were farmers. These small towns were usually far away from the larger cities. Farmers sent their crops to be sold in the city, but many people never saw a large city. They were born, grew up, lived, and died in the same small town. People did not usually move away to live in other towns. This way of life lasted until the late 1800s.

The Industrial Period

During the late 1800s, many machines were invented. These machines did work that people had had to do by hand before. For example, the cotton gin and the sewing machine changed the way that clothing was made. People no longer had to spin cotton, weave fabric, and sew clothing by hand. This change from the agricultural period to the industrial period is called the **Industrial Revolution**. But the Industrial Revolution created a new need as well. People were needed to work in the factories. New machines were creating all sorts of jobs.

Factories were built in large cities where there were many people. But even the biggest cities did not have enough people for the

The Industrial Revolution changed the way people worked.

factories. People had to come from the farms in order for there to be enough factory workers. Society changed a great deal as people who had been living on farms were offered new jobs in the city. Instead of growing crops, they were now busy making products with "new-fangled" machines.

During the agricultural period in the U.S., the population was spread out in small towns. People had close family ties and friendships. They also shared common values and beliefs. As more people began to live in big cities, society became more varied than it had been. People were freer to move. Not everyone was able to become as close to their neighbors as they had in small towns. They met a great variety of people from different racial, national, religious, and political backgrounds. They had fewer common values and beliefs. This made some people refer to America as the **melting pot**—the bringing together and blending of many different groups and cultures of people.

The industrial period has lasted more than one hundred years. We can still see a lot of it around us. There may be large factories in your city. Some of these factories produce steel, automobiles, clothing, or other items. The people who work in these factories live fairly close to them. They make their livings by making products.

But if we look inside the factories, we see evidence of a new age. Some of the jobs that people used to do are now being done by robots. And in the offices of the factories, paperwork is being done on computers. These are clear signs that the industrial period is giving way to a new period. In this new period, people will live, work, play, and interact in new and different ways.

In the Age of Information, factories look a little different than they did during the industrial period. This automated factory is monitored from a control room.

CHECK WHAT YOU HAVE LEARNED

1. Why did people move to the cities during the industrial period?
2. What do people mean when they say that America is a "melting pot"?
3. If we are entering the "Third Wave," then what were the first two waves?
4. Why were people afraid of the future after they read *Future Shock*?
5. How long did the industrial period last?

The Age of Information

The new period we are entering is the Age of Information. In this period, people will make their livings by handling information more than by growing crops or making products. This change is being made possible by computers. In factories and offices, computers are helping people do jobs more easily and efficiently. Let's take a look at the growing importance of information, and at how computers free us and help us to deal with it.

Robots: A New Way to Get Factory Work Done

Often, jobs that people did in factories were boring or repetitive. On assembly lines, people had to do the same thing over and over again. When people became tired or sick, their work was not always done correctly.

In the Age of Information, robots have taken the place of many of these human workers. **Robots** do not get sick or tired or bored. They do not mind doing the same thing over and over again. If their work is correct the first time, it is also correct the thousandth time. And they don't need light or air conditioning in their workplace. Robots help the manufacturer to make a better product for less money. They also free human workers to do other work that might be more interesting.

When you think about a robot, you may imagine human-looking metal "people." But robots do not really look like people—at least not yet. In fact, some robots look more like one large arm while others look like rolling bookshelves. Robots are

This robot is not afraid of being exposed to dangerous situations.

COMPUTERS IN OUR SOCIETY

really just programmable computers with moving parts. Their "output" is an action instead of a typed page. Everything the robot needs to operate is inside it, so it is not the same as a remote-control device. Also, a robot can do more than one thing over and over again. It can be given a different program, which will change what it does. And the robot is able to work with other objects. Its moving parts can move, hold, or change other objects. Some robots have sensory devices that allow them to sense things that a human is incapable of sensing. For example, a computer can detect a tiny object or a slight change in room temperature much more easily than a human can.

In factories, robots are used to paint cars, weld ships, make memory boards for other computers, and many other things. The government has plans to use robots as well. One very important job that robots have been used for is the inspection of microprocessor chips that go into computers. It takes human beings

Robots do not have to look like this famous "electronic man" and his cute friend.

Robots like this automated welder are being used in many plants to help build cars.

several hours to inspect one chip because the components are so tiny. Robots use sensory photographic lenses to do this job. The robot uses its camera to compare the chip to a picture of a perfect chip that it has stored in its memory. If the two chips are exactly alike, the new chip is accepted. This takes only a few minutes.

Robots do many other jobs that humans used to do. Robots can shear sheep or pluck chickens. Robots have been developed that sort fish brought in by a fishing boat. They can go into dangerous areas in the place of firefighters or police officers and can report back to their human chief about what they find.

New Ideas and Computers

Computers in Medicine

Medicine is a field in which computers are being used more and more often. For example, in Washington, D.C., a large library of medical information is stored on computers. This library is accessible by telephone to doctors all over the world. If a diagnosis is particularly difficult, physicians can access the Washington medical library. They can get the medical information they need within minutes.

Computer data banks also keep information on people who are waiting for organ transplants. When an organ donor is found, his or her blood type and other data are entered into the computer. The computer can match up the donor and the recipient. In these cases, the time saved by the computer can save the lives of those waiting for transplants.

Computers are also being used to monitor patients directly. In the emergency rooms of some hospitals, computer sensors are attached to the patient. The computer monitors the patient's heart beat, temperature, and other vital signs. They print out or display this information quickly and accurately.

Many doctors and hospitals use computers to keep medical records about their patients. Like any data base, this helps keep the information organized and up to date, and allows the doctor to look up important information quickly. A patient's health may depend on it.

But what happens to people who lose their jobs to robots? This is one of the most important questions we face as we move into the Age of Information. Some experts have predicted that within the next ten years we will see a 50 percent shift in the labor force. People will move from industrial (factory) jobs to technical jobs using or working with computers. This means that millions of people will have to leave jobs that they are familiar with. They may leave jobs they have been doing for years to take jobs that they are not trained to do. You will read more about this later in this chapter when we describe problems created by computers in the Age of Information.

The Importance of Information

As our society becomes more complicated, information is becoming much more important. During the agricultural period, each individual had to know about his or her farm, family, and community. The number of actual facts that the common man or wo-

COMPUTERS IN OUR SOCIETY

Factories are changing the tools they use to manage production.

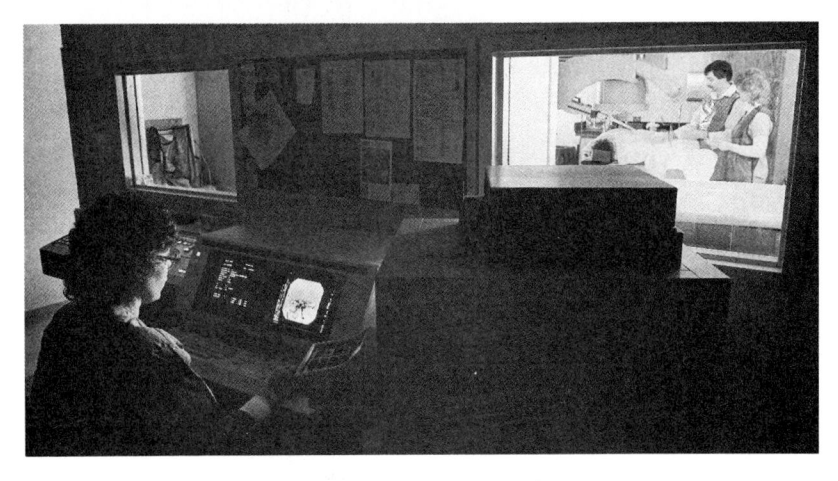

The computer is able to help save lives by analyzing medical information quickly and detecting possible medical problems before they cause harm.

man was expected to remember was really very small. In the industrial period, life became a little more complicated as people were expected to know about larger communities. People had to work with more complex machines and more information was needed in order to carry on daily life.

Specialists became common in many different types of work because no one person could learn all that was necessary to do a job well. During the agricultural period, for example, country doctors usually treated all kinds of ailments. They helped mothers give birth to babies and treated those babies for childhood illnesses. The same doctors treated accident victims in their towns and helped people deal with arthritis or heart trouble. As

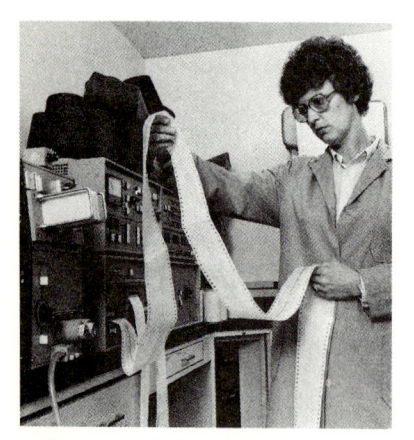

In the textile industry, computers are used to help test fiber strength and durability.

the medical profession became more complex, more young doctors became specialists in neurology, cardiology, or other areas of medicine. Like doctors, lawyers also usually chose specialties, such as corporate or business law. And businesses also began to need more information in order to operate as they grew from neighborhood offices to nationwide corporations.

As we enter the Age of Information, many people's jobs involve the gathering, processing, or using of this information. In fact, jobs that deal directly with information are quickly becoming more common than jobs involved directly with making things. And as robots take over more and more of the factory work, this trend will probably continue.

What do we mean when we say that people are working with information? Imagine a typical business office in the Age of Information. What are the workers doing? The marketing director might be looking over a list of 5000 names that was just received from the home office. The names are those of people who might be interested in the company's product. The marketing director will organize and work with this list to generate new sales. The secretary is looking over a company newsletter that must be typed. In it are graphs and charts that show the company's sales for the last month. The secretary must organize and work with this draft to make a final copy. One of the clerks is taking inventory of the stock in the supply room. The clerk is making a list that must also be organized and used by other people. Finally, a salesperson is meeting with a customer to explain the products that are sold by the company. In order to do this, the salesperson uses a list of information about the products. The salesperson may also be mak-

People and Computers

Steven Paul Jobs

Steven Jobs is an unusual success story. He attended only one semester of college. After that time, his interest in computers prompted him to work for a computer firm in California. When his friend Stephen Wozniak built a small computer, Jobs convinced him that computers for the small user would sell easily. Jobs and Wozniak quit their jobs and sold much of what they had in order to afford to build the first of their computers. They named the machine the Apple. The first Apple was produced in 1977, and since then several different models have been developed. Within five years, Apple Computer, Inc. had made over $664 million.

ing a list of the customer's questions so that the company can learn from them. Some of these questions may even lead to a computer-aided design revision of the product.

These people's jobs have become very difficult because of the large amounts of information that must be organized, changed, reorganized, and used. How can they deal with this information effectively? The tools that more and more offices are using to deal with this information are computers.

CHECK WHAT YOU HAVE LEARNED

1. Name three ways that robots are used in factories.
2. Name two jobs that work with information that have *not* already been mentioned in this chapter.
3. Why do most doctors become specialists?
4. In what way is a robot different from a remote-control device?
5. Name three reasons why an employer might prefer to "hire" a robot instead of a human being. Name two jobs a robot could not do.

Using Computers to Handle Information

One way that many people deal with the huge amounts of information that they must handle is with computers. Computers are used in business, banking, design, real estate, engineering, education, government—even crime fighting! In fact, there are very few jobs that do not use computers in one way or another. Let us look at some of the ways that computers help people in different jobs.

In business, computers can be used to keep track of bills and receipts. Some computer programs keep records of salespersons, special accounts, dates of payment, and so on. They automatically record in the account books amounts paid for services or products. Other programs can keep track of customers and may keep personal records on each customer. They can tell how much each customer owes and can calculate any late charges or other fees. Computers also keep inventory. Stores can enter information about their goods into the computer and the computer keeps a list of item numbers, item names, item cost, number of items, popular items, and so on. Some inventory records are hooked up

Managing information and communicating that information have become an important part of our lives today.

As computers become smaller and more manageable, they are also being used by many professionals outside of the office.

to electronic cash registers. This way, the computer keeps inventory by itself. Every time a purchase is rung up on the cash register, it is subtracted from the inventory.

Computers can also help with paying salaries. The names of employees, their social security numbers, addresses, jobs, salaries, and so on can all be entered into the computer. The computer processes the information and figures out taxes and other deductions. When the employee is paid, a statement of all the deductions can be listed on the check. This way, the payroll department's work is made much simpler.

Computers also help businesspersons to make schedules, calculate job costs, keep files, and prepare final documents. Computer data bases can take the place of complicated filing systems. For example, a computer can help real estate agents keep track of the houses on the market. An agent might enter many different pieces of information about each house into the computer. When a customer asks for a house with two bedrooms, the agent can have the computer print out information on all houses with two bedrooms. Another customer may ask for a house that costs a specific amount. The computer can print out a list of all houses in that price range. Word processing programs can help prepare final documents or letters. Anywhere large amounts of information are used or stored, computers can help.

Careers and Computers

Computer Technicians

Computer technicians install and maintain computer systems. They also add components or peripheral equipment. This means that they set up any new computer systems that customers purchase. They also perform routine checks and service to prevent the equipment from breaking down. They find out what is wrong with computers that fail to operate properly and repair equipment that is not working.

Computer technicians are vital to the industry because they keep the machines in good working order. Most computer users do not have enough technical knowledge to service and repair their own computer hardware. Without computer technicians, they would be at a loss when their equipment fails.

In the future, there will be a great demand for computer technicians. Employers will seek out people who can operate, analyze, develop, market, and repair computer hardware. These people must have a high degree of technical knowledge. They must get this from a university or technical school. As the demand for computer technicians increases, their salaries are likely to increase as well.

Training Specialists

Training specialists design ways to teach new users to operate their computer hardware and software. Training specialists design educational programs and teach classes that train other people to use computers and programs.

The training specialist must possess skills in communicating with other people. It is important to know how much the user already knows about computers and how much the user still needs to know. Finally, the training specialist is responsible for actually teaching users.

Training specialists may have degrees in educational technology or instructional design. Or they may have teaching experience. Besides having experience and skills in teaching, the training specialist must have a working knowledge of computer hardware and software. This career field is growing at a steady pace.

Technical Support Specialists

Technical support specialists are the people who assist users of hardware and software when they have questions about their computers or programs. Most hardware and software manufacturers provide a telephone number that customers can call if they have problems. When a customer calls the technical support department of a manufacturer, the technical support specialist talks with the customer to determine what the problem is. Then he or she advises the user about how to solve the problem. If a problem cannot be corrected by a phone call, the technical support specialist may need to travel to the place where the user has set up the computer. Therefore, this job may require some travel.

Many technical support specialists are trained by the companies that hire them. They must be completely familiar with whatever products the companies are marketing. The most important skill this professional must have is the ability to communicate with other people. Users may not know why they are having a problem. The technical support specialist must be able to help the user understand how and why a problem is occurring and how to correct and prevent this problem. Technical support specialists are the link between the people who develop computers and software and the people who use them.

Weather Forecasters
Meteorologists, often called weather forecasters, depend upon computers a great deal in their profession. Without computers to process information quickly and accurately, weather forecasting would be much less reliable. Computers control the weather satellites that constantly send data back to earth. Weather forecasters depend upon computers to receive and process regularly the thousands of pieces of data sent from satellites, weather stations, and airports. The computer is able to sort through the data quickly and find areas where there is a change in weather. It also can give the meteorologist an overall view of the weather in the local area, state, country, or world.

Computers help meteorologists give information about the weather to the public. Most television weather forecasters now use satellite weather maps that are controlled and enhanced by computers to show changing weather patterns. Many use computer-generated graphics to show what the weather will be like today, tomorrow, or next week.

Weather forecasting (meteorology) is a science that depends upon information for accuracy. The more information available, the better the chance of producing an accurate forecast. Computers make the processing of large amounts of information possible. The weather forecaster of today and tomorrow has to know both the science of meteorology and how to use computers to effectively process information.

Computers are used in engineering and architectural design. They can produce graphics to show what a product or design will look like. They can also do the necessary mathematical calculations to see if the product will work. The designer or architect can see the effects of a slight change in the design by changing it in the computer. The computer can then analyze the effect of the change. It can tell whether the design works better one way than another.

The government uses computers in many different ways. Computers are used for tax records, elections, and licensing. The government also collects information on all the people in the country. You will remember that the first punched-card data-entry system was used for the 1890 census. Since that time, census-taking has become dependent upon the use of computers.

Other Effects of Using Computers at Work

Using computers at work may also make other changes in our society. Here are some of the possibilities. People will no longer have to be close to factories or plants to do their work. More and more people may move to the country. This will be just the opposite of what happened during the industrial period.

As people move from large cities to smaller towns, two things may happen. First, the problem of overcrowding will be lessened. This means that we will probably have fewer problems with pollution than we have today. Also, some of our energy problems will be relieved if people do not have to commute from their homes to their offices each day.

Second, the nature of government may change to some extent. In a society in which most people live in large cities, government becomes centralized. In the United States, for example, the federal government is the central agency of the government. But as people move to small towns, the population will be more evenly distributed across the country. Local governments will become more important. Small communities may be more involved in the control of their own government.

There will be many changes, both in the lives of individuals and in our society, in the Age of Information. We cannot tell yet what all of the changes may be. One thing that seems to be certain, however, is that computers will play a large part in these changes.

In the future, many people may work in their homes and send their work to their office by using a modem.

It would be difficult indeed to manage the information about aerial surveillance of highway traffic without computers!

CHECK WHAT YOU HAVE LEARNED

1. How are computers used by engineers?
2. Briefly explain why a computer data base is more useful than a paper filing system.
3. Name three ways that a computer might be used in a typical business office.
4. What type of program helps the user to edit and prepare final documents?
5. During the Age of Information, many people may move out of the city. Name two advantages of this change.

Daily Life is Changing with Computer Skills

The Age of Information promises to be very different from the industrial period. Computers will change our daily lives almost as much as they change our workplace. They will affect the ways that we deal with our families, our homes, our friends, and our co-workers. Computer skills will be important for everyone to have.

Even though these ranchers do agricultural jobs, it is evident that they live in the Age of Information.

More and more people will eventually work at home, in *electronic cottages*.

The Electronic Cottage

In the future, many people may work at home. They will do their work on their computer and will send the work to their office by using a modem. When people work with their computers at home, they will be said to work in **electronic cottages**. This will make work easier in many ways. For one thing, people will be able to set their own work hours. They will not have to be at work at nine in the morning or leave at five in the afternoon. This will allow them to work when they are most productive. More importantly, they will not have to live close to work. This will change not only their work habits, but many other things as well. In the industrial period, people moved to the city to be closer to the factories and plants where they worked. In the Age of Information, we may see more people moving to the country to enjoy their leisure time.

Another important advantage of electronic cottages is that they allow parents to spend time at home with their children. When both parents work in an office, they must arrange some sort of day care for their children. They often have little time to spend with them after driving to the city and working long hours.

Since parents in an electronic cottage will work at home, they will be near their children, and family relationships may be much closer. In fact, children may learn a great deal by watching their parents work at home. They may even get some hands-on experience by helping their parents with their work.

Electronic Mail and Money Transfer

Before beginning their work, people may want to find out if they have any messages or mail. They will do this, too, through their computer. Mail will be sent electronically. After the user enters an identification password into the computer, he or she can view a list of the mail that has been sent. For example, the user may be told that there are three bills, two letters, and an advertisement waiting. The user can then decide to read one or all of the messages. A response can be sent just as easily. With **electronic mail**, messages can be sent almost instantly from one place to another.

The advertisement will be somewhat different from the ones we receive in the mail today. It will be made to view on the computer and will include computer graphics. At the end of the advertisement, it may ask the user if he or she has decided to try the product. If the answer is yes, the product can be ordered automatically. The user may decide to pay for it right away. Bills will be paid from home. The user will simply use the computer to transfer money from his or her own banking account to the account of the person being paid.

In the same way, the computer may be used to order products directly from the store. It may be possible to enter the name of the product into the computer. The computer can list stores that carry that product and prices at each store. The user may want to check the quality of the product brands by referring to recommendations (listed by the computer) of a consumer group. After deciding which brand to buy and choosing a store, the user can order and pay for the item directly through the computer.

Computers for Household Management, Learning, and Health

Because every household will have a computer, daily life may be very different. The computer may be used to prepare shopping lists, keep track of household items, leave messages for other family members, and many other things. It may control tem-

Managing a household has many responsibilities! Computers are beginning to help with many jobs in the home.

perature inside the house, opening and closing windows when it becomes too hot or cold. It may also be responsible for helping to plan diets, leisure time, or exercise routines.

For example, the computer may be programmed to keep track of daily nutritional requirements. At dinner time, the computer can account for the food already eaten that day. It can then tell what nutrients are missing and choose a dinner menu that includes those nutrients. It can then produce a recipe for the chosen menu and calculate the ingredients according to how many people are eating. The user simply has to follow the recipe, and the computer can be programmed to turn the appliances on and off so that the meal is perfectly timed.

The children in the family may spend much more time at home than at school. Much of their schoolwork will be done on the computer. Through computer aided instruction (CAI), the computer will help the teacher to present lessons. It will also test the students to see how much they have learned and will plan the next lessons according to their progress. The teacher will be able to

These students are learning to use computers in elementary school, because they are living in the Age of Information.

monitor their progress by viewing their lessons on her or his computer at home. Of course, the children will still attend school for some time each day. There are many things that are more fun to learn and do with a group.

Computers will also help people to stay healthier in the future. In addition to helping people to plan diet and exercise, they may also provide first-aid information. If an accident occurs at home, the computer will be able to tell someone how to handle the emergency. If a family member is sick, the computer may be able to analyze the symptoms and suggest treatment. The computer may measure blood pressure, temperature, and chemical makeup. The computer may even be able to tell what a person has had to eat by analyzing his or her body chemistry.

Computers for Better Citizens

In addition to helping people to plan, work, communicate, and learn, computers will also be used to help people vote in government elections. Instead of having to go to a central polling place, people will enter their votes into the computer. Voting will become both simple and convenient. This has many advantages for the elderly and for disabled people, who find it somewhat difficult to vote today. It will also make for a more representative society because more people will have a voice in decision making. It is important, too, that we will be able to easily express our opinions to people who represent us in government. With computerized electronic communication, we will be able to send messages to our representatives. This will allow the representatives to know what most of the voting citizens want them to do.

CHECK WHAT YOU HAVE LEARNED

1. What is an electronic cottage?
2. What are three advantages of the electronic cottage?
3. What might an advertisement be like in the future?
4. Name two ways that the computer might help to keep people healthier in the future.
5. Why might children spend less time at school in the future?

Problems in the Age of Information

There are many important questions that we must face as we enter the Age of Information. There are problems with robots replacing people in jobs. There are problems with illegal access to private information. And there are problems with other types of crimes committed with computers. We'll take a look at these problems in this section.

The Impact of Automation on Jobs

In the future, many jobs that are now done by people will be done by robots or computers. People will not be needed for the work of manufacturing some products, as they were in the industrial period. This means that many of the people who have been working in factories will have to leave or change their jobs. They may have to take jobs that they are not trained for.

This will create a problem that will have to be resolved. It will be necessary to have some people learn new skills. You have probably seen advertisements for technical and vocational schools, for example. These advertisements suggest that people get technical training so that they will have all the necessary skills for their jobs. Many people have taken this advice and are taking classes for computer-related careers.

The Future and Computers

Employment Data Bases

Many people are studying computers in order to get good jobs. But they might be surprised to find out that a computer will probably help hire them! Many companies are using computer data bases to find qualified applicants for openings.

When an applicant is looking for employment, he or she may choose to go to a computerized employment service. Here, the applicant fills out an application and information is entered into the computer data base. Companies that are interested in hiring someone may access these data bases. They may have very specific requirements. For example, one company may be looking for an applicant who lives in its city. Another company might want to look anywhere in the nation. The computer can sort the information to suit the company's needs.

After several applicants have been selected as possible choices, they may have another computer to face. Computers are being used to interview candidates as well. The applicant may come in and be asked a series of questions by the computer. Because the computer asks everyone the same questions, people may feel that they have been treated more fairly than if they were interviewed by a human being. And when they finally do reach the point of being interviewed by a human, the interviewer will be able to spend more time and attention on them.

Today, a job applicant usually has to go from office to office to submit her or his resume and make out applications. Or it may be necessary to search the want ads in the newspaper every day. In the future, however, it is possible that the hiring of new people may be done almost entirely by computer.

But there are many other people who find the field of computers new and different. They are reacting much as our great grandparents might have reacted to the "horseless carriage." These people may feel that computers are too complicated to understand and use. Or they may believe that computers make us less human. Some people think that computers are smarter than humans. Opinions about computers can change when people have the opportunity to work with them.

Some people who hold jobs in factories have special skills that are not the same as people in other kinds of jobs. Retraining to acquire new and different technical skills can be a challenge. It may be difficult because their job has not required that they be in a training setting. Imagine a factory worker who is forty years old and who has been working at the same job for twenty-two years. She graduated from high school before she began working. She is good at her job, and she has earned the respect of her coworkers. This factory worker is happy with her work, her home, and her family. It is very difficult for her to learn that her job will now be done by a robot. It may be very hard for her to go back to school after twenty-two years to learn a completely new skill. She must also consider responsibilities to her home and family while she is in school.

But our society has a responsibility to protect all its members. An effective way of helping people whose jobs are either eliminated or taken over by robots will have to be found. We are beginning to prepare for the change in labor. One way we are preparing for it is by offering courses in computers in schools to students at all levels. One definition of **computer literacy** is the ability to work with computers. Computer literacy may soon become a requirement for graduation from high school. This will ensure that young people being educated today will be able to live and work in the society of tomorrow.

CHECK WHAT YOU HAVE LEARNED

1. Why might computer literacy become a requirement for high school graduation?
2. Name two reasons why a person might not want to learn to use computers.
3. What is one problem that is caused by the change in types of jobs?
4. Why might a factory worker resist being retrained?
5. Why might someone want to get technical training?

Privacy

In the Age of Information, information has become very valuable. It is also much easier to keep information about individuals or companies. That means that it is also easier to abuse information.

The government is the single largest keeper and user of information. All sorts of government agencies keep computerized records about everyone in this country. For example, the Internal Revenue Service keeps records about our income and the amount of tax that we pay. The Department of Motor Vehicles keeps track of our cars, our driver's licenses, and our driving records. The Bureau of Vital Statistics records our births and our deaths.

Some people are worried that this information may be improperly used. Paper files can be kept locked up, but records stored on computers can be accessed by different computer terminals. We have read about computer "whiz kids" breaking into top-secret government records by figuring out an access code. There can be a great deal of harm done if the wrong person gains access to government information.

It is difficult to protect the privacy of individuals by making sure that unauthorized people cannot gain information about them. Part of the difficulty arises from the great volume of information that is kept. The government is not the only organization that keeps records about us. Until the mid-1970s, people could not even legally find out how much and what kind of information was being kept about them. The passing of the Privacy Act in 1974 brought the issue of protecting information to the public's attention. Security measures are being developed to protect the information being kept by the government and other organizations. However, there are no simple ways of protecting data.

What happens when the wrong person gets access to private information? Let's consider one type of information that people want to keep private: credit reports. Credit bureaus keep detailed records of people's bills and payment records. These records are used whenever people apply for loans to buy houses, cars, or other expensive items. If the credit report shows that a person has a good record of paying bills on time, then that person will have a better chance of getting a loan. If the credit report shows financial problems, then the loan may be denied. Most people think credit reports are very private. People must give written permission before anyone can obtain their credit report.

A person's good credit reputation could be hurt if someone who should not have access to a credit report got a copy of the report. At the very least, the person's privacy would have been invaded. At worst, the person could be denied credit that he or she was entitled to receive.

This becomes more of a problem when we multiply this situation by the number of data bases that contain information about many aspects of our lives. Some of this information is very private. For example, health records contain private information. So do reports of psychologists, schools, law enforcement agencies, and many other organizations. Careers, families, and lives can be damaged when this information falls into the hands of the wrong people.

Some disks are notched in such a way that information can be added to the disk. By covering over that notch, new information cannot be added. The disk can still be copied, however.

We as a society must give attention to the issue of protecting the privacy of individuals. We can do this by making sure that information stored in computers is secure. Paper files are easy to guard from theft. But electronically stored data is another matter. It can be accessed by many different methods.

Computer Crime

Theft of information is only one form of computer crime. There are literally millions of computers in our society. Any one of them can be used by someone who is dishonest and unethical.

There are many different types of computer crime. Some computer criminals do not commit crimes for the personal gain of money or information. Some people simply like the challenge of breaking into a security system. Some people have been known to break into a computer just because someone else dared them to do it or said that it couldn't be done. Unfortunately, they usually find out too late that it was a dangerous challenge to accept. When they find themselves facing criminal charges, they may wish that they had stuck to computer games for thrills.

The challenge facing us is to study the area of computer crime and to help control it. Experts say that computer crime now costs as much as $3 billion each year. As computers are more widely used and more valuable information is stored on them, the payoff of computer crime could increase. Also, greater numbers of people are being trained to program and work with computers. This means that more people will have the knowledge necessary to illegally access information stored in computers. In the next chapter, we will look at computer crime and prevention.

CHECK WHAT YOU HAVE LEARNED

1. What organization is the largest keeper and user of information about people?
2. Give some examples of information that is kept about most people in your country.
3. Why do some people consider committing computer crimes?
4. Name two bad things that can happen if the wrong person gains access to credit information.
5. Why is it difficult to protect the privacy of individuals when dealing with information stored in a computer?

WHAT YOU HAVE LEARNED IN CHAPTER EIGHT

We are living in an exciting age. Computers have become common in businesses, schools, government, and even private homes. And yet only a few years ago the first computers were just being developed. The rapid development of computers has marked the beginning of a new period of society. In order to understand this new period, we must first understand our society's roots.

Society really began in the agricultural period. This is when people began to grow their own food and live in one place. During the agricultural period, farmers stayed in one place long enough to form friendships. People usually lived in the same small town all their lives.

During the late 1800s, many machines were invented. These machines were able to do things that people had had to do by hand. Factories were created in which things were made in great numbers. This marked a change from the agricultural period to the industrial period. This change is known as the Industrial Revolution. Because people were needed to work in the factories, many people moved from their small towns to the city. This changed society a great deal as people met a variety of other people from different racial, national, religious, and political backgrounds. The industrial period lasted more than one hundred years.

We are now at the beginning of the Age of Information. In this new period, people will live, work, play, and interact in new and different ways. The factories are beginning to change, as robots take the place of some human workers. A robot is a programmable computer with moving parts. It can work with other objects. Robots do not necessarily look like humans. A robot can look like one huge arm or a rolling bookshelf. Robots are used in factories to do many things. For example, they are used to paint cars, weld ships, and make memory boards for other computers.

Even today, many jobs require the use of computers. Computers are important tools in business. They are used to keep records, pay bills, keep inventory, calculate job costs, and prepare final documents. They are used in engineering and architectural design. They are used by the government in a number of ways.

Daily life in the Age of Information promises to be very different from life during the industrial period. In the future, many people may work at home. They will do their work on a computer and send the work to their office by using a modem. This will allow them to live farther away from their office. It will be helpful to families because the parents will be able to be near their children during the day. When people work with their computers at home, they will be said to work in electronic cottages. They will also receive their mail through the computer. In fact, the computer will probably play a large part in many aspects of their daily lives.

But the Age of Information may also present some problems. As fewer and fewer people are needed in the factories, some workers' jobs are being replaced. They may leave or change jobs they have been doing for years to take jobs they are not trained to do. It will be necessary to retrain these people quickly. Another problem is that because information will become more and more valuable, there may be misuse of that information. As more and more people learn to use computers, prevention of computer misuse will be very important.

1. How long did the industrial period last?
2. What is a robot?
3. Name two ways that robots are being used in factories.
4. What major problem is caused by robots being used in factories?
5. What is an electronic cottage?
6. During what period did society really begin?
7. Name five ways that computers are used today.
8. Name two advantages of the electronic cottage.
9. Name two ways that the industrial period changed society.
10. How will people receive their mail in the future?

USING WORDS YOU HAVE LEARNED

1. When people work at home on their computers, they will be said to be working in an _____ _____ .
2. The Industrial _____ marks the change from the agricultural period to the industrial period.
3. In the future, people will probably get their messages through _____ mail.
4. The _____ period marks the beginning of what we call society.
5. A _____ is a computer with moving parts.
6. People will make their livings by handling information in the period called the _____ _____ _____ .
7. _____ _____ programs help prepare final documents or letters.
8. A _____ _____ specialist helps people who have questions about their computer hardware or software.
9. A _____ specialist teaches new users to use their computers.
10. A person who installs and maintains computer hardware and equipment is a _____ _____ .

EXERCISING YOUR WRITING SKILLS

A robot is a machine with a computer to control it. A robot might contain wires, gears, motors, arms, wheels, and mechanical grippers. Robots do many jobs that are dangerous or boring for humans to do.

Robots, however, are programmed by people. Pretend you are a robot, and follow this program to write a letter of the alphabet:

    Put your pencil point on the paper.
    Move left two inches.
    Move down four inches.
    Move right two inches.
    Move up two inches.
    Move left one inch.
    Remove your pencil point from the paper.

Write the following robot programs for a classmate to follow:

1. A program that will draw a number or a different letter of the alphabet.
2. A program that will take a piece of paper out of a notebook and put it in the wastebasket.
3. A program to get a pencil, go to the sharpener, and sharpen it.

UNDERSTANDING WHAT YOU HAVE LEARNED

MULTIPLE CHOICE

1. During the Industrial Revolution, many people moved to:
   a) small towns
   b) cities
   c) bigger houses
   d) agrarian culture
2. When people with different backgrounds met each other, this was called the:
   a) melting pot
   b) "new fangled" machines
   c) agricultural period
   d) Age of Information
3. The Age of Information:
   a) began in the late 1800s
   b) has not yet begun
   c) began in 1750
   d) is just beginning
4. During the agricultural period, most people lived in:
   a) mud huts
   b) glass houses
   c) small communities
   d) big cities
5. In business, computers can:
   a) keep inventory
   b) organize files
   c) help write reports
   d) all of the above
6. People who work in factories:
   a) will never lose their jobs
   b) may have to be retrained
   c) will starve
   d) may become robots
7. Computer literacy:
   a) is taught in many schools
   b) is learning how computers will replace robots
   c) will not help us prepare for the change in jobs
   d) was necessary fifty years ago
8. During the Age of Information, people will probably:
   a) move to the cities
   b) move away from the cities
   c) move to outer space
   d) none of the above
9. In the future, people may receive their mail:
   a) twice a week
   b) three times a week
   c) agriculturally
   d) electronically
10. Computer crimes may:
    a) become less common
    b) become less serious
    c) become important to prevent
    d) become impossible

COMPUTERS IN OUR SOCIETY

TRUE OR FALSE

1. There are many different types of computer crime.
2. During the agricultural period, many people moved to the city.
3. A robot always looks like a human.
4. During the industrial period, many people had jobs in factories.
5. A robot can do anything a human can do.
6. A human can do anything a robot can do.
7. Information has become very valuable.
8. The "Third Wave" refers to the Age of Information.
9. There are many absolutely safe ways of protecting computer data.
10. In the future, you will probably be able to order and pay for products from your home.

SHORT ANSWER

1. Name three ways that electronic cottages will change the way people live.
2. Name three ways that computers are used in business.
3. How long did the industrial period last?
4. Name two reasons why someone might be afraid of computers.
5. Name two ways that government might change in the Age of Information.
6. Who is the single largest keeper and user of information?
7. During what period did the "melting pot" occur?
8. Name two advantages of electronic mail.
9. Name two ways that computers may help people to be healthier in the future.
10. Name three reasons why a company might use robots rather than humans in its factories.

COMPUTERS IN THE FUTURE

So far, no one has been able to accurately predict what the future will be like. We can dream about it, make educated guesses about it, and try to plan for what might happen. We do know that computers will certainly be a part of tomorrow's world. The more we know about the computer and how it can be used to help us in improving the human experience, the better prepared we are to enter the future and make worthwhile contributions to it.

Advanced technology in transportation is responsible for some futuristic designs in moving vehicles. A prototype of a *maglev* rail system (**1**) (a train that glides above a guideway and is propelled by magnetic forces) may be able to operate at speeds approaching 400 miles per hour. Computers play an important part in all engineering and design phases of planning such a vehicle.

Tiny force sensors in the chip within a computer-operated robotic arm makes the gripper portion so touch-sensitive that it can pick up fragile items like this light bulb (**2**). Including sensory devices in integrated circuits (called *micromachining*) will bring about many new ideas for electronic control systems.

How can a computer "see?" Computer vision studied at Massachusetts Institute of Technology has produced this representation of a runner and separated the image into areas of contrast (**3**). The human eye and the concept of sighted vision is enormously complex—and the future holds much promise for progress in understanding sight.

COMPUTERS IN THE FUTURE

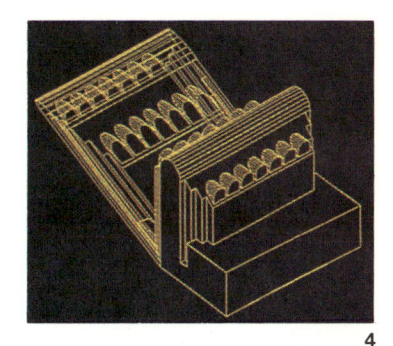

When anything new is added to the environment, certain changes must occur. A newly-constructed building, for example, will effect major changes on its surroundings—amounts of sunlight and shadow will change, wind patterns may vary, surrounding temperatures may drop, and views may be restricted. In order to solve these problems *before* construction begins, designers, city planners, and citizens can study computer-generated drawings (**4**). Future problems can be avoided, and future acceptable decisions can be made.

"My pet helped me with my homework last night." Will this ever be possible? Seriously, many experiments are conducted to learn how animals think and learn. Chimpanzees (**5**), dolphins, and gorillas, to name a few, have aided research that may change the way humans learn in the future. The field of artificial intelligence is growing, too — someday perhaps *machines* can think and learn.

Medical research of all types is growing. Tomorrow's accomplishments will be aided by special computer techniques. Three-dimensional graphics, for example, can visualize the human brain from any angle; drawings of computer-scanned sections are visually reconstructed, overlapped, and rearranged. (**6**).

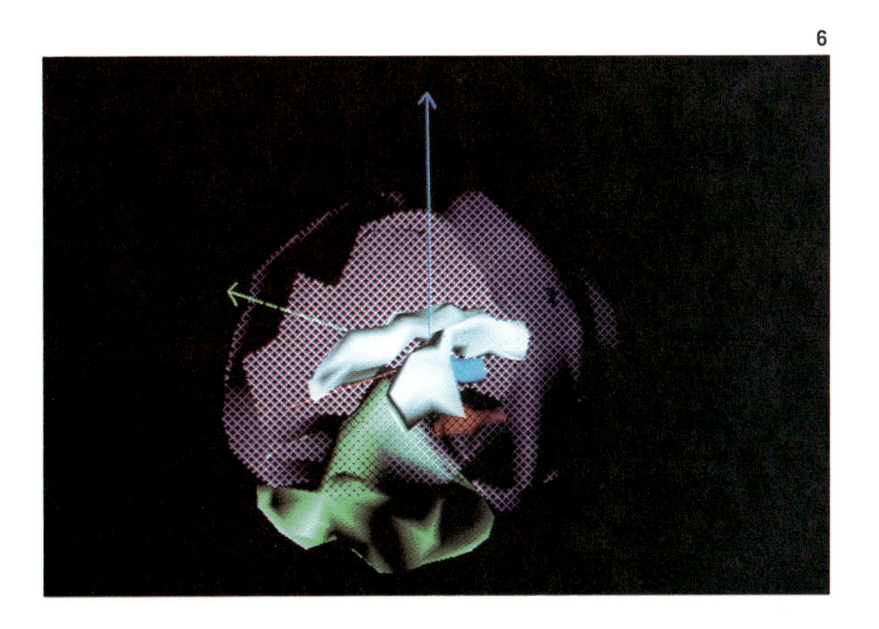

This aerial view of a solar station in a desert region of California shows the station buildings and equipment (in the center) surrounded by hundreds of reflective panels called *heliostats* (**7**). Each panel is part of a computerized system that is graphically displayed in color on a computer inside one of the buildings (**8**). Research and development of solar energy is an area of scientific study that is advancing with computer use.

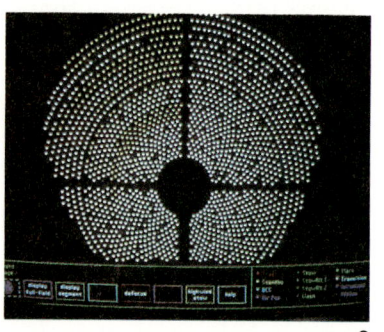

The human body is an amazing machine. For centuries, athletes have trained their bodies to overcome stresses and perform to the best of their abilities. But they may be able to do even more in the future. Performance analysis is now computerized (**9**), and biomechanics uses every

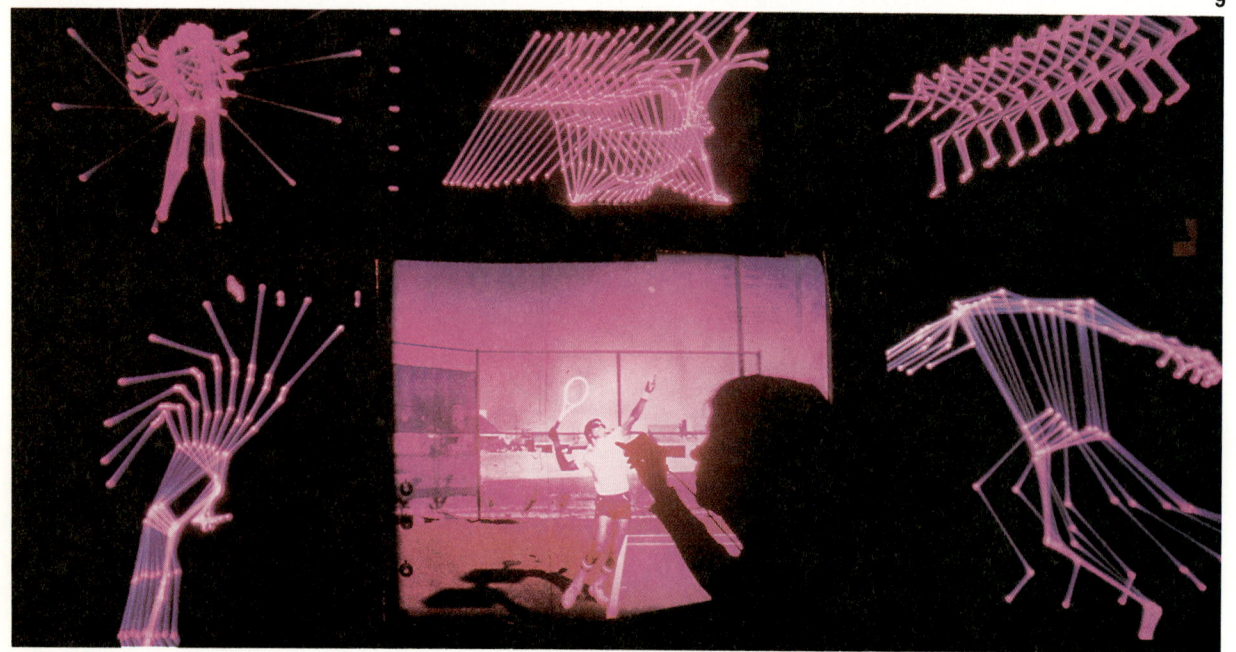

COMPUTERS IN THE FUTURE

aspect of computing to gain the greatest efficiency of movement in different sports.

Industrial robots and automation will play an important role in the world of the future. Even now factories and plants are converting to this type of mechanical labor (**10**). Some people are concerned about computerized machines taking the place of human workers. Others feel that the quality of life will be better because computers will help people and give them more time.

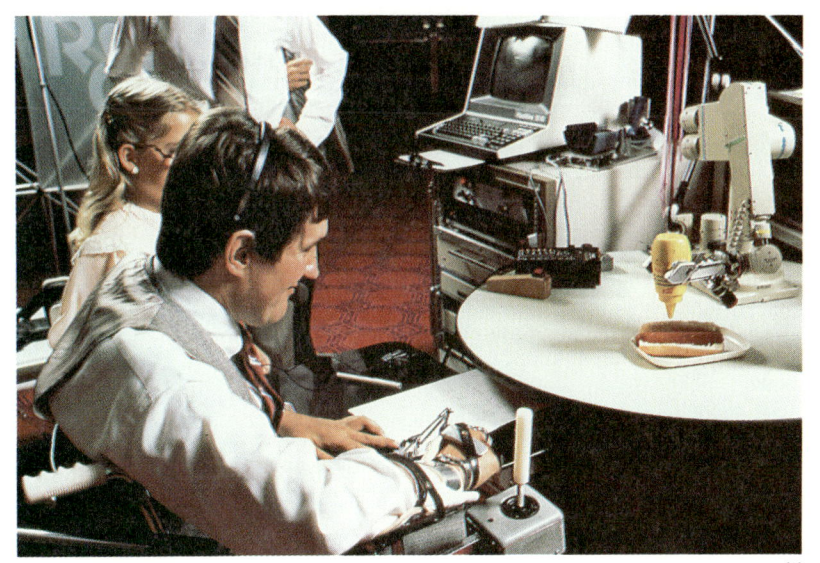

Routine things that happen every day can sometimes be major accomplishments when a person is disabled (**11**). Computers have greatly assisted in making the quality of life better—through such things as robotics, voice recognition, enhanced visual systems, and transportation aids.

Here is Omnibot, a personal robot (**12**). This computerized machine (or android—because it looks something like a human) can be pre-programmed. It "remembers" seven different programs, delivers objects (like snacks and beverages), and speaks. Omnibot even has a little alarm clock inside that can wake you up in the morning.

WHAT YOU WILL LEARN IN CHAPTER NINE

By the end of this chapter, you will be able to:

1. Explain the three major types of computer misuse today.
2. Identify several types of computer fraud, and be able to give examples of each type.
3. Name several security measures used to combat computer misuse.
4. Describe the difficulties involved with catching computer criminals.
5. Tell when invasion of privacy occurs and why it is an important problem.

Computer Ethics

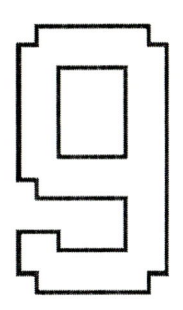

9

WORDS YOU WILL LEARN

backup copy
bootlegging
computer abuse
computer fraud
computer piracy
copyright
demagnetization
encryption device
ethics
password
private labeling
security measures
user's group

Computers are changing the way we live in so many ways and so quickly that it is sometimes hard for us to realize the full impact of computers on society. We have already looked at some of the ways that computers help us. They allow us to do our work much faster than we could without machines. They do not make as many mistakes as human workers do. They do work that is boring or dangerous for people to do. And they give us important information that we need to make decisions.

In fact, most of the changes that computers have brought about are helpful to us. Computers make our lives easier in many ways. But there is also a negative side to computers. As computers become more popular and more people learn to program and operate them, several new social problems are developing. It is a sad truth that some people use computers for improper purposes. Some use them to gain money illegally, to invade other people's privacy, or to vent their own frustrations. In this chapter, we will look at some of the ways that people use computers improperly or illegally. We will also see what is being done to prevent this from happening and explore how society might deal with these problems in the future.

Growth in world-wide sales of microcomputers by U.S. companies—figures for 1985 and future years are estimated amounts. Source: PREDICASTS, Inc.
PTS US FORECASTS

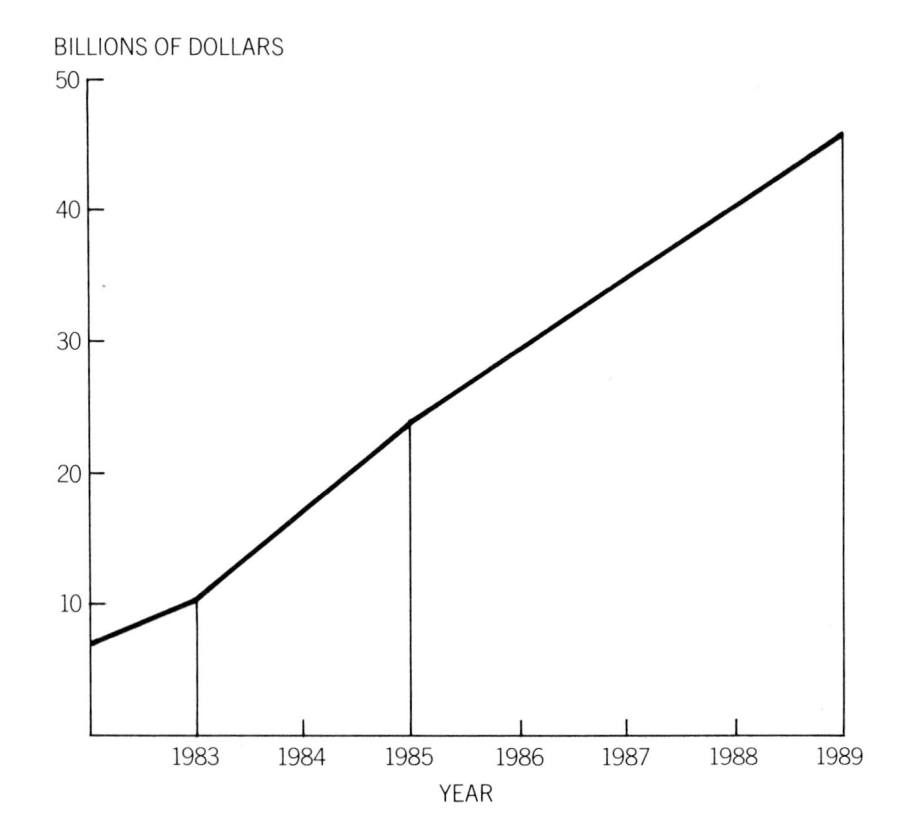

What Are Ethics?

This chapter is not really about crime. It is about the issue of computer **ethics**. The term *ethics* is defined in the dictionary as "a set of principles or values." Values and principles are beliefs we hold about what is right or wrong. When we behave ethically, we behave in a way that shows these values and principles.

Almost every day you are faced with ethical choices. In other words, you find yourself in a situation in which you must make a decision about how to act. For example, imagine that you are preparing to take a final exam in a math class. You have spent two weeks studying for the test and you feel sure that you will do well. Your best friend approaches you before the exam and asks if you will allow him or her to copy the answers from your test paper. Will you go along with this?

Many things will influence your decision. On the one hand, you have spent a lot of time and effort studying for this test. You may feel that someone who has not studied does not deserve to get a high grade by copying. On the other hand, this person is your best friend and you do not want to lose the friendship. And you have often been told by your teachers that cheating is dishonest. How will you answer your friend?

The choice that you make in this situation, and in many similar situations that you find yourself in, will depend on your values or ethics. If you believe in fairness and honesty, then you probably will not allow your friend to copy your answers.

People have to make ethical choices very often. The previous example is a decision that affects your friendship. But there are other types of ethical choices as well. For example, if you work in a store, you may have to decide whether or not to take home something that you want without paying for it. Or you may choose whether or not you will participate in an activity that may be dangerous or illegal.

Every profession has a code of ethics. This is a set of principles that determines how a person should behave. Lawyers must do everything they can to defend their clients in court. If they take bribes to do something that may hurt their clients' cases, they are being unethical. In the same way, doctors and nurses agree to do everything they can to save the lives of other people. If they hurt another person or if they do not help someone who needs medical attention, they are being unethical. Journalists must tell the truth to the best of their knowledge. If they write articles that they know are not accurate or true, then they are being unethical. Every career field has certain actions that are considered unethical.

Ethics in the Computer Field

People who work in the field of computers must also behave ethically. This is especially important for those who work with money or with private information. But the problem is that the field of computers is so new that there has not been time to develop a code of ethics. Lawyers, for example, have developed their ethics over hundreds of years. But until recently, very few people worked with computers.

The computer has no conscience of its own. The very thing that makes it so helpful to people also makes it an easy tool for criminals: the computer does whatever it is asked to do. It follows the instructions given it to the letter. It does not know, or care, whether it is stealing a million dollars or helping to find a cure for cancer. It is up to the people who use computers to make sure that computers are used for good purposes, not bad ones.

One of the reasons that computer crime is a problem today is that there are very few laws to prevent crimes like this. Our laws deal with crimes such as robbery, burglary, kidnapping, and blackmail. But computer crime is a new kind of crime. As it becomes more common, people are beginning to see the need for new laws against improper use of computers.

What exactly is improper use of computers? There are several ways that people use computers dishonestly for their own gain or to harm other people. These include computer fraud, piracy, computer abuse, and invasion of other people's privacy. Let us look at each of these problems in detail.

You realize, of course, that the position of company gremlin will be a thankless one. You'll be blamed for both hardware *and* software problems.

CHECK WHAT YOU HAVE LEARNED

1. What are ethics?
2. Name something that would be unethical for a journalist to do.
3. Why doesn't the computer field have a code of ethics?
4. In the test example, what decision would you make? Why?
5. Why has the computer been a possible tool for criminals?

Careers and Computers

Marketing Personnel

When a computer product is ready to be sold, it must be marketed. This means in part that the product, whether it is software or hardware, must be advertised. People who are interested in buying it must first hear about it. How well a product sells often depends on how well it is marketed. A very good product may not sell if it is not advertised correctly.

Marketing personnel are responsible for finding out who is probably going to be interested in their product. Then they must advertise the product in ways that appeal to those people. Marketing personnel also design advertising campaigns for magazines, television, radio, and other advertising media.

Marketing personnel may have college degrees in the field of marketing or another business-related field. It is helpful if they have some sales experience as well. In addition, they need to be able to speak and write clearly. Marketing personnel contribute their services to help sales that keep computer hardware and software companies in business.

Sales Representatives

Computer sales representatives often work closely with marketing personnel. Their job is to help customers buy computer hardware and software. Some sales representatives sell products directly to customers. This is called retailing. Other sales representatives sell products to hardware and software stores who will sell the products to their customers. This is called wholesaling.

In order to be successful, a salesperson must be able to communicate well with other people. It is important to be able to explain clearly to a customer why a certain product is better than another product. The computer hardware or software salesperson must also understand how computers work, and how the hardware and software work together. He or she must be able to explain technical details about a product to the customer.

The market for computers and software has grown very rapidly in the last several years. Qualified and knowledgeable sales representatives are likely to be in great demand for some time to come. Two advantages of this field are the chance to travel and the many opportunities for career growth.

Computer Lawyers

Within the field of law, there are many specializations. A lawyer can be a specialist in tax law, criminal law, corporate law, or domestic law, for example. A new specialization is developing: computer law. Lawyers who specialize in the area of computer law will help to protect businesses and individuals from people who misuse computers. They will also help to form a code of ethics for computer usage. They will help decide who should have access to information in our society. Lawyers must participate in the making of policies and laws. They must also uphold these laws. The area of computer crime offers a new challenge to lawyers. It is likely that many young attorneys will begin to choose computer law as a specialization.

Computer Fraud

Computer fraud is stealing by using a computer. It can involve stealing money, valuable goods, or time. Computer fraud is a growing problem in our society. This is not surprising since there are so many millions of computers used in businesses and homes across the country. As greater numbers of people learn to operate and program computers, computer fraud may increase.

What kinds of people commit computer fraud? The computer criminal usually has to know something about computers in order to use them to commit a crime. But computer criminals are not necessarily computer experts. In fact, some computer criminals don't know very much about the machines they use to commit their crimes. Other computer criminals are talented computer programmers. They know how to write clever programs that help them to steal money, goods, or computer time.

There is a problem with finding the people who commit computer crimes. Often, the criminal can hide his or her identity while the computer carries on its criminal activity. The computer criminal does not wear a mask and carry a gun like the robbers we see in movies. Instead, the computer criminal may wear a three-piece business suit. Or he or she may be a teenager in faded blue jeans.

Stealing Money or Valuable Goods

For example, two high school juniors were accused of shutting down a computer at a university by remote control. The computer was shut down for two days before the students sent a blackmail message to the university. The message said that the computer would be shut down again unless they were given a copy of a computer program worth $500. When they were asked why they did this, the pair replied that it was a challenge. Everyone had said that it couldn't be done. They wanted to prove that it could be done. But in the process they got themselves in a great deal of trouble. The students faced trial on charges of theft of services.

In another example, ten young people between the ages of fifteen and twenty-two used home computers to gain entry to computer banks at a government nuclear research laboratory. Employees of the laboratory detected the break-in. According to the authorities, no secret information was obtained by the ten young people. The idea for this incident may have come from a movie in which a young computer wizard manages to tap into the military's weapons control computer. The ten young people involved said that most of the ideas they used to break into the nuclear laboratory's computer system were their own. They said the break-in was easy to do. In fact, they admitted having gained illegal access to a number of other computer systems. This incident was investigated by the Federal Bureau of Investigation (FBI).

Some cases of computer fraud involve dishonest employees who use their employers' computers to commit crimes. One such case involved a bank teller who knew only how to operate a terminal. This teller used the computer to change records of accounts that had large amounts of money. He changed the total of the accounts to be less than the accounts actually contained. Then he took the amount he had subtracted from the accounts. For a long time, he kept other people from suspecting that he was stealing money. However, after three years his crime was found out. He had stolen $1.5 million!

Some computer crimes do not rely on the actual use of a computer. For example, one woman "tricked" the computer into thinking that she had paid off a large loan. When people get loans from banks, they are given coupon books to use when making monthly payments. With each payment, the person borrowing money returns one coupon. The coupons are coded so that the computer knows how to credit the payment to the proper account. The woman tricked the computer by sending in the wrong coupon with her first payment. This coupon was coded to tell the computer that the loan had been paid off. The mistake was not found for some time. When the bank found out about the error, it insisted that the customer pay the rest of the money that she owed.

Another case of computer fraud in a bank happened when a man used fake checking account deposit slips to cause other people's money to be added to his own checking account. Eventually,

Some computer criminals have altered computer-coded deposit slips in order to steal money.

customers began to complain to the bank that their deposits had not been credited properly. By the time the theft was discovered, the man had stolen $250 thousand.

Besides stealing money, some computer criminals steal other items of value. One young man decided to try this after he found old computer manuals and telephone equipment that the telephone company had discarded as garbage. Each day on his way home from school, he rummaged through the telephone company's garbage. Finally, he had the information he needed to order parts and equipment directly from manufacturers through a modem connected to his own computer terminal—and he identified himself illegally as a telephone company employee. He then re-sold the equipment he ordered and made quite a profit. His activity stopped when he was caught and arrested for stealing and reselling valuable equipment.

Computer fraud is not limited to banks and business. It happens wherever computers are used to do work that is important to more than one person. For example, a government employee working for the Department of Motor Vehicles made a great deal

Unauthorized use of discarded equipment can lead to computer fraud.

The Future and Computers

Biochips

As computer chips have gotten tinier and tinier, some researchers have become interested in building "biochip" computers. These computers would use organic molecules rather than silicon transistors. For this to work, scientists would have to develop a method of adapting proteins (by a process called genetic engineering) so that the proteins (instead of silicon chips) could actually do the computing.

Biochips would have two major advantages over silicon chips. The computing elements could be much closer together, and there would be new ways to process data. There are still many problems with the design of these "living" chips, and no one is quite sure if they will ever be possible. But the idea is serious enough that leading scientists and engineers have already held an in-depth conference to discuss the possibilities and advantages. What sounds like science fiction today may be growing on our computer desks tomorrow!

of money illegally. By altering a computerized list of people applying for driver's licenses, she was able to sell fake licenses to people who could not get driver's licenses legally. In a short period of time, she made more than $300 thousand. At the same time, she was responsible for more than 1000 unqualified people getting driver's licenses.

Police workers have been known to sell computerized lists of criminal records to employers who want to make sure that the people they are hiring do not have criminal records. This is private information and should not be sold. Health records have been sold to insurance companies for similar purposes. Since so much valuable information is stored on computers, people who have access to it can sell this information to other people who have some use for the data. Not only is this type of activity illegal, but it is also unethical. It is a serious invasion of the privacy of those people the information is about. We will discuss invasion of privacy in more detail later in this chapter.

CHECK WHAT YOU HAVE LEARNED

1. What is computer fraud?
2. Name two ways that an unethical person can try to make money selling information.
3. Give two examples of computer crimes that do not rely on the actual use of a computer.
4. Why is illegally selling information also unethical?
5. Explain how a coupon book helps banks keep track of payments.

Stealing Time

We have seen that computer criminals steal and sell valuable goods, information, and money. But another thing that computer criminals take advantage of is computer time. Using a modem and an unauthorized code word or number, the computer criminal can tap into a computer that belongs to another person or organization. He or she can use that computer for dishonest or unauthorized purposes. Computer criminals often tap into expensive and powerful mainframe computers. The cost of operating the computer is paid by the person who owns it. The computer criminal is, in effect, stealing from the owner of the computer.

One area where theft of computer time is a growing problem

is on college campuses. As they learn to operate and program computers, some students begin to use their knowledge in dishonest or unethical ways. For example, they may tap into student records to change grades, destroy other students' files, or send messages that may be offensive. Students might feel that breaking into the university's computer is an exciting challenge or prank. They don't realize that they could get into very serious trouble.

Many schools and colleges are seeing the need for rules and policies that prevent and punish computer misuse. In the past, colleges have not felt such a need because computers were not as available to students as they are today. But this is changing. Many colleges are seeing that it is time to include policies against tampering with university computer equipment. For example, one university will not allow students to use their computers to:

1. Copy another student's assignment for a computer programming class.
2. Look at another student's files.
3. Use computer accounts for unauthorized purposes.
4. Engage in "annoying and disruptive behavior," such as sending offensive messages.

Some colleges set up juries of administrators and teachers who deal with cases of misuse. As it becomes a bigger headache for colleges, computer misuse will become a more serious offense. Students may be expelled from colleges because they have tampered with computers.

Not all young people who steal computer time are college students. Some are younger. One high school student was caught tapping into a company's computer so that he could play computer games. Other criminals are professional people who use other people's computers to do their own work. No matter who the computer criminal is or what he or she steals, the result is the same: a great deal of money is lost each year to people who use the computer unethically.

CHECK WHAT YOU HAVE LEARNED

1. What harm does it do for one person to use someone else's mainframe computer without permission?
2. Name two good rules that a college might make to limit computer misuse.
3. In the future, what might happen to students who misuse computers?

COMPUTER ETHICS

4. What device might a computer criminal use to tap into someone else's computer?
5. How old are people who steal computer time?

Computer Piracy

So far we have explored ways that people have used computer hardware to steal items of value from other people. But another serious problem in the computer field is the theft of computer software. This type of theft is known as **piracy**. Piracy is the copying of a program without paying the person or company that legally owns the program.

All of the computer software on the market must be designed, written, and published by a software publisher. Computer programs are often time-consuming to design and write. Also, they must be documented. Someone who knows how to use the program must write instructions for people who do not know how to use the program. This is often called a manual. The process of producing software and the manuals that go with it is lengthy and expensive. Many professionals must work on it. For this reason, computer software and manuals can be expensive to buy.

Some people use the high cost of software as an excuse for pirating it. They say that if the cost of software were lower they would buy their own copies rather than make illegal copies. But what they do not realize is that software publishers have to raise their prices when people pirate their product. The losses that they suffer from illegal copies force them to charge more money. Higher costs are passed along to users who buy legal copies of software. Until piracy is controlled and prevented, software publishers will be forced to charge high prices for their software. Software pirates only make this problem worse.

Software piracy is not an uncommon computer crime. Software must be recorded on something that the computer can read. It is usually recorded on a disk or tape. Users often want to make backup copies of their software. A **backup copy** is simply an extra copy to protect their investment in case their original program is lost or damaged. Some software companies allow a user to make one backup copy in case the original is damaged. Disks and tapes are fairly inexpensive, and it is quick and simple to copy software from one disk or tape to another.

Sometimes groups of people engage in software piracy. For

Youngsters at computer camps and in user's groups can learn about the ethics and legalities of computer use.

example, there are many clubs for people who use computers. These clubs are known as **user's groups**. In some user's groups, it is a common practice to share the cost of a program and then make illegal copies for all of the members. Or one member may buy a program and then offer copies of it free of charge to the other members of the user's group. For example, if ten members share the price of a program that costs $500, the cost of the program for each person is only $50. But the company that publishes the program has lost $4500. That is how much more it would have made if each of the ten people had bought a legal copy of the software. In order to make up for that loss, the publisher has to raise the price of software even more.

Another way that piracy is done is known as **private labeling**. This is when unethical retailers buy a copy of the program, copy the program illegally, then sell the copies under their own private label. In this way, they can sell the program at a lower price. Private labeling causes a loss of profit to the publisher who made the product and sells it legally. A great deal of money is lost through private labeling.

Software **bootlegging** is another name for piracy. Bootlegging occurs on such a large scale that the loss from this criminal activity is several million dollars each month. Of this amount, about one third is lost in actual theft. The remaining two thirds represent sales opportunities that are lost to the software publisher. In the end, software publishers are forced to pass these losses along to their honest, paying customers. Everyone who buys software to operate on personal, business, or educational computers suffers because of this criminal activity.

Like books and magazines, computer software is protected by **copyright** laws. Copyright laws give the people who developed the software the exclusive right to sell it and to profit from its sales. These laws also prevent people who do not own the software from taking away the rights of the legal owner. When they are caught, software pirates can be charged with breaking copyright laws, which is a serious offense. They may discover that paying for a legal copy of the software would have been much cheaper for them than paying the penalties for piracy. The penalties are becoming stiffer as piracy increases.

What else can be done about software bootlegging? It is not an easy problem to cope with because programs can be copied quickly and simply. Also, copies made privately are hard to detect. The software publisher has no way of knowing when bootleg copies of a program are being made. If the publisher does discover that bootleg copies are being made and sold illegally, the publisher can sue the person making the bootleg copies. But taking legal action is expensive and time-consuming.

Computer software and written materials that go with it are protected by copyright laws.

New Ideas and Computers

Electronic Publishing

Some newspapers are beginning to publish electronic editions. A number of daily newspapers publish an edition that is not printed on paper but instead is reached through a modem and displayed on the reader's computer. One advantage of this is that each person reading the newspaper can choose those parts of the paper he or she is interested in from a menu (or list) on the CRT screen.

Other types of companies are considering how to take advantage of electronic publishing. It is likely that people will be interested in using their computers to get information that might change or vary from day to day. An example of this might be the phone book or a book of local advertisements. In fact, a phone company has tested an electronic edition of the yellow pages! It is likely that as electronic publishing becomes less expensive we will see more and more of it.

Publishers are actively looking for ways to prevent the illegal copying and selling of computer programs. In some cases, publishers can put serial numbers on programs. Then they can instruct the computer not to make copies of a program that has a serial number. This is one method of dealing with bootlegging, but it is not foolproof. It is likely that software publishers will find new and better ways of preventing bootlegging in the future.

CHECK WHAT YOU HAVE LEARNED

1. Explain how copying a program for friends can cost money to other software buyers.
2. What is a user's group? Are they all dishonest?
3. What is private labeling?
4. Name one way that publishers are controlling software bootlegging.
5. Why is it sometimes difficult to catch a computer bootlegger?

Computer Abuse

Computer fraud and computer piracy (including software bootlegging) are two ways that people use computers to steal money, computer time, software, and other valuable goods. But there is also another type of criminal activity. This activity is known as **computer abuse**, and it happens whenever a person intentionally damages computer equipment.

For years, science fiction books, movies, and stories have talked about what will happen when computers "take over." They paint a very grim picture of what society will become. They tell us about people becoming machines who can no longer think for themselves. They say that people will become the servants of computers. Of course, we know that computers do not think for themselves—they only follow the instructions of the humans who program them. But the stories have made many people afraid of computers. People who are afraid of computers may act out their fears by damaging computers with sharp objects, fire, and other methods.

Another reason that people abuse computers physically is frustration. In many offices and businesses, people are being ex-

COMPUTER ETHICS

pected to learn to use computers. This can be a very pleasant experience if the employee is given proper training and plenty of time to learn about and use the computers. But this is not always the case. Sometimes employers expect employees to train themselves without any help from others. This can be very difficult for the person who has never used a computer and does not know where to begin. Some people take out their frustration on the computer. They may damage the computer or do something that will shut the computer down temporarily.

It can sometimes be very frustrating to work with computers. Proper training can help eliminate this frustration.

"IT SAYS, 'WE ARE EXPERIENCING TRANSMISSION DIFFICULTIES. DO NOT TRY TO ADJUST YOUR SET.'"

Even people who do not work directly with the computer can become frustrated with it. Many businesses now use computers to keep track of customer records. Customers may have trouble with having errors on bills corrected. When they report the problem, they may be told, "The computer must have done that." If they are not able to resolve the problem, their frustration may lead them to damage computer equipment.

Besides destroying the physical equipment that makes up the computer system, people may try to destroy records that are stored on a disk or tape. There can be many reasons for wishing to destroy company records. A common reason is that the person destroying the records may want to cover up information that is in the records. Or the person may want to disrupt a business's activities by destroying all the information it needs to function.

Fire can destroy records. Another way to destroy records is through **demagnetization**. Demagnetization is a way of erasing data stored on a magnetic tape or disk. This is a very serious crime because it can cause great losses in money. Demagnetization also causes great losses in time that must be spent to restore records that have been destroyed. If the records cannot be restored, then valuable information can be lost forever.

Most cases of computer abuse can be traced to feelings that some people have when they encounter computers in their offices, banks, schools, and homes. These people feel afraid, frustrated, or angry. It is always a good idea for people to take breaks from the computer when they feel tired or frustrated. Finding ways of coping with the stress that computers can cause in humans is a good way to prevent computer abuse.

CHECK WHAT YOU HAVE LEARNED

1. Explain why it is unwise to ask employees to train themselves to use computers.
2. Why are some people afraid of computers?
3. What is demagnetization?
4. Name one way to prevent computer abuse.
5. Make up two examples of people who might want to destroy records kept on computer disks or tapes.

Invasion of Privacy

The age of computers has also been called the Age of Information because information is becoming more and more valuable. In the past, the goods and services that people produced were more valuable than information, but this is changing rapidly. We are finding many uses for information that we did not have before. This is because computers have given us the ability to process and store a great deal of information. There is a high price tag associated with information, and whenever there is a lot of money to be made there is also crime and unethical behavior. One common form of crime in the Age of Information is the invasion of privacy. This is the illegal buying and selling of records about people.

Stop and think for a moment about all of the records about the average person that are stored on computers across the country. The government is a major keeper of personal records. For example, the Bureau of Vital Statistics keeps birth certificates for all babies born in the U.S. each year. Schools keep educational records from kindergarten through graduate school. The government keeps records for driver's licenses, police records, health records, income records for tax purposes, and many other records. But the government is not the only keeper of records about us. Insurance companies, hospitals, businesses with whom we have credit, clubs to which we belong, and many other groups or organizations have information about us. They are likely to store this information on computers.

Credit bureaus, for example, keep records of how much credit people have. They keep track of how much people pay to the institutions they owe money to and whether or not they make payments on time. These records are used by people who are considering giving them credit. If a person applies to a bank for a personal loan, for instance, the bank will probably ask a credit bureau if that person is a good credit risk. If the credit bureau says that the person has a history of making payments on time, then the credit will probably be approved. By the same token, if the credit bureau says that the person is a bad credit risk, then probably the loan will not be made. If the information that the credit bureau passes along is incorrect, then the person requesting a loan could be unfairly turned down.

Many schools now keep computerized records of students' grades and other information. These records are confidential and are to be seen by authorized school personnel, the student, and his or her parents only. Such records are valuable in helping school personnel make decisions about student placement in classes that meet the needs of that student.

Many people don't like the fact that some personal records about them are being kept by others without their permission. They feel that it is too easy for unauthorized people to get to this information and learn more about them than they want to have known. This is certainly possible. We mentioned earlier that records about criminal activity and health are sometimes illegally sold to other people. This could have terrible results for the person that the information is about.

Until recently, people did not have the right to look at many of the records that are kept about them. But in 1974 the government passed the Freedom of Information Act. This law makes it easier for people to get copies of records that the government and other organizations keep about them. If they find mistakes in these records, they can try to have them corrected.

Before a bank or other institution can ask a credit bureau for information about your financial history, you must give the bank written permission to get this information. This protects you from unauthorized people looking at your records. However, there are many ways for unethical people to get access to your records. They can buy them from people who keep the records. For example, an unethical employee of a credit bureau might be bribed into selling credit bureau records to someone who has no right to the information.

Why would anyone want to buy information about another person illegally? Because the information has some value. People can be blackmailed when information they do not want known falls into the hands of an unethical person. Mailing addresses can be sold to companies who want to send out advertisements. (This is usually done legally, but it can be done illegally as well.) Information can be used to hire and fire people and to determine whether people should be given credit. Some of these uses can be legal. They can only be legal, however, if the person whose records are being examined has given permission for others to obtain that information.

Who should have access to information? How much information about a person should be stored on computer? These are questions that our society needs to answer as computers become more common. It is difficult to decide who should have access to information and what kinds of information ought to be stored on computer. But if we do not try to make these decisions, we face the loss of our privacy—a dangerous consequence.

CHECK WHAT YOU HAVE LEARNED

1. What law makes it possible for you to get copies of records about you?
2. What must a bank or other institution have before it can get a copy of credit records?
3. Explain how credit records can help banks.
4. Give two examples of illegal or unethical use of information. They do not need to be examples talked about in this chapter.
5. Explain why it is important to have access to information that is kept about us.

Preventing Computer Misuse

We have looked at four specific ways in which people misuse computers for their own personal gain: computer fraud, piracy, computer abuse, and invasion of privacy. We must find effective ways of preventing this type of activity.

Businesses are becoming more aware of the need to protect their computers and the information they store. The methods that they use to try to prevent dishonest people from misusing computers are called **security measures**. Let us look at some of the common security measures that businesses use today to help prevent computer crime.

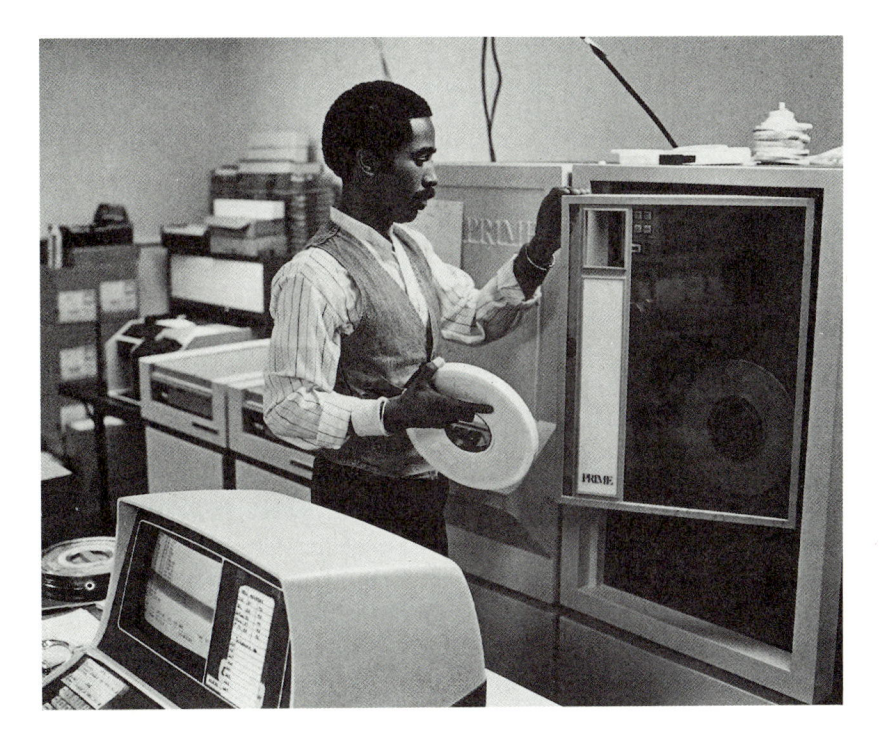

This computer operator has authorized access to the computer room.

Security Measures

Probably the most common security measure against computer misuse is to make sure that only authorized people have access to the computer room. In a small company with only a few employees this is simple. Everyone knows who should and who should not be in the computer room. But it can be more of a problem in a company that has a large number of employees. Larger companies may insist that their employees wear identification badges, often with photographs attached. This makes it easier to be sure that no one enters the computer room who is not supposed to be there. Only people who need access to the computer to do their work, such as computer operators, are permitted in the area around the computers.

The use of **passwords** is another common method of prevention. A person must know the password to get onto the computer. The password is only known by authorized users. This way, unauthorized users cannot get access to material they are not supposed to have. There are three basic types of passwords used to authorize people to use computers. They are:

1. Something the person has, such as a key or card.
2. Something a person knows, such as a code word or number.
3. Something about a person, such as a fingerprint or a voice print (the particular sound patterns of each person's speech).

Employees can be given keys or cards that allow them to enter the computer room. When the key or card is inserted into a security device, the door to the computer room opens. This is not a foolproof system, though. Objects such as cards or keys can be lost, stolen, or sold to other people.

Code words can also be used to keep unauthorized people from using the computer. Instead of words, some companies use numbers. The computer can be programmed to ask the user for a code word or number. If the user does not know the word or number, he or she cannot use the computer to do work or look at records. But code words and numbers present a similar problem to that of keys and cards. Code words and numbers can be forgotten or given to other people besides those who are supposed to use them. They must be changed on a regular basis to prevent unauthorized people from finding them out and using them. And when an employee leaves a company, his or her password should be removed from the list of authorized passwords. Otherwise, the employee could continue to use the company's computer.

Probably the safest kind of password is one that depends upon something about a person that another person cannot copy or imitate. For example, a person's fingerprint can be used to allow or deny that person access to a computer room. There are also devices that recognize voice prints. Or the computer can be programmed to ask a series of personal questions that only the authorized person knows the answer to. These might include "When is your husband's birthday?" and "What is your youngest child's name?" It is very difficult for security systems like these

Security measures sometimes include the use of special cards or codes to gain entry to the computer room.

People and Computers

Marvin Minsky

Marvin Minsky is one of the leading pioneers in the area of artificial intelligence. Born in New York City in 1927, he studied genetics, physics, and intelligence at Harvard and Princeton universities. After he became interested in how brain cells work, Minsky built one of the first learning machines in 1951. Marvin Minsky is now a professor at the Massachusetts Institute of Technology.

He helped Seymour Papert to develop educational computers, and has also done a great deal of work in artificial intelligence. He wants to create machines that have common sense and even a sense of humor. Marvin Minsky's contributions will be very important as we develop machines that have more human qualities and that can make better and more logical decisions.

---

to be tampered with by people who have no right to use the computer.

Another way to protect information is to use an **encryption device**. After data is entered into a computer, an encryption device can be used to scramble the data into a code. This code cannot be read by just anyone. Only a person who has access to the decoding program can read and use the data after it has been unscrambled. The problem with devices like this is that they

This encryption device automatically codes or decodes any data that is stored on disks or transmitted through phone lines.

complicate the process of using the computer. But this can be worthwhile if the data stored on the computer is very private or sensitive.

Businesses have a growing awareness of the problems caused by computer crime. They are taking stronger actions to prevent such crime from taking place. They are being far more careful about the people they hire to work with computers. Some companies may require that a person take lie detector tests or fill out lengthy questionnaires about personal ethics. They decide whether or not to hire that person based on her or his answers. Businesses are installing better security systems. They are also changing them frequently (for example, giving employees new passwords) to keep people from figuring out the system and breaking into the computer.

Computers can help security guards to do their job.

Laws Against Computer Crime

Businesses are also much more likely to press charges against people they find misusing computers. In the past, some businesses were hesitant to report computer crime. They did not want anyone to know that their security system had been broken into. But today businesses realize that it is important to expose things like this. It is necessary to track down the persons involved. The loss of information by theft is a serious crime. Information developed for a business belongs to that business—unauthorized use by someone else or some other business is against the law. Even though information may not be confidential, time and money is required to replace it. In the future, it will be much more difficult to get away with computer-related crime than it has been in the past.

As a society, we must find ways to deal with people who use computers in unethical ways. Computer crime costs us a great deal of money. It is even threatening our personal privacy and security. We must first develop and then live by a code of computer ethics. It is possible that computer crime will increase in the future. But methods of coping with it will increase as well. A great deal of attention will be given to inventing new security measures and passing laws against computer crime.

Unfortunately, not all laws deal specifically with computer crime. This has presented a problem in prosecuting computer criminals. Often, laws that cover more traditional forms of crime such as robbery and burglary cannot be applied to computer cases. But the growing awareness of this problem of computer crime will make lawmakers more eager to control it. Tough laws may be one way to discourage people from using the computer for dishonest purposes.

CHECK WHAT YOU HAVE LEARNED

1. Name two types of passwords.
2. What is the major problem with using a key or card as a password?
3. What problem might a prosecutor face when trying a computer criminal?
4. What is an encryption device?
5. Why were some businesses reluctant to report computer misuse until recently?

WHAT YOU HAVE LEARNED IN CHAPTER NINE

Most of the changes that computers have brought about are helpful to us. But there is also a negative side to computers. It is a sad truth that some people use computers for improper purposes. Some have used them to gain money illegally, to invade other people's privacy, or to vent their own frustrations. These practices are unethical. That is, they violate our beliefs about what is right.

We are faced constantly with ethical decisions. For example, we may be tempted to read our sister's diary or to tear up our report card so our parents won't see it. We may have to decide whether or not to tell the truth when confronted with a difficult situation. The way we respond to these challenges will depend upon our ethics. Every profession has a code of ethics. A lawyer must defend a client as well as possible, and may not tell anyone what the client has said privately. A doctor must try to save lives and must keep clients' records secret. A journalist must try to tell the truth. People who work with computers must also behave ethically. But the field of computers is so new that there is not an established code of ethics. Computer misuse is the use of a computer for unethical or illegal purposes.

One type of computer misuse is computer fraud. Computer fraud is the stealing of money, valuable goods, or computer time by using a computer. An example of this might be a bank teller who uses the computer to take money from other people's accounts and deposit it to his or her own. In this case, the computer criminal is stealing money. Computer criminals steal time when they tap into a more powerful computer without the owner's permission. The owner of the larger computer must pay to operate the computer. People who use the system without permission are stealing computer time. Rules and laws about the stealing of computer time are becoming very strict.

When a computer user copies a software program without permission, it is called computer piracy. Some people say that computer software is too expensive to buy. But they do not realize that software publishers have to raise their prices to make up for the losses they suffer from computer piracy. Sometimes computer programs are sold with private labeling. This is when a store owner buys a piece of software and then copies it illegally. The store owner can then sell many copies at a lower price. The software publisher, who has paid for the development and marketing of the software, does not get any of that money. Millions of dollars a month are lost through computer piracy. This software bootlegging affects not only the software publisher but also the honest paying customers.

Sometimes people become angry or frustrated when they are working with a computer. Or sometimes they are afraid of the "machine without a heart." People who are having trouble dealing with computers sometimes damage computer systems. Other people sometimes destroy software or computer information in order to hide something that is in the records. Physical destruction of computers or software is known as computer abuse.

Computers are often used to keep records about people. They keep records of births, hospitalizations, income taxes, bank payments, and so on. This information is important. But people do not usually want just anyone to see their records. When unauthorized people see records about other people without their permission, this is an invasion of privacy. We have a right to see information that is kept about us. We must also be asked before those records are shared with anyone else.

There are several ways to keep unauthorized users from using computers and the information they contain. One way is by using a password. A password is a method of gaining access to the computer that is only available to authorized users. A password might be a key or identification card. Or it might be a special code word or number. Finally, it could be a voice print or fingerprint of the authorized user. Another way is by using an encryption device. An encryption device changes the data in the computer to a code that can be read only by authorized users. New ways to stop computer criminals are being invented as businesses become more aware of the problems with computer crime. Laws are being made stricter to discourage people from using the computer for dishonest purposes.

1. How much money is lost because of computer piracy?
2. What does an encryption device do?
3. Name three situations in which ethics might help you make a decision.
4. Name one reason that people damage computers.
5. Why is there no established code of ethics for computer users?
6. Name two types of passwords.
7. What is an invasion of privacy?
8. What does stealing computer time mean?
9. Name three types of computer misuse.
10. Who has the right to see information that is kept about us?

USING WORDS YOU HAVE LEARNED

1. _____ is the physical damaging of computers or computer software.
2. If I make a copy of my favorite program to give to my friend, I am guilty of computer _____ .
3. One way to destroy software by erasing it is called _____ .
4. A club for people who use computers is called a _____ group.
5. When retailers make copies of a program and sell the copies under their own label, they are guilty of _____ _____ .
6. A _____ is a book of instructions that accompanies a piece of software.
7. People who use a computer to take money from bank accounts are engaging in computer _____ .
8. _____ are our beliefs about what is right or wrong.
9. A code word or number can be used as a _____ if it is only known to authorized users of the computer.
10. A device used to scramble the data on the computer into a code is called an _____ device.

EXERCISING YOUR WRITING SKILLS

John, Mark, and Jill have a computer at home. They enjoy using it for playing games, doing their homework, and experimenting with new ideas. They were working at it one day when John found a way to tap into the records of a credit bureau.

"Wow!" said John. "Do you realize what this means? I'll finally have something on Mr. Hodgkins at school. Just wait till the next time he gives me his lecture on Responsible Behavior. He's two months overdue with his bank loan!"

"You can't use that," said Mark. "In fact, you shouldn't even be looking at it. This gives me the creeps. It's like spying."

"Don't be silly," said Jill. "We're just having a little fun. And you better not tell anyone or none of us will be able to use the computer again. Mom would really be mad. Besides, we're not hurting anyone. What *we* know won't hurt them."

"It still gives me the creeps," replied Mark. "I'm getting out of here."

Mark went downstairs and began to think. If he told on the other kids, none of them would be allowed to use the computer. Besides, he didn't want to be a tattletale. But on the other hand, what the kids were doing didn't seem right.

What do you think Mark should do? Why? Is it really hurting anyone for the kids to be looking up records from the credit bureau? Who is it hurting? Do you believe it is more important for kids in a family to stick together or for people to keep their private records private? Finish this story with an ending that reflects what you believe to be right.

UNDERSTANDING WHAT YOU HAVE LEARNED

MULTIPLE CHOICE

1. Whether or not you cheat on a test will depend upon:
   a) your mother
   b) your ethics
   c) your friend
   d) the test
2. Someone who steals money by using a computer is guilty of:
   a) computer fraud
   b) computer ethics
   c) computer abuse
   d) computer time
3. Computer piracy is:
   a) very rare
   b) very difficult
   c) only possible with a mainframe
   d) not a difficult computer crime
4. People who abuse computers are usually:
   a) crazy
   b) poor
   c) frustrated
   d) young

5. Copyright laws:
   a) give buyers the right to copy materials
   b) prevent people from copying materials without permission
   c) prevent the publishers from copying the materials
   d) give bootleggers the right to copy materials
6. When a person leaves a company, that person's password
   a) should be given to a new employee
   b) should not be changed
   c) should be changed only if the person cannot be trusted
   d) should always be changed
7. Software bootlegging:
   a) does not happen very often
   b) is another name for piracy
   c) makes the price of software go down
   d) is not a serious crime
8. Demagnetization is one way of:
   a) destroying files
   b) safeguarding files
   c) catching computer criminals
   d) using a password
9. The best way to cope with the stress that computers can cause in humans is to:
   a) get frustrated
   b) get rid of the computers
   c) damage the computer
   d) try physical exercise during a break
10. Stealing computer time:
    a) is not really hurting anyone
    b) costs the computer owner money
    c) is a type of computer abuse
    d) is an example of invasion of privacy

TRUE OR FALSE

1. Everyone in a company should be able to work with the computer.
2. It is best to let employees train themselves on the computer.
3. Computer piracy is not a difficult computer crime.
4. Some computer criminals do not realize how serious their crimes are.
5. Demagnetization is a way to steal money from banks.
6. There are several different types of passwords.
7. Computer criminals are always expert computer programmers.
8. Businesses are not very aware of computer crime.
9. An encryption device is used to code data.
10. Our laws on computer crime are very complete.

SHORT ANSWER

1. Name three types of computer misuse.
2. Give an example of an unethical act.
3. What law gives us the right to see information kept about us?
4. Name two types of passwords.
5. What is a user's group? When are they unethical?
6. Give an example of invasion of privacy.
7. Why might a person use demagnetization?
8. What are two types of computer fraud? Give examples.
9. Why is it sometimes difficult to catch a computer criminal?
10. Why is it sometimes difficult to prosecute a computer criminal?

WHAT YOU WILL LEARN IN CHAPTER TEN

By the end of this chapter, you will be able to:

1. Explain new directions in computer science.
2. Define artificial intelligence.
3. Name two processes by which computers can make choices.
4. Describe some of the applications of artificial intelligence.
5. Describe probable future advances in the field of robotics.

The Future and Beyond

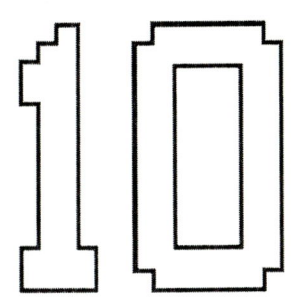

10

WORDS YOU WILL LEARN

artificial intelligence
backward chaining
expert system
fifth generation
inferring
robotics
search trees
time-sharing
vision system

The past several chapters have taken a close look at some of the ways that computers are used in our world today. We have only to look around wherever we go to see that computers have become very powerful tools in our lives. In this chapter, we will try to imagine how computers will be used in the future.

The Fifth Generation of Computers

Computer technology develops at a very fast pace. This means that the computers that we use in our jobs and in our homes will be very different ten or twenty years from now from the computers we know today. In what ways will they be different? From looking at the way computers have changed since the 1940s, we can make a few guesses about what tomorrow's computers will look like and how they will operate.

First, it is likely that the computers we will use in the years ahead will be smaller than the computers we use today. Think back for a moment to our discussion of the early computers such as Mark I. First-generation computers were extremely large. Special rooms had to be built to house them. Today we are in the fourth generation of computers. We are used to seeing computers that fit easily on a desk top or in a briefcase. We even use computers built into household appliances such as microwave ovens. It is easy to see that computers are becoming smaller and smaller.

The fact that they are becoming smaller does not mean that

First-generation computers, such as the UNIVAC, were extremely large and slow to process information. Fifth-generation computers will be very different!

computers are slower or less powerful, though. In fact, just the opposite is true. Today's smaller computers are much faster than their larger grandparents. As new types of memories are developed, more memory can be built into smaller machines. More memory means more power and speed. Remember how yesterday's automobiles seemed slow when compared with the speed and power of today's cars? We can also assume, then, that tomorrow's computers will make today's computers look slow by comparison.

Computers in the future are also likely to be "smarter" than the computers we use today. This will come about as computer scientists work to develop **artificial intelligence** (AI for short). Computer systems using AI are often called the **fifth generation** because they will be very different from fourth generation systems. Computers that possess artificial intelligence will be able to learn and remember, much as humans do. These systems will be able to make some types of decisions that previously could be made only by people. This will make them far more powerful than today's computers. Fifth generation computers will be knowledge processors, capable of learning from the information given them and using that knowledge to more effectively manipulate data. Today's computers can do little more than to follow the instructions that humans give them.

Robots will also be far more developed than those of today. Because they will have artificial intelligence, they will be able to learn and remember. This means that they will be much more effective as tools. They will be able to help in business, industry, and even around the house. As they become less expensive, they will also become more common. In the near future, robots in the home may be as common as television sets.

FRED (Friendly Robotic Educational Device) is a small robot that has a 57-word vocabulary, the ability to move in any direction, and drawing capabilities. It is controlled by a hand-held communicator, or it can be programmed by a computer.

CHECK WHAT YOU HAVE LEARNED

1. Name three ways that computers may be different in the future.
2. What will artificial intelligence enable computers to do?
3. What will make computers of the future faster and more powerful?
4. Will smaller computers of the future be able to do less than larger computers of today? Why or why not?
5. How will the fifth generation of computers differ from the fourth generation?

Artificial Intelligence

Remember from our discussion of how a computer operates that the computer is no more than a machine that follows the instructions that humans give it. It does not think, feel, react, decide, or solve complicated problems as we do. Not yet, at least. Scientists in the field of artificial intelligence are working to give computers the thinking power that humans possess.

Computers have become important links between people. Will they become even more important as they become "smarter"?

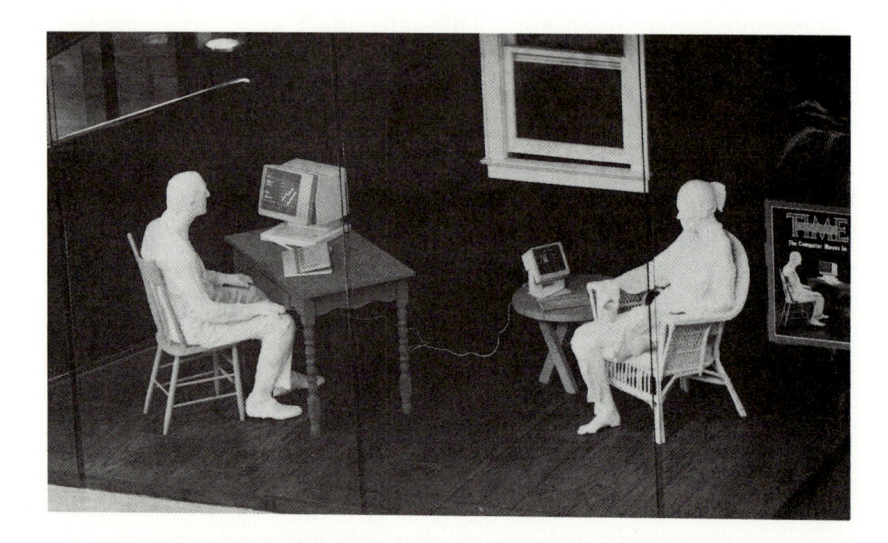

Artificial intelligence is usually defined as the ability to imitate the way humans think. Computers and robots with artificial intelligence will be able to make decisions and solve problems. As computers become better at imitating human reasoning, they will no longer be limited to simple calculation but will enter the area of intelligent behavior.

Human Thinking vs. Computer Thinking

In order to talk about AI, we have to first discuss how the human mind works. This is not easy because it is an area where even the experts disagree. No one knows for sure how the human mind arrives at conclusions as it does. But we can begin by pointing out some of the differences between the way humans think and the way computers operate.

Let's say that we are playing a guessing game. You must guess whether a piece of fruit is a grape, an orange, or a banana. You

THE FUTURE AND BEYOND

New Ideas and Computers

Intelligent Computers

The development of artificial intelligence is progressing rapidly. Many companies are involved in developing artificial intelligence programming, and they are racing to produce systems that are useful and that will pay for themselves once they are put to use. Already, expert systems have been developed for use in many areas, including medicine (to diagnose illnesses and recommend treatment), investment management, and petrochemical exploration.

For example, one of the early artificial intelligence products was the Prospector system. This system was very useful in helping geologists discover a molybdenum deposit in eastern Washington state. The expert system was able to suggest the most promising drilling sites for exploratory drilling. Exploratory drilling can be very time-consuming, expensive, and risky, so having as much information as possible from an expert system before actual drilling begins is extremely useful.

Some researchers are working on an expert system "shell." This would enable people who are not AI programmers to develop their own expert systems. This type of program, like other AI programs, includes an **inference engine**. An inference engine is a program for reasoning about the facts and knowledge in an expert system, and forming opinions or making decisions based on these facts or knowledge.

AI researchers are also developing more ways to allow computers to "sense" the world around them. This ability is useful, for example, in the planning of an orbiting space station or space probe. Although artificial intelligence is still in the research and planning stages for the most part, we may see more and more "smart" computers in our lives in the next few years!

cannot see, touch, or taste the fruit in order to make your decision. But you do know one fact about it. It is not round.

Immediately you know that of the three choices—grape, orange, or banana—the fruit is a banana. You know this on the basis of one fact: the piece of fruit is not round. This seems like a very simple guessing game. But stop for a moment and think about how you knew which fruit to guess. You have seen many grapes, oranges, and bananas, and from this experience you know that grapes and oranges are round. Probably no one ever told you this. You observed it for yourself by looking at these fruits. You were told that the piece of fruit you were guessing was not round. So you automatically eliminated grapes and oranges as choices and decided on the correct answer—a banana.

What would happen if you asked a computer to solve this same problem? First of all, you would have to find a language for asking the computer this problem. The computer, remember, does not understand natural—or human—language. Second, the computer would be baffled by the question. Computers cannot tell the difference between grapes, oranges, and bananas. Besides, they have not learned from experience that bananas are not round while grapes and oranges are.

We tend to think of computers as superbrains because they can add, subtract, multiply, and divide numbers at terrific speeds. But the computer cannot tell the difference between grapes, oranges, and bananas even when it is given an obvious clue! Sometimes the computer doesn't seem so intelligent, after all.

This is just one example of the differences between the way humans think and the way computers operate. There are many areas in which the human mind differs from the computer. For example, let's imagine that we are trying to decide where to spend our summer vacation. We have two choices. We could go to Iowa and visit our best friend who moved there in the middle of the school year. Or we could go to the coast of Mexico and take scuba diving lessons. We have to take many different factors into consideration. On the one hand, we miss our friend. We would like to spend some time catching up on the latest news since the friend moved. On the other hand, we always wanted to learn scuba diving. The coast of Mexico is supposed to be a beautiful and exciting vacation spot. How will we make the decision?

It is not a simple matter. To some extent, the decision depends on how much we miss our friend who now lives in Iowa. If we cannot stand to be apart, then we will probably go to Iowa and leave scuba diving for the next summer. But we may also have to consider other factors, such as money. The trip to Iowa would cost less than scuba diving lessons in Mexico. It may be best to travel to Iowa this summer. Then we could spend next year saving up for a trip to Mexico. If money is no problem, we may decide to spend some of our vacation in Iowa and the rest in Mexico.

What will happen if, after we have made our decision, someone offers to take us to London? Then we will have to begin the decision-making process all over again. We will have to consider again what we want to do, what is most practical to do, and what others want us to do. Human decisions can be very complicated. They often rely as much or more on emotions than on facts.

The computer differs from us in that it has no emotions. It can base decisions only on very simple facts. In other words, it cannot make distinctions between a good decision and a better decision. It cannot recognize that a decision may be good in one situation but bad in another. The computer operates strictly on the basis of logic, which is an organized system of reasoning. But this system does not always work for humans.

For instance, imagine that a friend of yours has just painted a picture. She asks your opinion of it. You dislike the colors, and you think that the horse looks more like a rocking chair than an animal. If you responded based on logic, as the computer would, the process would be something like this:

> Premise: My friend wants to know my opinion of the painting.
> Premise: I hate the painting.
> Conclusion: I will tell my friend that I hate the painting.

But just as you open your mouth to tell your friend how ugly her painting is, something occurs to you. If you tell your friend what you think, you will hurt her feelings. You might even risk losing the friendship. At the same time, you don't want to lie to your friend. So you might try to avoid hurting your friend's feelings. You say, "It certainly looks as if you spent a lot of time painting that picture." Unlike the computer, you know how to be kind.

Sometimes the fact that a computer has no emotions can be very helpful. In an emergency, humans sometimes panic and fail to make decisions that will resolve the problem quickly. The computer, by comparison, can evaluate the situation calmly. It can decide on a course of action and solve the problem in a matter of seconds. In certain situations, this could save lives and prevent great damage. This is one reason why AI is receiving so much attention.

The task that the AI scientist faces is to find a way to teach computers to "think," or to imitate the way humans think. But this is not an easy task. Computers think in binary terms. This means that they can only make yes or no decisions. They can only operate in terms of if-then logic. In other words, the computer thinks, "If a certain event occurs, then I will take a certain action." But consider all the questions that people have to answer that require more than a yes or no:

> Which college do I want to go to?
> Should I become a doctor or an engineer?
> Is my friend angry at me?
> Do I want to read a book or listen to the stereo?
> Should I order a hamburger or a pork chop?
> Which team will I back in the World Series?

This supermarket robot is preparing sliced meats for its customers.

The list could go on forever. These are questions that even supercomputers cannot answer as effectively as a human can. Our minds consider many facts and feelings that computers do not possess. The work of AI scientists is to give computers the powers of the human mind.

CHECK WHAT YOU HAVE LEARNED

1. What is artificial intelligence?
2. Name two reasons why a computer probably cannot answer a simple riddle.
3. What are two things that might influence a human decision?
4. When is it helpful to have a machine that lacks emotion?
5. Computers think in binary terms. Why does this make it difficult to teach them to make some decisions?

How Does AI Work?

Much artificial intelligence programming has been done in the area of game playing. Checkers, chess, and backgammon have been popular games to teach the computer to play. Programs for these games all follow the same basic pattern:

THE FUTURE AND BEYOND

1. Provide the computer with an enormous number of facts about different moves. Explain their relationships to other moves.
2. Provide the computer with information about the situation it is currently in, the game it is playing at present.
3. Provide the computer with a way of comparing the choices of moves it can make to see which move is best.

These programs enable the computer to use its memory ability to full advantage. In a very short time, the computer can compare many different moves and decide which move to make. It does this by one of two processes: **search trees** or **backward chaining**.

In a search tree, the computer assigns a score (or a number) to different moves. A good move may receive a high score while a bad move receives a low score. The computer can then search through the many moves in its memory. It checks to see which move gets the highest score. That is, with the search tree it searches for the move that is best in a certain situation.

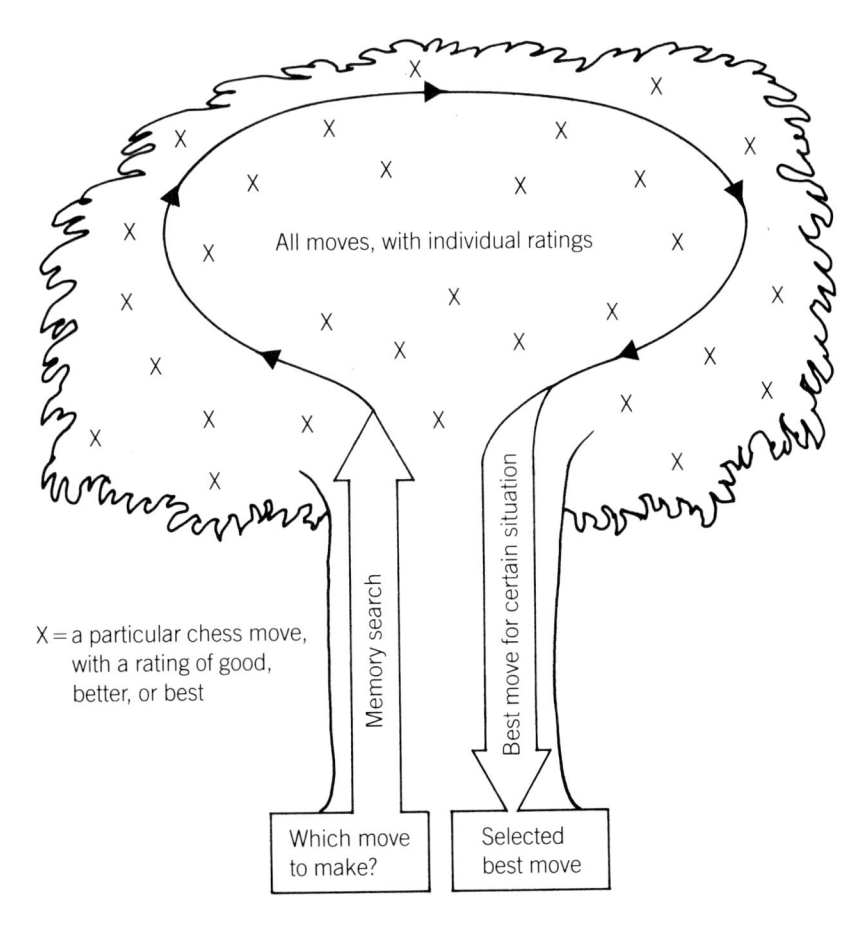

Using a search tree to find the best chess move in a certain situation, the computer memory is searched of all its previously stored and rated moves. Each arrowhead in the diagram indicates that a decision has been made to select a good (rather than bad) move. Then, the memory search continues for an even better move. When the search finds the most appropriate move, the computer selects it as the best.

X = a particular chess move, with a rating of good, better, or best

All moves, with individual ratings

Memory search

Best move for certain situation

Which move to make?

Selected best move

Starting with the goal of winning a game in upper left, the computer memory looks back through all the good moves it has been programmed to play in the past. The best move in a particular situation is chosen, and becomes a "link in the chain" to lead back up to the goal of winning the game.

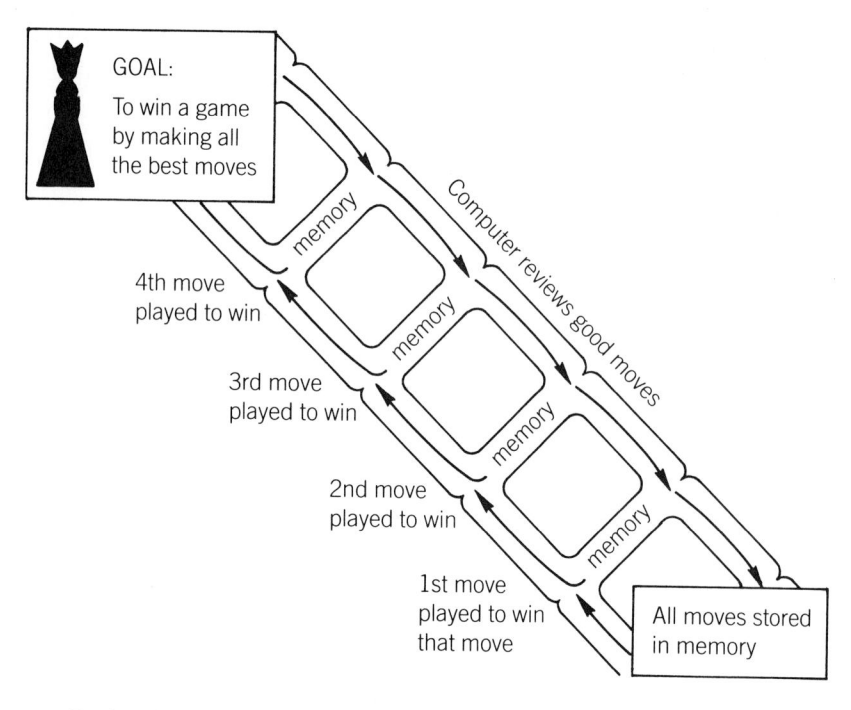

GOAL: To win a game by making all the best moves

Computer reviews good moves

4th move played to win
3rd move played to win
2nd move played to win
1st move played to win that move

All moves stored in memory

In backward chaining, the computer begins by defining its goal. In the case of a game, the goal is to win. But the computer knows that in order to reach the goal, it must follow a series of steps. Beginning at the goal, it looks backward through the chain of events that will lead to its goal. This is backward chaining. Then it takes an action that is likely to lead it successfully to its goal—winning the game.

The computer can do this more quickly and systematically than human players can. The computer can consider all of the moves that have been programmed into it. Then it chooses the best move. Because the human mind works in a more random manner, the human player may overlook a good move.

AI programming today uses either search trees or backward chaining to give computers the ability to make choices. The programmer must feed a vast amount of data into the computer. This way it will have all of the information it needs to "make a decision." In a way, this is similar to the process that humans go through as they grow up.

When you were born, you knew very little about the way the world operates. You only knew how to cry to get someone's attention when you needed something. As you grew, you gained more experience in the world. You learned certain facts. For example, you learned that a stove can be very hot. You learned that it can burn you if you touch it. The experience of burning your hand taught you not to touch the stove again because you remember the pain of the burn.

Without artificial intelligence, the computer cannot remember facts like these. Because the computer is not human, it would just go on touching the stove and getting burned time after time. This is because each time the computer is turned off it "forgets" all of the data in its memory. Imagine what your life would be like if each night while you slept you forgot everything that you had learned in your life. You would have to begin again each morning to learn the simplest things like walking and talking. This is the problem the computer faces.

When computers are able to remember what they have done before and use that information to solve similar problems, they will have become knowledge processors. Let's look again at the example of the computer programmed to play chess. Each time we play a game with that computer, it goes through the same processes using search trees or backward chaining, as if it has never played before. If the computer could remember previous games and situations it would be able to move quickly when like or similar positions occurred. It would be able to automatically discard many possibilities. If it lost a game it would know to try a different sequence of moves the next time a similar position occurred. Not only would the computer become quicker as it played, but it would also become a much better chess player.

To give the computer artificial intelligence, the AI programmer must first program in vast amounts of information so that the computer has a basis for decision making. Then he or she must find some way to make the computer understand the current situation it is in. Let's use our example of the stove. When you were a child, you learned that the stove in your home was hot when it was turned on. From this, you figured out that the stove in your grandparents' house was probably also hot when turned on. This process is called **inferring**. Inferring is using the facts in one situation to make decisions about another similar situation. For example, you used the facts about the stove in your parents' house to make a decision about the stove in your grandparents' house. A major goal of AI research is to teach the computer to infer, or to apply facts from one situation to another situation. This is an important part of the learning process.

AI research has a long way to go before it produces computers that can imitate the human mind. But in the process of finding ways to make computers more intelligent, AI researchers have made many contributions to computer technology. Next we'll take a look at some of the by-products of AI research.

CHECK WHAT YOU HAVE LEARNED

1. What is the major difference between a knowledge processor and a data processor?
2. Give an example in which inferring helped you to learn something.
3. What is the difference between a search tree and backward chaining?
4. Why can't a computer without artificial intelligence learn from experience?

By-Products of AI Research

The concept of **time-sharing** is a by-product of AI research. Time-sharing means that several users can share the use of a large computer system at the same time. The users cannot tell that anyone else is using the same computer. Time-sharing has brought computer power with its access to a large amount of data into the hands of people who could not afford to buy or maintain their own computer systems. The concept of time-sharing was developed by John McCarthy at the Massachusetts Institute of Technology, where a great deal of AI research is done. McCarthy is the same computer scientist who designed the LISP programming language for artificial intelligence.

Another AI by-product is the **vision system**. A vision system allows a machine to "see" much as humans see. In fact, a vision system is often referred to as an electronic eye. Vision systems are used in industrial machines that build objects. They can be used in quality control. For example, robots with vision systems are used in producing computer chips. The robot has a photograph of a perfect chip in its memory. It can compare each chip that is made to the photo of the perfect chip. It can check to see whether the new chip matches the perfect chip. If the chip matches the photo, then the robot approves it. If not, the chip is rejected as a faulty chip. Robots can do this more effectively than human workers who cannot see the tiny circuits on the chip without some sort of magnification.

Vision systems were developed by AI researchers. They realized that computers had to be given senses if they were to think like humans. We gain much of our knowledge about the world through our eyes by looking at things. Vision systems give computers and robots the same ability to see.

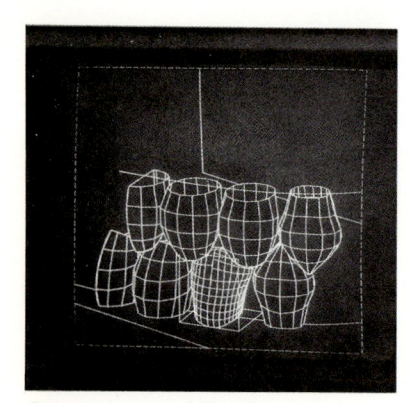

Computers are aiding dentistry. A tooth crown can be made by inputing the exact shape required—a machine fashions the new tooth in minutes.

THE FUTURE AND BEYOND

Computerized machines help the sight-disabled by reading books aloud.

Vision systems can also aid people with visual impairments. For example, there are now computerized reading machines. These machines scan words on the page of a book with normal print and then read the words aloud. This is very helpful to blind persons who must depend on Braille to read. Reading machines and many other devices with vision systems can make people's lives easier and more enjoyable.

A popular new kind of computer program is the **expert system**. This type of system can turn the computer into an expert on almost any subject. In effect, the expert system is a problem-solver much like a human expert. With an expert system, the computer can consider the facts in a given situation. Then it can advise humans of the best action to take.

An expert system is made up of several parts. One part gives the computer a knowledge base that is complete, up to date, and supplied by experts in the particular field. This knowledge base contains facts along with assumptions, beliefs, theories, and rules used in that field. Another necessary part of an expert system is the capacity for interaction between the computer system and human experts. With this interaction, new information, theories, and rules can be generated by the computer and validated by the experts.

One expert system known as Puff helps doctors and other medical personnel to diagnose respiratory diseases. The Puff

People and Computers

Donald Knuth

Donald Knuth is a professor at Stanford University and one of the foremost authorities on computer programming. His research into algorithms—the instructions that computers follow to carry out a task—won him the National Medal of Science in 1979.

Dr. Knuth realized at a very young age that he had an unusually systematic mind. When he was in the eighth grade, he took part in a contest. The challenge was to find out how many words could be formed with the letters in the name of a candy bar—Ziegler's Giant Bar. Dr. Knuth invented a way to search the dictionary for words and found more than 4500 words included in the letters of the name Ziegler's Giant Bar. That was 2000 more than the Ziegler's company had found! He won the contest and was awarded a toboggan, a TV set for his school, and a Ziegler's Giant Bar for everyone in his class. His meticulousness and logic have since combined to make him one of the world's most respected computer scholars.

Over a span of twenty years, Dr. Knuth has written three volumes of *The Art of Computer Programming*, and he hopes to complete four more. *The Art of Computer Programming* is an encyclopedia of information that surveys the entire field of computer science. Dr. Knuth is a very important figure in the ongoing development of computer technology. Mathematical formulas developed by Dr. Knuth have been important contributions in the development of new and valuable computer languages such as Aldes and Algol.

Donald Knuth enjoys playing his pipe organ as well as working with computers.

---

program contains a huge amount of information—a data bank. (A data bank is a large amount of information that can be used by more than one data base.) This information is about breathing disorders. The computer can use this information to determine what problem a patient has. A doctor can enter information about a patient's symptoms into the computer, and Puff will consult the information in its memory to try to decide what is wrong with the patient. Puff does this all very quickly, and it is correct in 80 percent of the cases it diagnoses. This is a good record for a computer that has never been to medical school!

The main advantage of expert systems is that they can act very quickly once they are given all the facts. A problem, though, is that giving the computer the facts—writing an expert system—takes a very long time. It can take two to three years and millions of dollars to develop a useful expert system. Once developed, however, the expert system provides constant access to a data bank. The data bank contains expert knowledge on any subject that it has been programmed to include.

Writing an expert system requires a great deal of careful planning. The programmer must work with others to determine exactly what the expert system is expected to do. The goal of the expert system must be stated very clearly and precisely. Then the programmer must decide how much and what kind of information the expert system will require to make its decisions. Computers do not yet "learn from experience." Until they do, expert system programmers will have to provide every bit of information that the expert system needs. Eventually, AI scientists hope that computers will be able to learn from their past experiences. When they can do that, they can gather their own information.

Once the programmer decides how much and what kind of information is required, the necessary information must be found. This is usually provided by a human expert in the field in which the expert system will be used. For example, a medical doctor helped to provide the data bank that enables Puff to diagnose respiratory diseases.

After the data bank is built, the programmer must design some way for the expert system to compare the facts in its data bank to the facts in whatever situation it finds itself in. When it is asked for advice, the expert system considers the present situation and then scans its memory for similar conditions. Then it recommends some answer or action based on the information in its data bank.

Expert systems can be used in every field of human work where computers are used. This can be anything from medicine to education to business to government. They are expensive and time-consuming to develop, but once they are developed expert systems are extremely useful. They can put many kinds of expertise at the fingertips of people who need this information to do their work.

An architect can consider many different views of a building he has designed and may make changes quickly and easily on the computer.

A three-dimensional "wireframe" computer figure helps designers evaluate proposed designs for car interiors. The figure on the left tests an instrument control location. The figure on the right emphasizes angles of body movement.

CHECK WHAT YOU HAVE LEARNED

1. Give one reason why expert systems are very rare.
2. What is time-sharing? Why is it helpful?
3. How can a computer with a vision system help someone who is visually impaired?
4. Would an expert system like Puff be helpful in diagnosing or treating new diseases? Why or why not?

Applications of AI

The list of applications for artificial intelligence is endless. AI promises to revolutionize the field of computers. It will do this in a way that is difficult to imagine today. One AI expert has compared the computers we use today with the potential development of artificial intelligence computers in the future. Today's computers are simple, like bicycles—tomorrow's AI computers will be complex, like fine-tuned automobiles.

AI computers will be powerful tools in every field that you can imagine. They will be especially powerful because they will learn more and more about a field as they are used. AI experts talk of designing computers that will even be able to program themselves!

Imagine the changes that AI could bring about in schools. Many schools now use microcomputers in the classroom. They use them to help students learn to operate computers and to run computer-aided instructional software. But many of the computer programs used in classrooms are simple drill-and-practice programs. These only give students practice in subjects they have already learned. AI computers in the classroom could interact with students. They could develop an idea of how quickly a certain student learns. They could introduce new material at a pace appropriate to each student. AI computers will be better able to present subjects to students. They will do more than merely test students on subjects they have already learned.

We have already seen how expert systems like Puff can be used in hospitals to help save lives of patients. Imagine what would happen if we added AI to a program like Puff. We would have a program that could learn from each patient diagnosis that it made. It could also continuously add to its data bank to make sure that it had all the information it needed to make accurate diagnoses. AI computers could also be used in surgery to provide advice on the

Careers and Computers

Computer Scientists

Computer scientists help to invent new ways for us to use the computer. They are always trying to discover methods of making the computer a better tool. They make it smaller, faster, and more powerful. The computer scientist may work on a new memory technology, design a new way of allowing computers to communicate with each other, or invent new ways for computers to process information. The main task of the computer scientist is research and experimentation.

Computer scientists are quite often hired by companies that manufacture new computers and software. They generate ideas that other development personnel, such as engineers and programmers, will put into action. In order to do this, they must have a very high level of technical knowledge. In fact, it is not uncommon for a computer scientist working for a major corporation to hold a doctorate degree in computer science.

Because of the extensive training and education required to design new applications of the computer, computer scientists usually receive top salaries. They have a wide range of jobs to choose from because they are in great demand. The computer scientist is one of the most respected professionals in the field. The computer scientist also has the excitement and pride of knowing that the work he or she does helps to shape the age of computers in which we live.

Architects

Architects perform many functions that include designing and drawing plans for buildings, bridges, and so on, that are needed in today's and tomorrow's world. The computer is an important tool for architects. Computer-aided design (CAD) is helping architects in many ways. By using computer-generated drawings, the architect is able to view each stage in the construction of a building. By simply pushing a button, the architect can test whether a staircase is more pleasing to the eye in one spot or another. He or she can look at the planned building in relation to the surrounding environment. These are things that might have taken architects and drafters a long time to draw before. Now they take only a few seconds as the computer draws them on the CRT screen.

One significant advantage of the computer is the machine's ability to draw three-dimensional curves. Curves are very hard to draw to scale by hand, but the computer can draw curves as easily as it can draw straight lines. This makes it a very valuable tool for architects. It will be even more valuable to architects in the future.

latest surgical techniques, and keep track of the patient's condition throughout the surgery.

AI will also be extremely useful in business environments. The amount of information a business needs to keep track of is always growing. An AI computer could monitor the progress of a business. It could use the information it gained to update all sorts of records and even programs without the need for humans to enter data into the computer. Computers that possess artificial intelligence will function more like human experts than as mechanical tools. Businesses will be able to rely on advice from AI computers to help in making wise business decisions.

AI computers in homes will take over more household functions than today's personal computers can perform. AI computers will learn from experience and so will grow, in effect, with their users' needs. It is likely that AI computers will be used in every facet of our lives. They will probably make the computers we use today seem very primitive.

With vision systems and optical fiber cable, the computer is able to "copy" many things and transmit them via a cable network.

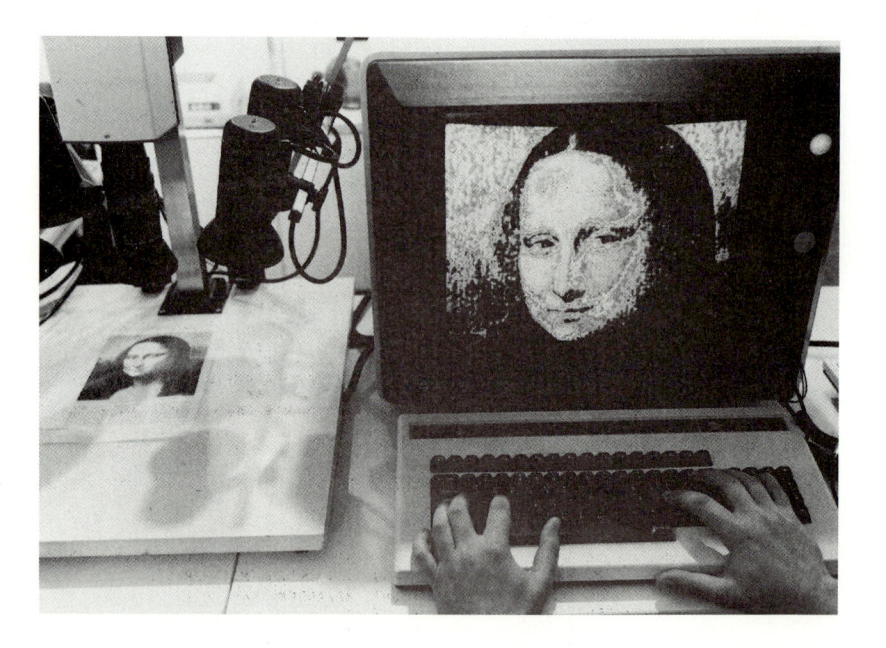

CHECK WHAT YOU HAVE LEARNED

1. Describe how AI programming would improve an expert system like Puff.
2. Name one reason why an AI computer would be a good tool for a teacher.

3. Name two ways in which AI computers will be useful in business.
4. Describe an advantage of AI computers for use in the home.
5. Why will AI computers be very powerful?

Future Applications of Robotics

Robotics is the science of designing and building robots. It is closely related to the field of artificial intelligence. In an earlier chapter, we explored different kinds of robots and some of the uses they serve today. The science of robotics is relatively new. Many exciting developments are taking place today, and many more are just around the corner.

Perhaps the most promising area of development in robotics is in giving robots artificial intelligence. Robots today do precisely what they are instructed by humans to do. Like most computers, they can do nothing more on their own. For example, some robots inspect computer chips to make sure they are built correctly. These robots must look at an image of a perfect chip in their memory each time they inspect a chip. Each time a robot looks at the image, it is as if the robot is seeing the image for the first time. It has no memory of having performed this task many times before. It also does not learn to perform better with experience.

Robots with artificial intelligence would be much more versatile tools in industry. They would constantly gather data about conditions around them. They would use this data to make better decisions in the future. They could take over more tasks that humans perform today.

Many people find this idea to be very exciting. We can teach robots and computers to take over more of our routine work. This way, we can concentrate on what humans do best: bringing creativity and innovation to our world. Humans possess many characteristics that cannot be programmed into or taught to a computer. This is what will keep people in control of computers. When we use robots to do tedious or boring work, humans are freed to spend more time doing work that is more interesting and challenging to them.

In the future, robots will be used in even more ways than they are used today. We already know that robots are useful for work that is repetitive, boring, or dangerous. But a job often requires

Robots can be used to help with many things like production or security patrol today. As artificial intelligence is developed, what will they be able to do tomorrow?

judgments based on past experiences. For example, we might imagine a worker thinking to herself, "The last time I did this under these conditions it didn't work well. Maybe I should try something else." As people learn to do their jobs, their job performance improves. Without artificial intelligence, it is impossible to program a computer to "know" all of the things that these people have learned on the job. But intelligent robots could take on many jobs that robots today cannot do. As they did their jobs, they could learn from each experience. This way, they would learn to do their jobs better as they worked.

Intelligent robots could be very helpful in jobs that require judgment and decision making but that are difficult or dangerous for humans to perform. Some jobs require that the worker come

---

The Future and Computers

Microprocessors in Cars

In the fuel-conscious 1970s, big high-performance engines in cars were replaced by smaller, less powerful engines. However, cars are now being developed with small engines that can perform just as well as the larger engines of a few years ago. This increase in efficiency is being made possible by computers that are being built into cars. The automobile industry has entered the computer age.

Microelectronics is appearing under the hoods of cars. Microprocessors now control such functions as engine ignition and fuel flow. There are devices available to monitor the battery and the fluid levels of the car's systems. These devices let the driver know when replacement or maintenance is needed. There is even a sensor that keeps track of what problems have occurred in the engine. This sensor can relay that information to people who repair the car.

There are devices that sense rain on the windshield and turn on the wipers. Windows can be kept defrosted and defogged by a computer-controlled heating unit on the windows themselves. The driver can unlock the car by punching a combination on an electronic keypad on the door rather than by using a key in a keyhole.

Inside the car the microprocessor allows keyless ignitions, voice-activated radios and telephones, and synthesized speech to alert the driver to hazards or problems. Has a car asked you to fasten your seatbelt lately? Another device that is appearing is an onboard computer complete with CRT and keyboard that can help the driver navigate and even show the present position of the car and its destination on a map. There is even a magnetic-field sensor that registers the position of a car in relation to the north and south poles. So a computer may keep us from getting lost when we are driving!

in contact with dangerous chemicals or extreme temperatures. For example, firefighting is a job that requires a great deal of judgment but is also extremely dangerous. In the future, we may call a fire-robot to put out a fire! Because robots will be capable of collecting much more specific data than humans, their decisions in some cases may be better because these decisions will be based on much more complete information than is available to humans.

Another exciting area of robotics is aids for the disabled. Robots often perform many tasks that disabled people cannot do for themselves. Intelligent robots could do even more. For example, an intelligent robot with voice recognition could do many errands for a disabled person. The person would only need to tell the robot what to do. Robots in the field of medicine may be able to monitor a patient's symptoms around the clock—they may automatically refer physicians to an appropriate expert system if a critical situation develops, and notify emergency hospital personnel at the same time.

Today, robots are used mainly in large factories because they are still quite expensive to design, build, and maintain. We can compare this situation to the early computers, which very few people could afford. But today many people use microcomputers in their homes. It is becoming rare to find a business that does not have at least one computer. The same trend will probably occur with robots.

In fact, there are now some inexpensive kits on the market to build small robots. As the field of robotics advances, robots will become more common. We will probably use them in our homes to do gardening, home maintenance, and other routine tasks. This will free us to enjoy more leisure time. Intelligent robots will be able to perform a wide range of tasks that we do not want to do or do not have time to do ourselves. Imagine how nice it will be to have a robotic arm do our dishes and a robotic gardener mow our lawns!

CHECK WHAT YOU HAVE LEARNED

1. Define robotics.
2. How can AI robots help the disabled?
3. Name three ways that robots might be used in our homes in the future.
4. Why do few people have robots today?
5. Why will people always be in control of computers?

The Future and Beyond

Computers have already become a major force in business, education, health care, and home maintenance. As they become smaller, smarter, and less expensive, computers will be even more a part of our everyday lives. They will be as common and as necessary to our society as the electric lightbulb. And they will probably affect our lives in many ways that we can only dream about now.

As we think about the future, we realize that the science of computers and robotics is no longer science fiction. Exciting new discoveries are taking place every day. Computers are being explored in many different ways and for uses in almost every area of life. When we dream about our robot butler and our automatic car, we are not just dreaming about the impossible. When we think about the blind seeing and the paraplegic walking, we are not just wishing. When we think about life in the future, we are not thinking about some faraway fantasy. In the world of computers, the future is only days away.

WHAT YOU HAVE LEARNED IN CHAPTER TEN

Computer technology develops at a very fast pace. The computers we use ten or twenty years from now will be very different from the computers we know today. It is likely that they will be smaller but more powerful and faster. They will probably also be "smarter" than the computers we use today.

Many researchers are working on the development of artificial intelligence. Artificial intelligence (usually called AI) is the ability to imitate the way humans think. Computers today do not think, feel, react, decide, or solve complicated problems as we do. Scientists in the field of AI are working to give computers the thinking power that humans possess.

We think of computers as superbrains because they can do arithmetic very quickly. But the computer cannot answer a simple riddle or give an opinion. It has difficulty making very simple decisions. In designing a computer to play a game, for example, the programmer must give the computer an enormous number of facts. The programmer must provide some information about the situation the computer is presently in. He or she must then give it some way of comparing possible choices so it can see which is best.

To make a choice, the computer uses one of two processes: search trees or backward chaining. In a search tree, the computer gives a number to different moves. The computer can then search through the moves in its memory to find one with a certain number. With the search tree, the computer searches for the move that is best in a certain situation. In backward chaining, the computer first defines its goal. In a game, the goal is to win. Beginning at the goal, the computer looks backward through the chain of events that will lead it to its goal. Then it takes an action that is likely to lead it to that goal.

As we grow up, we learn about our surroundings by experiences that we have. We learn that a stove is hot when we burn ourselves on it. But we do not have to touch each stove to find out if it is hot. After a few experiences with hot stoves, we figure out that all stoves that are turned on are probably hot. This is called inferring. It is the process of using the facts in one situation to make decisions about another similar situation. This is an important part of the learning process. The computer cannot yet infer. This is a major goal of AI research.

AI research has a long way to go. But it has already given us some important advances. It has given us time-sharing, which means that several users can share a computer system, and access to its large amount of data, at the same time. It has also given us vision systems, which are like "electronic eyes" that allow computers to "see" much as humans do. And it has given us expert systems. Expert systems are programs with huge data banks that enable the computer to consider a given situation and to give advice about that situation.

Artificial intelligence will change computers a great deal. With AI, computers will be able to learn and remember. Computers will become more powerful because they will learn more about a field as they are used. When AI programs are used with robots, the robots will become extremely useful both in industry and in the home. In the future, robots will also probably become less expensive. We will soon have reasonably priced robots to help us run our homes.

1. What is artificial intelligence?
2. How does backward chaining work?
3. Name two advantages of artificial intelligence.
4. Name two advances that AI research has brought about.
5. What is time-sharing?
6. Name three ways that computers will probably change in the future.

7. Give an example of something you have learned by inferring. Use a new example not mentioned in this chapter.
8. What is a search tree? How does it work?
9. Name two things that humans can do that computers cannot do yet.
10. What is an expert system? How is an expert system useful?

USING WORDS YOU HAVE LEARNED

1. I fell in the water two times. Both times I tried to breathe and I choked. I can _____ that it is not wise to breathe underwater.
2. In a _____ _____ , the computer assigns a score to different moves and then looks for the move that gives it the highest score.
3. _____ _____ is the ability to imitate the way humans think.
4. Using _____ _____ , the computer looks backward from a goal to choose a path of events that will lead to that goal.
5. A _____ system allows the computer to "see" much as humans see.
6. An _____ system is a problem-solver with an enormous data bank.
7. _____ allows several users to share the use of a large computer system at the same time.
8. _____ is the science of designing and building robots.
9. Artificial intelligence may allow computers to _____ and remember.
10. _____ systems are called "electronic eyes."

EXERCISING YOUR WRITING SKILLS

Form with classmates into small discussion groups, and brainstorm answers to finish this sentence:

"I would like a computer that could _____ ."

When you have fifteen answers that tell what a computer could do, stop and decide which suggestion you like best. Prepare to sell your idea to the class as if a computer with such powers already existed. Write an advertisement for your new computer. The ad should describe the computer's special features and the benefits buyers will get from owning it. Read your advertisement to the class.

When all presentations have been made, discuss if each idea is practical or possible. If possible, predict how many years it will be before each idea actually becomes a product.

UNDERSTANDING WHAT YOU HAVE LEARNED

MULTIPLE CHOICE

1. Artificial intelligence will allow computers to:
    a) gain mastery over human beings
    b) become emotional
    c) learn, remember, and make decisions
    d) become smaller
2. In the fifth generation of computers, computers will become:
    a) smaller, faster, and smarter
    b) smaller, slower, and smarter
    c) larger and more complex
    d) smaller but less powerful
3. Robots are used mainly in factories because:
    a) they are only useful in manufacturing
    b) they are very expensive
    c) they are very dangerous
    d) they would clutter up houses

THE FUTURE AND BEYOND

4. In the future, robots may be able to:
   a) do the gardening
   b) do the dishes
   c) do the housework
   d) all of the above
5. We are inferring when we:
   a) use experience to make a decision about similar situations
   b) use experience to make a decision about the exact same situation
   c) decide something by logic alone
   d) decide something emotionally
6. When the computer looks backward from a goal to trace a best path, it is using:
   a) vision systems
   b) time-sharing
   c) backward chaining
   d) search trees
7. Puff is an example of a(n):
   a) vision system
   b) expert system
   c) time-sharing device
   d) robotic device
8. Computers think in:
   a) semester terms
   b) romantic terms
   c) decimal terms
   d) binary terms
9. It is helpful to have a machine that lacks emotion when:
   a) you are choosing clothes
   b) you are deciding on a vacation spot
   c) you are in an emergency situation
   d) you are reading a book
10. When a computer is turned off, it:
    a) "forgets" everything in its memory
    b) stores everything in its memory
    c) erases its system
    d) none of the above

TRUE OR FALSE

1. Time-sharing was developed by John McCarthy.
2. A robot that is being used to check computer chips has a photograph of a perfect chip in its memory.
3. Puff is an example of an expert system that is correct 100 percent of the time.
4. AI will affect all computers except those in educational settings.
5. A search tree is one process computers can use to make choices.
6. Robots will never be practical for the home.
7. Computers are definitely smarter than people.
8. Human decisions are often influenced by emotion.
9. Artificial intelligence research has a long way to go.
10. Backward chaining assigns a high number to the best move, then searches out the highest numbers.

SHORT ANSWER

1. What are the two basic processes computers can be programmed to use to make choices?
2. Name two ways in which AI will improve the performance of computers.
3. Name two difficulties in the development of AI and explain them.
4. Why aren't robots used in homes today?
5. Give three of your own examples of questions that today's computers could not answer.
6. Name two developments that have come from AI research.
7. Define artificial intelligence.
8. Name one way that AI computers will be helpful in schools.
9. How will AI robots help industry to become more productive?
10. There are many ways that tomorrow's computers will be better than today's. What improvement are you most excited about? Why?

Glossary, Index, Acknowledgments

Glossary

abacus The first small counting machine. An abacus is a wooden frame on which beads are strung on thread to represent numbers.

accountant A person who keeps records of the financial matters of a business, organization, or person.

accounts payable All of the money that a business owes to other businesses, organizations, and people.

accounts receivable All of the money that the customers of a business owe to the business.

Age of Information The social and economic period we are now entering, in which people make their livings by handling information more than by growing crops or making products.

agricultural period The social and economic period in which most people made their livings through farming, and during which most people lived in small communities rather than large cities.

algorithm A step-by-step outline of the calculations the programmer wants the computer to perform.

application software Programs that tell the computer how to do specific jobs for the user.

arithmetic logic unit (ALU) The portion of the central processing unit that does all of the calculating for the computer.

artificial intelligence The ability to imitate the way humans think. Computers with artificial intelligence will be able to learn, make decisions, and solve problems.

assembler A program that translates assembly language into machine language.

assembly language A computer language that uses letters of the alphabet to represent the different arrangements of binary machine code.

authoring language A computer language that allows users who do not know programming languages to program in human language.

backup copy An extra copy of software that is made (with the software publisher's permission) in case the original program is lost or damaged.

backward chaining A computer program in which the computer reaches a certain goal by beginning at the goal and looking backwards through the chain of events that will lead to the goal.

BASIC (Beginner's All Purpose Symbolic Instruction Code) A high-level computer language that is easy to learn and very popular in business, schools, and homes.

binary Consisting of two. The binary number system has only two digits (0 and 1), as opposed to the decimal system that has ten digits (0 through 9).

bit A single piece of information (0 or 1). A bit is the smallest piece of information that can be read by a computer.

bootlegging The copying of a program without paying the person or company that legally owns the program. Bootlegging is also known as software piracy.

bottom-up programming Writing a short computer program without any planning. This type of program does only one specific task.

bus In a computer, circuits that pick up messages from parts of the computer and deliver them to other parts. Computer buses travel at 186,000 miles per second.

byte Small units of information, usually made up of eight bits.

cathode ray tube (CRT) A vacuum tube, similar to a television tube, that displays computer information (see monitor).

cell The place in a spreadsheet for a specific piece of information. A cell is in one row and one column only.

central processing unit (CPU) The part of a computer that controls the overall activity of the computer composed of the control unit, ALU, and primary storage unit.

chip A wafer-thin piece of silicon on which many tiny transistors are put together to form integrated circuitry.

COBOL (COmmon Business-Oriented Language) A high-level computer language designed to be used in writing programs for business.

code Actual computer instructions used in programming.

column A vertical space into which information may be entered.

compiler A program that translates programs from high-level languages into machine language.

computer A machine that takes in information and processes it in some way.

computer abuse Intentionally damaging computers or computer equipment.

computer-aided design (CAD) Use of the computer to help in the planning or designing of new products.

computer-aided instruction (CAI) Use of the computer to help in teaching students.

computer fraud Stealing with the use of a computer. This can involve stealing money, valuable goods, or time.

computer literacy Knowledge of and ability to use computers.

computer-managed instruction (CMI) Using the computer to help in grading papers or keeping track of grades and students' progress.

computer piracy The copying of a program without paying the person or company that legally owns the program. Computer piracy is also known as bootlegging.

control unit The part of the central processing unit that acts like a supervisor in an office, controlling the other parts of the computer system and regulating the work they do.

copyright The right that is given to the people who develop software or other original material to be the only people who sell it and to profit from its sales. Copyright laws protect people from having their product ideas stolen, or a product duplicated without permission.

counter A program feature that keeps track of how many numbers have been stored in, or removed from, a given location in the computer's memory.

cursor A pointer of light on the computer's screen that indicates where the next entry will be made.

cybernetic interface device An input device that is being developed with which the computer will be able to understand our thoughts without our even having to say them out loud.

data base A computerized method of organizing and storing information from which the information may be easily retrieved.

data item A piece of specific information in a data base that is filled into a field.

decision symbol In flowcharting, a diamond-shaped symbol that indicates a place in a program where the computer needs to decide which of two branching routes to take. The computer makes its decision based on tests to see what conditions exist.

debug To correct the mistakes in a program so that it runs the way it is supposed to.

dedicated word processor A computer that is specifically designed for use as a word processor.

demagnetization A way of erasing data stored on a magnetic disk or tape.

disk drive The device by which information stored on a diskette is entered into a computer.

diskette Round platters made of a plastic called Mylar, on which information is stored on a magnetic surface.

display To show data.

documentation A method of supplying information about a program (within the program lines) to the programmer or user.

electronic cottage The term used to describe where people will work when they work with their computers at home and send their work to a main office by using a modem (instead of commuting to an office each day).

electronic mail The method of sending mail and messages through a computer rather than using a paper postal system.

encryption device A part inserted in a computer used to scramble information into a code that is entered into a computer, so that only a person who has access to the decoding program can read and use the data.

ethics A set of principles or values, or beliefs that we hold about what is right or wrong.

expert system A program that turns the computer into an "expert" on a specific subject by supplying the computer with a complete knowledge base and a system for analyzing new information.

field A space where specific information is stored in a data base.

fifth generation Computers that will use artificial intelligence and be very different from fourth generation computers.

file A collection of records in a data base.

flowchart A drawing, made up of different symbols, that is used to plan a computer program.

font A set of type all of one style or shape of lettering. Italics is an example of a frequently-used font.

form letter Letters that leave blank spaces where names or other specific information should be. These blank spaces are filled in by hand after the letter has been copied.

formula A set of directions that tells a computer how to arrive at the number that is to be entered into a specific cell in a spreadsheet.

Forth A programming language that is especially popular in engineering and graphics applications.

FORTRAN (FORmula TRANslator) One of the early computer languages, designed to make writing mathematical formulas easier.

function keys Keys on the computer keyboard that perform routine tasks when pressed.

generation One stage in a developing sequence, born from the last and giving birth to the next.

graphics A computer feature that allows a user to make drawings for display or printing.

hard disk A hard computer disk that increases the computer's memory. It is usually fixed inside the computer by the computer manufacturer.

hardware The physical equipment of the computer system. Terminals, keyboards, disk drives, tape drives, printers, and the central processing unit are all hardware.

high-level language A language that is more similar to human language than machine or assembly language. Programs are easier to write in high-level languages, but must be translated by compilers (or interpreters) for the computer to understand them.

industrial period The social and economic period in which most people made their livings by making products, usually in factories. During the industrial period, most people moved into or close to big cities.

Industrial Revolution The term used to refer to the great changes that took place when society changed from the agricultural period to the industrial period.

inferring Using the facts in one situation to make decisions about another similar situation.

initialize In programming, to set the counters and other variables at zero.

input The method by which instructions and information that the computer needs are put into the computer.

input/output symbol In flowcharting, a parallelogram-shaped symbol that indicates places in the program where data is either entered, printed out, or displayed.

integrated software Programs that can communicate with each other, so that information that is in one program may be used with another program.

interface A connection by cable between the computer and input and output devices.

justify To make all of the lines of a page begin or end at a specific point on the page. Printed books are usually justified at both the left and the right margins.

key In a data base, a field by which the information may be organized and retrieved.

keypunch A method of computer data entry in which small holes in cards represent numbers and letters to the computer.

kilobyte (K) 1024 bytes of information. Computer memory is usually measured in kilobytes.

large-scale integrated circuitry (LSI) A type of integrated circuitry in which many tiny transistors are put on a chip. Also, each chip can do a number of different jobs.

ledger A special book in which people may keep records of their sales, income and payments, or other numerical information.

LISP (LISt Programming) A computer programming language used in the field of artificial intelligence.

logarithms Mathematical manipulations that make it possible to do multiplication and division by doing a series of additions and subtractions.

Logo A programming language designed to help children learn mathematics and computer programming.

loop (1) a portion of a computer program that repeats itself several times or until a certain condition is met; (2) the act of repeating itself.

machine language A language made up of different arrangements of bits. Machine language is easy for the computer to understand, but difficult for humans to use.

magnetic core memory Memory made of some magnetic material that can hold electrical charges. The computer can read the electrical charges as numbers.

magnetic ink character recognition (MICR) An input method that works by recognizing characters printed with a special magnetic ink.

magnetic tape Tape on which information is recorded that can be entered into the computer by a tape drive. The pattern of electrical currents on the tape makes up a code that the computer can translate into instructions and information.

mainframe The largest and fastest computers in use today. A mainframe has very large memory, works very quickly, uses more than one input and output device, and uses disks or tape for secondary storage.

main routine The routine in a program that tells the computer what subroutines to perform and when to perform them.

melting pot A term used to refer to the United States, because many different groups and cultures of people came together and their groups "blended."

memory That part of the computer system that stores information or instructions.

menu A list of choices from which the computer user may choose what he or she would like to do with the program being used.

merge To put together two documents, as with a list of names and a form letter.

microcomputer A computer that is designed to fit on a desk top. Its small size makes it very convenient to use, but it usually has less memory than minicomputers or mainframes.

microfiche Permanent readable copies of data that have been reduced in size and photographed onto thick film stored as flat cards.

microfilm Permanent readable copies of data

that have been reduced in size and photographed onto thick film stored in long rolls like filmstrips.

microsecond   One millionth of a second.

minicomputer   A computer in the middle range of computer power, smaller than mainframes but larger than microcomputers.

modem   A small box that connects to, or is built into, a computer and that has a place to put a telephone handset or to attach a telephone cord. With a modem, computer information can be sent from one computer to another over telephone lines.

monitor   Cathode ray tube—it is the part of a terminal that displays information.

mouse   A small, moveable, box-like device that may be used instead of a keyboard on some computers to input data and instructions into the computer.

nanosecond   One billionth of a second.

networking   A connection of computer systems at different locations that exchange data.

optical character recognition (OCR)   A method with which computers can "see" characters and marks. An example of OCR is the bar code reader used in stores.

output   The manner in which the computer displays its work in some way that humans can understand and use.

Pascal   A programming language introduced in the early 1970s that is easy to learn and use.

password   A word, code, number, key, fingerprint, or voice print that is used to gain access to the computer. The password allows only authorized users to gain access to the data on the computer.

payroll   The amount of wages that each employee in an organization has earned.

peripheral   Hardware devices that attach to a computer and may assist with input, processing, or output of information.

picosecond   One trillionth of a second.

PILOT   An authoring language that allows people who do not know computer programming to write their own programs.

plotter   A device that prints hard copies of processed information. The plotter uses data from the computer to guide pens across paper to draw images.

printer   A device used to print information from a computer onto paper.

printout   A paper copy of information that has been generated by the computer.

private labelling   When unethical retailers buy a copy of a program, copy the program illegally, and then sell the copies under their own private label.

procedure   A routine in Logo.

processing   The handling, changing, and storing of information.

process symbol   In flowcharting, a rectangular figure that indicates a place in the program where the computer must do a calculation.

program   A set of instructions that the computer follows when it is processing information.

programmable read-only memory (PROM)   A chip that is similar to the ROM chip but that can be programmed once. Most PROM chips cannot be erased.

programming language   A language that helps humans to communicate with computers and in which programs are written.

proofread   To read a written paper carefully to be sure that there are no errors in punctuation or content.

prototype   A model of a new product that is made from the plans to see if the object or machine will operate correctly and safely.

programming languages   Special languages that help humans communicate with computers.

pseudocode   A method of planning a computer program in which the instructions are written down in a human language before they are coded into programming language. Pseudocode is like an outline of the program.

random-access memory (RAM)   A method of storing information that can be erased and rewritten whenever the user needs to store different information. Also called direct access, data stored through random access may be retrieved quickly because the computer goes immediately to the spot to find it.

read-only memory (ROM) A method of storing information which allows the computer only to read information. The manufacturer of a ROM chip puts information onto it and the information cannot be changed.

record In a data base, a collection of several fields that are all about the same thing or person.

register A tiny memory space, the size of one computer word, in which the computer stores a word until it is ready to use it.

relational data base A fairly complex data base that is organized in a way that makes it unnecessary to repeat any information at all.

REM statement A statement in a computer program that simply reminds the programmer of what is happening at that point. REM is short for "remark."

return In a computer program, the word that causes the computer to return to the main routine from a subroutine.

robot Programmable computer with moving parts; some robots are capable of working with other objects.

robotics The science of designing and building robots.

routine Part of a computer program that completely performs one specific task.

row A horizontal space into which information may be entered.

security measures The methods that are used to try to prevent dishonest people from misusing computers.

search trees Computer programs in which the computer reaches a goal by assigning a score to different moves and then searching its memory for the move with the highest score at each turn.

sequential access A method of finding data by sorting through all of the data that has been stored from beginning to end. Sequential access may take a long time.

shared-logic word processor A computer that is used for word processing and for other tasks.

simulation The process in which the computer pretends that something is happening and the computer user can practice what to do in that situation.

software A set of instructions, or program, that is part of the computer system, and that allows the computer to do a particular job.

spreadsheet An electronic ledger that can help to plan, account for, or manipulate numerical information.

stand-alone word processor A computer that is specificially designed for use as a word processor—also called a dedicated word processor.

statement One line of a computer program. Each statement tells the computer what to do.

statistics The collection and analysis of numerical information.

subroutine A routine in a program that performs one specific task and then returns the computer to the main routine.

supervisor That part of the computer's operating system that tells the computer what order to do the jobs in, how and when to accept input or send output, and that gets instructions for a specific job from the tape or disk where they are stored.

syntax The order and arrangement of words in a specific language.

system software (operating system software) A set of rules or instructions that help the computer's operating system. For example, a program that tells the computer how to accept input information is part of the system software.

tape drive The device by which information stored on magnetic tapes is entered into the computer.

terminal A typewriter-like keyboard and a screen or printer at which the computer operator may input or view information.

terminal symbol In flowcharting, an oval-shaped figure that indicates the beginning and ending points of a program or routine.

text Written material.

time-shared word processor A microcomputer linked to a larger computer so that several people can do word processing at the same time.

without being able to tell that anyone else is using the same computer.

top-down structured programming A system of planning computer programs in which the job the computer is to do is broken down into smaller and smaller steps. The programmer begins at the top of the chart with what the program will do, then moves down the chart, dividing the job into smaller tasks.

update To change, correct, or add to data that has been entered before.

user's group A gathering of people (a club, for example) who use computers.

variable Something that can change within a computer program. For example, the price of an entry might be different each time the same program is run, so price is a variable.

very large-scale integration (VLSI) Integrated circuitry even smaller than large-scale integration, in which greater numbers of microscopic circuits are put onto chips. With VLSI, chips contain as many as 300,000 units.

vision system An "electronic eye" that allows the computer to "see" in somewhat the way humans see.

voice recognition device An input device that accepts data that is spoken rather than typed or recorded on disk or tape.

window An area of the screen that shows the user information from a specific program. Windows are often used with integrated software.

word One or more bytes which the computer takes as one unit in its memory.

word processing A computerized system that helps the user to write, edit, store, copy and/or print a written document.

Index

Abacus, 15–16
ABC computer, 20, 24, 30
Abuse of computers, 272–274, 283
Access
  direct, 48
  restriction of, 277–280, 283
  sequential, 48
  types of, 48
Accountant(s)
  computer use, 13, 155, 172, 185
  ledger use, 168
Accounting, computers in, 155–157, 163, 172, 185
Accounts payable, 155–156, 163
Accounts receivable, 156–157, 163
Accuracy, computer, 5
ADA language, 15, 58, 60, 68
Address of a word, 58–59
Advertising, computer in, 242
Age of Information, 227, 230–240, 245–249, 250–251
  agriculture in, 240
  artificial intelligence and, 297, 300, 308–309
  factory in, 229
Agricultural period, 227–228, 250
Agriculture, computer in, 240
AI. *See* Artificial intelligence.

Aiken, Howard, 20
Airlines, data-base use, 153
Airplanes
  computer-aided design of, 203
  computer testing of, 11
Algorithm, 90–91
ALU (arithmetic logic unit), 46–47, 68
Analysis of problem, 195–196, 221
Analysts, computer, 81, 178, 206
Analytical engine, Babbage's, 18, 19
Android, 257
Animal learning, 255
Animal thinking, 255
Animated art, 122, 155
Animation, computer-generated, 155
Apple computer, 234
Application program(s), 104
Application programmers, 81–83, 206–208
Application software, 83–86, 104
Architects, computer use, 301, 303
Architectural design, computer in, 191, 238
Arithmetic, in businesses, 12
Arithmetic logic unit (ALU), 46–47, 68

Arrows, in flowchart, 201, 221
Art, animated, 122, 255
Artificial intelligence (AI), 66, 91, 99–100
  applications of, 302–305, 309
  future, 290–302, 308–309
  games and, 294–295, 309
  how it works, 294–298
  LISP language in, 99–100
  research by-products of, 298–301, 309
  robot application, 305–307, 309
Assembler, 60
Assembling of computers, 134–135
Assembly language, 60, 68, 94
Assembly lines, 228, 229, 231, 232
Association of Computing Machinery, 195
Astronomy, simulation in, 172
Atanasoff, John, 20, 30
Atanasoff-Berry computer (ABC), 20, 24, 30
Athletes, simulation in training of, 178
Authoring languages, 94–103, 105
  PILOT as, 102–103, 105
Automation, 257
  jobs and, 245, 251

INDEX

Automobiles
  CAD in, 300
  computer testing of, 11–12
  early and advanced, 226
  microprocessors in, 306

Babbage, Charles, 18, 19, 58
Babbage analytical engine, 18
Backgammon game program, 295
Backup copies of software, 269
Backward chaining, 25, 296, 309
Bacon program, 91
Bank statement, as spreadsheet, 180
Banking, computer use in, 129, 155–158, 163, 180–181
Bar codes, 44, 67
Base 10 number system, 15
BASIC language, 60, 67, 68, 98–99, 105
  key words in, 209
  programming in, 208–212, 222
  writing the code in, 216–217
BASIC program, 98
Berry, Clifford, 20, 30
Billing, spreadsheets in, 174
Binary, defined, 56–57
Binary code
  EDVAC use, 24
  UNIVAC-I use, 25
Binary number system, 56–57, 68
Biochips, 266
Biomechanics, 256
Bit, defined, 57
Blind persons
  reading with computer, 299
  voice synthesis use, 54
Booth, Andrew, 22
Bootlegging software, 270–271, 282–283
Boredom, computer lack of, 6, 30
Bottom-up programming, 200
Britten, Kathleen, 22
Broker, data-base use, 151
Bubble memory, 66
Budgets
  computers in, 9
  spreadsheet use for, 181, 185
Bugs, 90–91, 105. *See also* Debugging.
Buses, speed of, 59
Businesses
  artificial intelligence in, 304
  computer crime in, 280, 283
  computer use in, 12, 30, 68, 325
  data-base use in, 151, 153, 155–158, 163
  spreadsheet use in, 168–170, 173–174, 177, 179, 184–185
  word processing in, 12
Byron, Ada, 18, 58
Byte, defined, 58

CAD. *See* Computer-aided design.
CAI. *See* Computer-aided instruction.
Calculations, in spreadsheet, 169
Calculators
  early, 15–16
  mechanical, 16–17
Calculi, 15
Carbon-paper copies, 112
Cards
  Hollerith, 20
  Jacquard, 18
  keypunch, 37
  speed of, 38
  UNIVAC use, 25
Careers
  computer-related, 8, 63–64, 81–83, 127, 178, 206–208, 237–238, 263–264, 303
  opportunities in software, 103
Cassettes, storage on, 147
Cathode-ray tube (CRT), 40, 51
  outputting, 50
  screen, 68, 89
Cells, spreadsheet, 175, 185
Census
  computers in, 12–13, 19, 20, 30, 238
  data-base use in, 152
Centering text, 115, 119, 130

Central processing unit (CPU), 46–47
  arithmetic logic unit in, 68
  memory boards in, 49
Changes, in word-processed letters, 110, 115, 116, 118
Changing fonts, 120–121, 130
Changing text, 112–113, 115–120, 130
Changing type size, 121, 130
Character(s), 53
  magnetic-ink recognition of (MICR), 45–46, 67
  optical recognition of (OCR), 44, 45, 67
Checkers program, 295
Chess program, 294–295, 297
Children
  computer camps for, 209, 270
  computer learning and use, 170
  education for computers, 244
  electronic cottage life, 241–242
  learning keyboarding, 126
  programming by, 100–102
Chimpanzee at keyboard, 255
Chips, 26–29, 31
  biochips, 266
  circuit drawings, 73
  circuit masks, 73
  digitizing circuits, 73
  kinds of, 68
  "living," 266
  making of, 72–75
  memory, 68
  packaging of, 73, 75
  size of, 72
  wafer containing, 26, 73
  wiring of, 75
Choices, intelligence aspect, 291–292, 309
Circuit(s). *See* Chips; Integrated circuitry/Integrated circuits.
Circuit boards, 134
Citizenship, computer and, 244–245
Clean room, 26, 49, 74
CMI. *See* Computer-managed instruction.
COBOL language, 60, 67, 68, 96–97, 105

INDEX

COBOL program, 96–97
Code(s), 105, 212
   bar, 44, 67
   program, 90
   pseudocode and, 93, 105
Code words, for computer protection, 278, 283
Columns
   ledger, 169
   spreadsheet, 168, 185
Comments, in FORTRAN program, 96
Compilers, 59, 195
Computer(s), 1 *and throughout*
   access into, 48, 79, 277–280, 283
   advantages and disadvantages of, 260, 282
   capacity, 2–4
   decision-making, 289, 309
   defined, 2, 4, 29
   early, 226
   electronic, early, 20–22
   generations of, 22–29, 31. *See also* First (etc.) generation of computers.
   history of, 3, 15–29
   limitations of, 194, 196, 221, 292, 308, 309
   mainframe, 61–62, 68
   micro-, 31, 65–68
   mini-, 62–65, 68
   modern society, 224–253
   personal, 128, 130
   popularity of, 3–7
   portable, 236
   preventing misuse of, 277–281, 283
   security use of, 280
   "smarter," 289–291, 308–309
   super-, 29, 61–62, 288–289
   talking to, 199
   testing of, 136
   types of, 61–66, 68
   uses of, 2–14, 29–30
   working of, 56–61
Computer-aided design (CAD), 11, 30, 203, 303
   architecture, 301
   automobile, 300
   graphics in, 88

Computer-aided instruction (CAI), 7–9, 30, 243–244
   military use of, 13–14
Computer art, 122, 155
Computer camps, 209, 270
Computer consultants, 127
Computer crime, 249, 251, 262, 281–283
Computer ethics, 258–285
Computer fraud, 264–269, 282–283
Computer language, 59–60, 78, 105. *See also* Language.
Computer law, 263, 282–283
Computer literacy, 247
Computer-managed instruction (CMI), 7–9, 79
   military use of, 13–14
Computer operators, 63
Computer piracy, 269–272, 282–283
Computer programs. *See* Programs.
Computer scientists, careers, 303
Computer skills, daily life and, 240–245
Computer surveillance, 14
Computer system, diagram, 51
Computer technicians, 237
Computer thinking, 293, 308–309
Computer time, stealing of, 267–269, 282
Consultants, computer, 127
Control system, electronic, 254
Control unit, in CPU, 68
Convenience, computer, 6
Copies
   made at terminal, 125
   multiple, 112, 130–131
Copying, 115, 304
   prevention of unauthorized, 248
   text, 123
Copyright laws, 271–272
Correcting text, 115–117, 130
Corrections, word processor and, 112, 130
Cost
   computer, 6, 28, 30–31
   mainframe, 61

   microcomputer, 65–66
   minicomputer, 62, 64
Counters, 16, 213
Counting, 15–16
Counting board, 16
CPU. *See* Central processing unit.
Credit bureaus
   computer use, 248
   permission to release data, 276, 283
   records of, 275, 283
Crime, computer, 249, 251, 262, 282–283
   laws against, 281, 283
Criminal records, computer theft of, 267
CRT. *See* Cathode ray tube.
Cursor, 39, 110
   what it does, 110–111
Cybernetic interface device, 44

Data
   displaying of, 150, 163
   entering in data base, 149, 162
   organization of, 140–141, 162
Data base(s), 138–165
   advantages of, 145–147, 162–163
   display, with fields, 156
   employment and, 246
   fields in, 143, 156
   organization of, 143–145, 162–163
   privacy and, 248
   relational, 142
   setting up and using, 148–150
   what they are, 140–142, 162
   where used, 151–163
Data-base management system, microcomputer, 150
Data-base program, 84–85
Data-base specialists, careers, 153
Data-base system, 84
Data compiler, 195
Data-entry operators, 63–64
Data item, 143, 162
   example in data base and fields, 143

Data processing, 5, 30
Data storage, government, 12
dBase II, software, 150
Debugging, 82, 91, 105, 206
  line numbers and, 97
Decimal number system, 15
Decimal point, 16
Decision(s), ethical, 261, 282
Decision making, 292, 309
  computer-assisted, 141
  data-base use in, 154
  spreadsheet use in, 166–187
Decision-making computers, 289, 309
Decision-making symbol, 201–202, 221
Dedicated word processor, 124, 131
Demagnetization, 274
Dentistry, computer in, 290
Deposit slips, stealing with, 265
Design
  computer-aided (CAD), 11, 30, 88, 203, 200, 300, 301, 303
  computerized, 198
  spreadsheets in, 184
Designers, software, 82
Development, careers in, 8
Dialects, talking with a computer, 199
Dictionary stored in memory, 115, 117
Difference engine, 19
Digital watch, 28
Digitization, 122
  chip circuits, 73
Direct access, 48
Disabled persons
  computer help for, 257
  robot aids for, 307, 308
  telecommunications use, 129
  voice devices and, 43
  voice synthesis use, 54
Disadvantages of computers, 260, 282
Discomfort, computer freedom from, 6
Disk(s), 39
  data storage on, 147, 162
  editing of, 128
  filing on, 113
  hard, 50, 68
  storage of, 163

Disk drive, 19, 39
Diskettes, 39, 50, 67, 68
  magnetic, 39
  speed, 39
Display, 150, 163
  on CRT screen, 190
  of information, 150
  of tissue-sample images, 189
Displaying data, 150, 163
Doctors, computers and, 9, 30
Documentation, 209
Document storage, 113
Dot matrix characters, 53
Dot matrix printing, 52–53
Drawing(s), computer generated, 255
Drawing flowcharts, 214–215
Drill-and-practice software, 7–8
Driver's licenses, data bases for, 154
Dumb terminals, 42
Dust-free factory, 49
Dust table, as calculator, 15

Early calculators, 15–16
Early computers, 226
Eckert, John Presper, 20
Editing
  telecommunications and, 128
  word processing and, 126–128, 131
EDSAC, 24
Education. *See also* Schools.
  simulation in, 171, 185
  spreadsheets in, 179
EDVAC, 24
Elections
  computer use in, 13, 25, 30, 238
  data-base use in, 152
  spreadsheets in, 182
Electrocardiograms, analysis of, 10
Electromagnetic computers, 20–21
Electromechanical computer, 20, 23
Electronic computers, early, 20–22
Electronic control system, 254
Electronic cottage, 241, 250
Electronic eye, 298, 309

Electronic housekeeper, 243
Electronic mail, 242, 251
Electronic mailbox, 129
Emotion, computer freedom from, 293
Employment, data bases on, 246
Encryption device, 279–280, 283
END, key word, 209
END statements, 210
Engineer(s), data bases and, 142
  program, careers, 206–207
  simulation use, 171
Engineering, computers in, 11, 190, 238
ENIAC, 20–24
Entering data, in file, 149, 162
Errors, computer, 5
Ethical decisions, 261, 282
Ethics, 258–285
  what they are, 261–262
Experiments, computer, 9
Expert systems, 291, 299–301, 309

Factories
  old and modern, 228, 229
  robots in, 229, 230–232, 234, 307, 309
  tool advances, 233
Farms, computer use on, 64, 191
Fear, computer freedom from, 6
Federal Bureau of Investigation, 265
Fields, 143, 162
  creating, 148–149, 162
  example in data base, 143
Fifth-generation computers, 29, 61–62, 288, 289
Files, 143–144, 162–163
  creation of, 148, 162–163
  data-base, 146
  paper, 145–147, 163
  privacy in, 248
  record and, example, 144
Filing, 140, 141, 162–163
  on disks, 113
Filing system, data-base program as, 84
Financial planning, 87
Finding, 119–120, 130

INDEX

Fingerprints, password function, 278, 283
Firefighting, robot job, 307
First-generation computers, 23–25, 30, 288
Flowchart(s),
   drawing, 93–94, 105, 214–215
   examples of, 201, 205, 214, 215, 218, 219
Flowcharting, 200–202, 221–222
Fonts, changing, 120–121, 130
Form letters, 117
FORMAC, 195
Formed characters, 52–53
Formula, spreadsheet need for, 175
Forth language, 60, 99, 105
Forth program, 99
FORTRAN, 60, 67, 95–96, 105
FORTRAN program, 96
Fourth-generation computers, 27–29, 31, 288
Fraud
   computer, 264–269, 282–283
   discarded equipment used in, 266
FRED, robot, 289
Freedom of Information Act, 275–276
Frustration
   computer freedom from, 6, 30
   human, with computers, 277, 283
Function keys, 40, 113, 130
Future, computers and, 28, 66, 91, 254–257, 286–311

Games, artificial intelligence and, 294–295, 309
Generations, computer, 22–29, 31
GOSUB, key word, 209
GOSUB statements, 210
GOTO, key word, 209
GOTO statements, 210
Government,
   computers in, 12–14, 30, 68, 238, 247–248

   data-base use in, 152–154, 163
   effects of computers on, 239
   spreadsheet use in, 179–180, 185
Graphics
   computer-aided design of, 88
   medical research and, 255
   merging with text, 121–122
   movie use of, 155
   simulation in, 170–172
Graphics tablet, on CRT screen, 190

Hard copy, data storage on, 189
Hard-copy terminal, 40
Hard disks, 50, 68
Hardware, 36–56, 60
   input, 36–46, 67
   output, 67
   processing, 36–50, 67
   storage, 36–50, 67
Health maintenance, computer-aided, 242–244
Health records, computer theft of, 267
Heliostats, computer control of, 256
High-level languages, 60, 68, 94, 105
History of computers, 3, 15–29
Hollerith, Herman, 19, 20, 152
Hollerith tabulating system, 20
Homes
   artificial intelligence in, 304, 309
   buying in, 242
   computer-aided management of, 242–244
   data bases in, 162–163
   languages for computers in, 98
   robots in, 307, 308, 309
   spreadsheet use in, 170, 173, 181
   work in, 239, 241–242
Hopper, Grace Murray, 195
Horseless carriage, 226
Human thinking, 293, 308–309
Human-to-machine language translation, 95

IF . . . THEN, key word, 209
IF . . . THEN statements, 211
Impact printing, 52
Income taxes, computers and, 13, 188
Industrial period, 228–229, 250
Industrial Revolution, 28, 228–229, 250
   calculators and, 18–19
   factory in, 228
Industry, spreadsheets in, 184
Inference engine, 291
Inferring, 297, 309
Information
   Age of. *See* Age of Information.
   finding, 138–165
   importance of, 232–235
   merging, 117–118, 130
   storage of, 12, 30, 140–141, 162
   value of, 274–276, 283
Information handling, computer use for, 235–237
Information management, 236
Information processing, 5, 30
Initializing, 212
Input, 36, 67
INPUT, key word, 209
Input hardware, 36–46, 67
Input/output symbol, 200, 201, 221
INPUT statements, 210–211
Inputting, 36, 50
Inspection
   of computers, 134
   robots for, 231, 298
   wafer, 74
Instruction by computers
   computer-aided (CAI), 7–9, 30, 243–244
   computer-managed (CMI), 7, 79
Instruction to computers
   FORTRAN program, 96
   software as, 78
Insurance business, data bases in, 158–159, 163
Integrated circuitry/Integrated circuits, 27, 31, 47–48, 68

sensory devices in, 254
large-scale (LSI), 27–29
very large-scale (VLSI), 29, 47–48
Integrated software, 87–90, 104–105
Integration, very large-scale (VLSI), 29
Intelligence, artificial. *See* Artificial intelligence.
Intelligent computers, 291, 309
Interface(s), 59
Interface device, cybernetic, 44
Internal Revenue Service, 247–248
  data base, 154
  spreadsheet use, 179, 185
Interviews, computer-conducted, 246
Inventories, 42–43
  computer keeping and control of, 9, 235–236
  CRT screen showing, 89
  in data bases, 157–158
Invoice, display, with fields and data items, 157

Jacquard, Joseph Marie, 18
Jacquard loom, 18
Jobs
  Age of Information and, 234–235
  automation and, 245–247, 251
  computer effect on, 243–247
  robots and, 231–232, 245–247
Jobs, Steven Paul, 234
Justifying text, 119, 130

K (kilobyte), 59
Kemeny, John, 98
Key(s), 144, 162
Keyboard, computer, 40, 111, 113, 130
Keyboarding, children learning, 126
Keypunch, 38

Keypunch cards, 37
Keypunch machine, 37
Keypunching
  defined, 18
  Jacquard, 18
Kilobyte (K), 59
Knitting industry, 203
Knuth, Donald, 300
Kurtz, Thomas, 98

Labor force, robots and, 231, 232, 251
Laboratory technicians, programming by, 207–208
Language(s). *See also* names of languages: ADA, BASIC, COBOL, Forth, etc.
  assembly, 60, 68, 94
  authoring, 94–103, 105
  categories of, 94, 104–105
  computer, 59–60, 78, 105
  high-level, 60, 68, 94, 105
  home use of, 98
  machine, 60, 68, 94
  microcomputer, 67, 98
  programming, 26, 27, 68, 94–103, 105, 196–197, 222
  schools, 98
  structure of, 199
  talking with computer, 199
  types of, 59–60
Language translators, 80, 104
Large-scale integrated circuitry (LSI), 27–29
Large-scale integration, very (VLSI), 29, 47–48
Laser characters, 53
Laser printing, 52
Lashlee, Hal, 150
Law, computer, 263, 282–283
Law-enforcement officers, 82–83
Lawyers
  computer, 263
  data-base use, 151
Learning
  animal, 255
  computer-aided, 242–244
  machine, 255
Ledger, 172

accountant with, 168
columns and rows in, 169
spreadsheet vs., 85, 168–169, 185
Leibnitz, Gottfried, Wilhelm von, 17
Leibnitz calculator, 17
LET, key word, 209
LET statements, 210
Letters
  form, 117
  word-processor changes in, 110, 115, 116, 118, 120
Librarians, data-base careers, 153
Libraries, computer use in, 9, 188
Licensing, computers in, 238
Limitations, computer, 194, 196, 221, 292, 308–309
Line(s), in flowchart, 201, 221
Line numbers
  in BASIC program, 98
  in COBOL code, 97
LISP language, 99–100, 105, 298
LISP program, 100
Literacy, computer, 247
Logarithms, calculators based on, 16
Logic, computer basis, 293
Logic unit, arithmetic (ALU), 46–47, 68
Logo language, 67, 100–102, 105
  writing code in, 217–220, 222
Looping, 213
Lovelace, Ada Byron, 18, 58
LSI (large-scale integrated circuitry), 28–29

McCarthy, John, 298
Machine(s)
  industrial, 228–229, 250
  learning, 255
Machine language, 60, 68, 94
Machine thinking, 255
Maglev rail system, 254
Magnetic core memory, 22, 23, 29

INDEX

Magnetic diskettes, 39
Magnetic ink character recognition (MICR), 45–46, 67–68
Magnetic numbers, 45
Magnetic tape(s), 38–39, 67
 speed, 38, 39
 storage of, 38
Magnetic tape unit, 38
Mail, electronic, 242, 251
Mailbox, electronic, 129
Mailing lists, 13, 117–118, 130, 152, 163
Main routine, 204, 221
Main storage, 47, 68
Mainframe computers, 61–62, 68
Manufacturing, computers in, 6, 11, 30
Marince, Rob, 43
Mark I computer, 20–21, 288
Marketing personnel, careers, 263
Masks, chip circuits, 73
Mauchly, John W., 20
Mechanical calculators, 16–17
Media specialists, careers, 153
Medical records, computers keeping, 232
Medical research, graphics in, 255
Medicine
 computers in, 4, 9, 30, 189, 232, 233
 data banks in, 232
Melting pot, 229
Memory, 2, 68
 bubble, 66
 magnetic core, 22, 23, 29, 47
 programmable read-only (PROM), 48, 68
 random-access (RAM), 48
 read-only (ROM), 47–49
 semiconductor, 27, 47
Memory boards, 48–49, 68
Memory chips, 68
 programmable read-only (PROM), 68
 random-access (RAM), 68
 read-only (ROM), 68
Menu, 148
Merging information, 117–118, 130

Merging text with graphics, 121–122
Meteorologists, computer use, 238
MICR (magnetic ink character recognition), 45–46, 67–68
Microcomputers, 31, 65–68
 data-base management system for, 150
 languages for, 67, 98
 sales growth, chart, 260
 speed, 66
Microfiche, 53
Microfilm, 53
Micromachining, 254
Microprocessors, in autos, 306
Microseconds, 5
Minicomputer(s), 62–65, 68
Minicomputer system, 64
Minsky, Marvin, 279
Missing persons, data bases and, 154
Mistakes, computer, 5
Misuse of computers, 277–281, 283
Modem, 40–42, 67
 computer-to-computer communication, 126
Money transfer, electronic, 242
Monitor, 40
Monitoring of patients, 232
Motor vehicle departments
 computer theft in, 266–267
 computer use, 154
Mouse, 39, 122
Movies, graphics in, 155
Moving text, 123, 130
Multiple copies, 112–113, 122, 130–131
Music synthesis, 54–55
Music synthesizers, 54–55, 68

Nanosecond, defined, 5
Napier, John, 16–17
Napier calculator, 16
National Aeronautics and Space Administration (NASA), 188
National Crime Information Center (NCIC), 82
Networking, 42

Number(s)
 binary, 56–57
 magnetic, 45
Number systems, 15
Numbered lines, in BASIC programs, 208
Numbering, steps in, 202
Numbering of pages, 115
Numeric values, speech and voice, 42

OCR (optical character recognition), 40, 44, 45, 67
Omnibot, 257
Operating system, 79–80, 104
Operating system software, 79, 104
Operations
 basic, 67
 careers in, 8
 personnel in, 63–64
Operators
 careers, 8
 computer, 63
 data entry, 63–64
Optical character recognition (OCR), 40, 44, 45, 67
Optical character recognition device, 45
Orbiting Astronomical Observatory, 172
Organization
 of data, 140–141, 162
 of spreadsheet, 185
Output, 36, 67
Output hardware, 36, 50–56, 67
Outputting, 50, 68
Overheating of computers, 20–21, 24, 25, 30–31

Packaging
 of chips, 73
 of computers, 137
Paper files, 145
 disadvantages of, 145–147, 163
Paper tape, 20
Papert, Seymour, 100–101, 279

Pascal, Blaise, 17, 98
Pascal calculator, 17
Pascal language, 17, 60, 67, 68, 98–99, 105, 217–220, 222
Pascal program, 99
Passwords, 278, 283
Payrolls
  computers and, 236
  data bases in, 157
Peripherals, 36
Personal computers, 65, 128, 130
Piaget, Jean, 101
Picoseconds, 5
Pictorial symbols, 200, 221
PILOT, 67, 102–103, 105
Piracy, computer, 269–272, 282–283
Planning
  business, spreadsheet in, 184
  computer use in, 255
  solution of a problem, 198–200, 221
Plotter, 53–54
Police work, 82–83
  data-base use in, 154
Political spreadsheet, 182
Portable computer, 236
Portable terminals, 83
Prediction, spreadsheet use for, 173
Present society, 227–230, 250
PRINT, key word, 209
Printers, 40, 52–53
  outputting, 51
Printing, 111, 130
  computer use for, 4
  ways of, 52–53
Printouts, 13, 68
  at terminal, 125
Privacy
  computers and, 247–249, 251
  data bases and, 248
  invasion of, 274–276, 283
  violation of, 267, 282–283
Privacy Act (1974), 248
Private labeling, 270, 283
Problems
  analysis of, 195–196, 221
  defined/defining, 194–195
  feed to computer, 196
  solving by programming, 212–220

statements of, 194–195
steps to solve, 194–196, 197, 221
Procedures, Logo routines, 217–218
Process symbols, 200, 202, 221
Processing, 2, 67. *See also* Word processing.
Processing hardware, 36–50, 67
Processors, 46–47, 68
Professions
  data-base use in, 151
  ethics of, 261–262, 282
Professionals, spreadsheet use, 170
Program(s), 2, 29, 78
  application, 104
  software as, 78
  utility, 80
  writing of, 86, 104–105
Program analyst, 206
Program code, 90–91
Programmable read-only memory (PROM), 48, 68
Programmer(s)
  application, 81, 83, 206–208
  careers, 8
  system, 81–82, 206
Programmer analysts, careers for, 178
Programming
  BASIC, 98, 208–212, 216–217, 222
  bottom-up, 200
  careers in, 9
  college students' use of, 214
  tools for planning, 200, 221
  solving a problem by, 212–220
  steps to, 192–193
  top-down structured, 92, 105, 200, 221
  what it is, 196–198
Programming languages, 26–27, 68, 94–103, 105, 196–197, 222. *See also* Languages.
  feed to computer, 196
  second-generation computers, 26
  third-generation computers, 27
Programming personnel, 81
PROM chip, 47–48, 68
Proofreading, 116

Prototype, 2
  simulated, 11
Pseudocode, 93, 105, 200–202, 221
  example of, 202, 203
  relation to code, 93, 105
  writing, 212–213, 221–222
Psychology, computer use in, 14
Publishers, software, 82, 87
Publishing, word processing in, 126–127, 131
Puff, expert system, 299–300, 302

RAM (random-access memory), 47–48, 49
RAM chips, 48, 68
Random access, 48
Random-access memory (RAM), 47–48, 49
Random-access memory chips (RAM), 48, 68
Ratcliff, Wayne, 150
Read-only memory (ROM), 44–48, 49
  programmable (PROM), 48, 68
Read-only memory chips (ROM), 48, 68
  programmable (PROM), 68
Reading machine, 299
Real estate business
  computers in, 236
  data bases in, 158–159, 163
  example of data base, 159
  spreadsheets in, 181–182
Records, 62, 143
  destruction of, 273–274, 283
  file and, example, 144
  government, 275, 283
  invasion of, 275, 283
  privacy protection, 247–249
  updating, 149
Register, 58
Relational data bank, 142
Relay connectors in computers, 22
REM, key word, 209
REM statements, 209
Research, 9, 14, 30
  simulation in, 171–172, 185

INDEX

spreadsheet in, 183
Reservation clerks, airline, 153
Retailing, careers in, 8
Retraining, 245–247
Return, meaning, 204–205
RETURN, key word, 209
RETURN statements, 210
Robot(s), 6, 101, 257, 288
   artificial intelligence and, 305–307, 309
   assembly line, 232
   capacities of, 231, 250, 305
   computer control of, 11–12
   disabled persons and, 307, 308
   factory, 229, 230–232, 234, 307, 309
   fearlessness, 230
   future, 66, 289, 309
   home, 307–309
   imaginary, 231
   inspection by, 231
   jobs and, 231–232, 245–247
   kits for making, 307
   labor force and, 231–232, 251
   personal, 257
   supermarket, 294
   touch sensitive, 254
   welding by, 191
Robotics, 56, 305, 307
   future applications, 305–308, 309
Routines, 200, 221
   Logo language procedures, 217–218
ROM (read-only memory), 47–48, 49
ROM chips, 47–48, 68
Rows
   ledger, 169
   spreadsheet, 168–169, 185
Royalty, programmer's, 82
Runaway children, data bases and, 154
Running the program (BASIC), 216–217

Sales representatives, careers, 263
Sammet, Jean, 195
Sand table, as calculator, 15

Satellite orbits, 188
Satellite telecommunications, 146
School(s)
   artificial intelligence in, 302
   computer education in, 244
   computer use in, 7–10, 30, 68, 103, 188
   data bases in, 161–163
   languages for, 98, 102. *See also* Languages.
   Logo language in, 102
   records, 275–276, 283
   simulation in, 185
   spreadsheets in, 179
   telecommunications in, 129
   voice synthesis in, 54
   word processing in, 125, 131
Schooling, at home, 243–244
Science
   computers in, 9–10, 30
   data-base use in, 160, 163
   spreadsheet uses in, 170, 179, 183, 185
Scientists, programming by, 207–208
Screen
   cathode ray tube (CRT), 40, 51, 68
   touch-sensitive, 122
Search tree, 295–296, 309
Searching, 115, 119–120, 130
Second-generation computers, 25–26, 31
Secondary storage, 47, 48, 68
Secretarial services, word processing and, 127
Security of computers, 248–249
Security measures, computer protection by, 277–280, 283
Seeing, computer, 255
Semicolons, in Pascal program, 99
Semiconductor factory, 49
Semiconductor memory, 27, 47
Sensory devices, integrated circuits with, 254
Sequential access, 48
Shared-logic word processor, 124, 130–131
Silicon wafer, 26, 74
Simon, Herbert A., 90
Simulation, 9, 30, 171–172, 190

   in astronomy, 172
   in military training, 14
   in schools, 171, 185
   in space research, 172
   in testing, 171
   uses for, 171–172
Simulation software, 9
Sinclair, Clive, 176
Size of computers, 6, 30–31
Skills, computer, in daily life, 240–245
"Smarter" computers, 289–291, 308–309
Social sciences, computers in, 14
Society
   computer effects on, 239–241
   present, 227–230, 250
Sociology, computer use in, 14
Software, 7, 78–105
   application, 83–86, 104
   basics of, 78, 104
   career opportunities, 103
   instructions, 78
   integrated, 87–90, 104–105
   kinds of, 7–9
   mail-order, 150
   operating system, 79, 104
   system, 79–83, 104
   tutorial, 7, 8
   types of, 78–90, 104–105
Software designers, 82
Software publishers, 82, 87
Soil samples, computer gathering of, 10
Solar electricity station, 256
Solution, planning for, 198–200, 221
Soule, Samuel W., 111
Space program, CAD and CAM in, 188
Space research
   simulation in, 172
   spreadsheets in, 183
Space travel, computers in, 10
Special effects, computer generated, 155
Specialists, in the Age of Information, 233–234
Speed
   bubble memory, 66
   buses, 59
   cards, 38

computers, 20–21, 23–26, 30–31
diskettes, 39
magnetic tape, 38, 39
mainframe computers, 61
microcomputers, 66
small computers, 48–49
Spelling, checking of, 4, 115, 117, 130
Sports, computer analysis in, 256
Spreadsheets, 84–86, 179
advantages of, 172–174
bank statement as, 180
banking use of, 180–181
business use of, 168–170, 173–174, 177, 179, 184–185
decision making and, 166–187
organization of, 185
school use of, 179
setting up, 174–177
uses of, 177–185
Stand-alone word processor, 124, 131
Statements
bank, 180
problem, 194–195
program, 208–212
Statistics, 14
data-base, 152
Stealing, computer misuse for, 264–267
Steps
numbering of, 202
problem-solving, 194–196, 221
Storage
data, by government, 12
devices for, 47, 48, 147, 163
document, 113
information, 12, 30, 140–141, 162
magnetic tape, 38
main, 47, 67, 68
secondary, 47, 48, 68
text, 111
Storage hardware, 36–50, 67
Stores, telecommunications in, 129
Structured programming, top-down, 92, 105, 200, 221

Students
data-base use, 151, 163
telecommunications use, 129
Subroutine, 203–205, 221
Supercomputers, 29, 61–62, 288–289
Supermarket robot, 294
Supervisor, 79–80, 104
Surveillance, computer, 14
Syntax, in computer language, 208, 222
Synthesis
music, 54–55
voice, 53–54
Synthesizers
music, 54–55, 68
voice, 55, 68
System(s)
careers in, 8
diagram, 51
System analysts, 81
System personnel, 81
System programmers, 81–82, 206
System software, 79–83, 104

Talking with a computer, 199
Tape(s), 68, 147
magnetic, 38, 39, 67
paper, 20
Tape drive, 38
Tape unit, magnetic, 38
Tate, George, 150
Tax records
computerized, 238
software for, 13
Teachers
computer benefits, 9
data-base use, 161
spreadsheet use, 170, 185
word processing and, 128–131
Teaching, computers in, 4
Technical support services, careers in, 8
Technical support specialists, 237
Technical writers, 82
Technicians, computer, 237
Telecommunications
editing and, 128

satellite, 146
uses, 129
Television set, as terminal, 51
Terminal(s), 39–40, 51
dumb, 42
hard-copy, 40
portable, 83
printout at, 125
television screen as, 51
Terminal symbols, 200, 221
use of, 201, 221
Testing
computer in, 30, 234
computer review of, 190
computer use for, 190
simulation in, 171
Text
centering, 119, 130
changing, 112–113, 115–117, 119–120, 130
copying, 123
correcting, 115–117, 130
justifying, 119, 130
merging with graphics, 121–122
moving, 123, 130
word processed, 110
Thinking
animal, 255
human vs. computer, 290–294, 308–309
machine, 255
Third-generation computers, 26–27, 31
Time, stealing, 267–269, 282
Time-shared word processing, 123–124, 130
Time-sharing, computer, 298, 309
Tiring, computer freedom from, 6, 30
Toffler, Alvin, 227
Top-down structured programming, 92, 105, 200, 221
flowchart example, 205
Touch-sensitive screen, 122
Traffic control, 239
Training
computers in, 13
simulation in, 171
Training specialists, 237

INDEX

Transistors, 25–29, 31
Translation, human-to-machine language, 95
Translators, language, 80, 104
Turtles, 100, 102
Tutorial software, 7, 8
Type size, changing, 121, 130
Types of software, 78–90, 104–105
Typewriter
  direct printing, 113
  disadvantages of, 124–126, 130
  word processor compared with, 111–114, 130

UNIVAC, 288
UNIVAC-I, 24–25
Updating
  of data base, 144
  of records, 149
Use(s) of computers, 2–14, 29–30
User-friendly computers, 122
User groups, 270
Utility programs, 80

Vacuum tube(s), 11
Vacuum-tube computer, 20, 23–25, 30
Variable, 210
Very large-scale integrated circuits (VLSI), 47

Very large-scale integration (VLSI), 29
Video games, 28
Vision, computer, 255
Vision system, 298–299, 304
Vital Statistics, Bureau of, 275
  data base, 152
VLSI (very large-scale integrated circuits), 47
VLSI (very large-scale integration), 29
Vocabularies, computer language, 208, 222
Voice patterns, 42, 43
Voice prints, 43
  password function, 43–44, 278, 283
Voice-recognition device, 42–44, 68
Voice synthesis, 53–54
  blind and, 54, 299
Voice synthesizers, 68
  in use, 55
Voting, computers in, 13
Vulcan software, 150

Wafer
  chips on, 26
  inspection of, 74
  silicon, 26, 74
Weather forecasters, computer use, 238
Window, in software programs, 89
Wiring, chips, 75

Words, computer, 58–59
Word processing, 30, 84, 110–111, 130
  advantages of, 110, 112–114, 125–128, 130–131
  changes in letter, 110, 115, 116, 118, 120
  computer use for, 4
  editing and, 126–128, 131
  in publishing, 126–127, 131
  in schools, 125, 131
  time-shared, 123–124, 130
  uses of, 110, 124–128, 130–131
  who uses, 110, 124–128, 130–131
Word processing program, 83–84
Word processors, 112
  dedicated, 124, 131
  kinds of, 123–124, 130–131
  printout at terminal, 125
  "stand alone," 124, 131
  tasks it can do, 115–123, 130–131
  typewriter compared with, 111–114, 130
  users of, 110–133
  writers and, 126–131
World War II, computer development and, 20
Wozniak, Stephen, 234
Writers
  technical, 82
  word processing and, 126, 131

Zuse, Konrad, 22

Photo Acknowledgments

Cover:	C&I Photography	23 bottom:	Gary G. Bitter		Publishing Company
xii:	Los Alamos National Laboratory	25:	IBM Archives	52:	Motorola, Inc./ Four-Phase Systems
2 top:	Arthur Grace/Stock, Boston	26:	Western Digital Corporation	53 top right:	Imagen Corp., Santa Clara, CA
2 bottom:	Brian Payne/Black Star	27:	National Semiconductor	53 bottom:	CalComp
3:	Hewlett-Packard Company	34:	Frieder Michler/ Peter Arnold, Inc.	55 left:	The Disabled Children's Computer Group, Berkeley, CA, courtesy of The Rehabilitation Engineering Center, The Smith-Kettlewell Institute of Visual Sciences
4:	IBM	37:	IBM		
5:	Control Data Corp.	38 top:	IBM		
6:	MTS Systems Corporation	38 bottom:	Dennis Brack/ Black Star		
7:	IBM	39 top:	Wayland Lee*/ Addison-Wesley Publishing Company		
9:	Tom Tracy				
10:	Matrix Instruments, Inc.	39 bottom:	Apple Computer, Inc.	55 right:	Renee Lynn/Peninsula Times Tribune
11:	Prime Computer, Inc.				
12:	Wang Laboratories, Inc.	40:	Wayland Lee*/ Addison-Wesley Publishing Company	58:	Culver Pictures
13:	*San Francisco Chronicle*			62:	Prime Computer, Inc.
15:	Wayland Lee*/ Addison-Wesley Publishing Company	41:	Codex Corporation	64:	Wang Laboratories, Inc.
		44 top:	Synapse		
16:	The Bettmann Archive	44 bottom:	Wayland Lee*/ Addison-Wesley Publishing Company	65:	IBM
17 top:	IBM Archives			72 top:	AT&T Bell Laboratories
17 bottom:	IBM Archives				
18 top:	The Bettmann Archive			72 bottom:	Intel Corporation
18 bottom:	The Science Museum, London	45:	National Semiconductor	73 top:	National Semiconductor
19:	National Portrait Gallery, London	47:	© Mike Streff	73 center:	National Semiconductor
		49 top:	Ellis Herwig/ Stock, Boston		
20:	IBM Archives			73 bottom:	National Semiconductor
21 top:	IBM Archives	49 bottom left:	Motorola, Inc.		
21 bottom:	Sperry Corp.	49 bottom right:	Wayland Lee*/ Addison-Wesley	74 top left:	Intel Corporation
23 top:	IBM Archives				

PHOTO ACKNOWLEDGMENTS

74 top right:	NCR Corporation
74 center:	Intel Corporation
74 bottom left:	NCR Corporation
74 bottom right:	NCR Corporation
75 top:	NCR Corporation
75 bottom:	National Semiconductor
76:	Los Alamos National Laboratory
84 top:	Hewlett-Packard Company
84 bottom:	Apple Computer, Inc.
85:	Honeywell Inc.
87:	Apple Computer, Inc.
88:	Chrysler Corporation
89:	Xerox Corp.
101:	Ellis Herwig/Stock, Boston
102:	Apple Computer, Inc.
103:	Christina Thomson/Woodfin Camp & Associates
108:	Los Alamos National Laboratory
112:	Wayland Lee*/Addison-Wesley Publishing Company
114 left:	Wayland Lee*/Addison-Wesley Publishing Company
114 right:	IBM
122:	Hewlett-Packard Company
125:	Hewlett-Packard Company
126 top:	Christina Thomson/Woodfin Camp & Associates
126 bottom:	Gregory Heisler/Gamma-Liaison
134 top left:	Hank Morgan/Rainbow
134 top right:	Mitzi Trumbo
134 bottom:	Hank Morgan/Rainbow
135 top left:	Mitzi Trumbo
135 top right:	Mitzi Trumbo
135 bottom left:	Mitzi Trumbo
135 bottom right:	Mitzi Trumbo
136 top:	Apple Computer, Inc.
136 bottom:	Hank Morgan/Rainbow
137 top left:	Hank Morgan/Rainbow
137 top right:	Apple Computer, Inc.
137 bottom:	Dan McCoy/Rainbow
138:	Los Alamos National Laboratory
141:	© 1982 Sidney Harris. Created for *Discover*.
142:	Bell Helicopter Textron, Inc.
144:	Gary Gladstone/The Image Bank
146:	Wayland Lee*/Addison-Wesley Publishing Company
147:	Wayland Lee*/Addison-Wesley Publishing Company
148:	D. W. Hamilton/The Image Bank
150:	Amdek Corporation
151:	Sylvia Johnson/Woodfin Camp & Associates
154:	Xerox Corp.
155:	Xerox Corp.
157:	Texas Instruments, Inc.
158:	Wells Fargo Bank—Tim Davis Photography
159:	Aronson Photographics/Stock, Boston
160:	Peter Menzel/Stock, Boston
161:	Software Publishing Corp.
166:	Los Alamos National Laboratory
168:	Culver Pictures
169:	Xerox Corp.
170:	David Burnett/Contact Press Images
173:	Hewlett-Packard Company
174:	Sylvia Johnson/Woodfin Camp & Associates
180:	Wells Fargo Bank—Tim Davis Photography
181:	Charles Gupton/Stock, Boston
183:	Michal Heron/Woodfin Camp & Associates
188 top left:	Guido Alberto Rossi/The Image Bank
188 top right:	Walter Bibikow/The Image Bank
188 bottom:	Michal Heron/Woodfin Camp & Associates
189 top left:	Matrix Instruments, Inc.
189 bottom left:	Dan McCoy/Rainbow
189 right:	Gabe Palmer, Palmer/Kane Inc./The Image Bank
190 top left:	Control Data Corp.
190 top right:	Jay Freis/The Image Bank
190 bottom:	Control Data Corp.
191 top:	Hellmuth, Obata & Kassabaum, Inc.
191 bottom left:	IBM
191 bottom right:	Automatix, Inc., Billerica, MD
192:	Los Alamos National Laboratory
196:	Ira Berger/Woodfin Camp & Associates
198:	Michal Heron/Woodfin Camp & Associates
199:	Aronson Photographics/Stock, Boston

PHOTO ACKNOWLEDGMENTS

203:	Bill Grimes/Black Star
206:	© 1982 Otha Collins. First published in *Creative Computing Magazine*.
209:	Tannenbaum/Sygma
214:	Massachusetts Institute of Technology, photo by Calvin Campbell
224:	Los Alamos National Laboratory
226 top:	American Motors
226 bottom:	Pontiac Division, General Motors
227:	State Historical Society of Wisconsin
228:	Culver Pictures
229:	Michael Hayman/Black Star
230:	Diego Goldberg/Sygma
231 top:	© Lucasfilm Ltd. (LFL) 1977. All rights reserved.
231 bottom:	Chrysler Corporation
233 top:	Ellis Herwig/Stock, Boston
233 bottom:	Office of Information Services, University of Wisconsin-Madison
234:	Michal Heron/Woodfin Camp & Associates
236 top:	John Coletti/Stock, Boston
236 bottom:	Texas Instruments, Inc.
239 top:	Xerox Corp.
239 bottom:	Tim Carlson/Stock, Boston
240:	David Burnett/Contact Press Images
244:	Diego Goldberg/Sygma
248:	Wayland Lee*/Addison-Wesley Publishing Company
254 top:	The Budd Company
254 bottom:	Transensory Devices, Inc., Fremont, CA
255 top left:	Dan McCoy/Rainbow
255 top right:	Hellmuth, Obata & Kassabaum, Inc.
255 bottom left:	Matrix Instruments, Inc.
255 bottom right:	Bill Nation/Sygma
256 top left:	Peter Menzel
256 top right:	Peter Menzel
256 bottom:	Dan McCoy/Rainbow
257 top left:	Diego Goldberg/Sygma
257 top right:	Sepp Seitz/Woodfin Camp & Associates
257 bottom:	Tomy Corporation. Omnibot is made and sold by Tomy Corporation.
258:	Los Alamos National Laboratory
262:	© Anthony Cresci
266 top:	Diego Goldberg/Sygma
266 bottom:	© 1982 Sidney Harris. Created for *Discover*.
270:	Tannenbaum/Sygma
271:	Wayland Lee*/Addison-Wesley Publishing Company
273:	© Anthony Cresci
277:	Christopher Morrow/Stock, Boston
278:	Rusco Electronic Systems
279:	Western Digital Corporation
280:	Ellis Herwig/Stock, Boston
286:	Los Alamos National Laboratory
288:	Sperry Corp.
289:	Androbot, Inc.
290:	Radio Shack, a division of Tandy Corporation
294:	UPI/Bettmann Newsphotos
298:	Christian Vioujard/Gamma-Liaison
299:	Office of Information Services, University of Wisconsin-Madison, photo by Norman Lenburg
300:	Lianne Enkelis © *Discover* Magazine 9/84, Time Inc.
301 top:	CalComp
301 bottom:	Chrysler Corporation
303:	Presley Development Company, developers of Ahwatukee
304:	Christian Vioujard/Gamma-Liaison
305:	Androbot, Inc.

Photographs provided expressly for the publisher.